Christianity and Society

Christianity and Society

by

NELS F. S. FERRÉ

Essay Index Reprint Series

BOOKS FOR LIBRARIES PRESS
FREEPORT, NEW YORK

To
BERNARD JOHNSON POND,
a constantly ready and wise friend,
and to all other Christian laymen who carry concrete concern
for a new and better social order

INTERNATIONAL STANDARD BOOK NUMBER:
0-8369-1924-6

LIBRARY OF CONGRESS CATALOG CARD NUMBER:
78-117791

PRINTED IN THE UNITED STATES OF AMERICA

Contents

Preface

This book completes the first volumes of a series which I hope to be privileged to write, at least to satisfy a craving of my life to see for myself more fully the truth which I find authentic and presently relevant. *Christianity and Society* is Volume Three of *Reason and the Christian Faith,* which, in turn, is Part I of the proposed series. It is not a study of the specific methods or of the concrete choices of social action, but a discussion of the total bearing of the Christian faith on social solutions.

Most of the material used in the book was prepared in connection with the Denio, the Earl, the Cole and the Hoff Lectures, to enumerate them chronologically, and I am still warmly thankful for the many courtesies of the administrations, faculties and students at Bangor Theological Seminary, The Pacific School of Religion, the School of Religion of Vanderbilt University, and Bethany Biblical Seminary.

Dean Walter G. Muelder of Boston University School of Theology and my colleague, Herbert Gezork, have been kind enough to read and to criticize the manuscript, but they are free of all blame for form and content! The last chapter was also read and constructively criticized by two other colleagues, Wesner Fallaw and John Billinsky. I owe them all many thanks for their frankness in constructive criticism. In the production of the book I was graciously helped by Miss Barbara Winne and by the courteous concern of President Harold Tribble, a great leader and friend, who made available facilities of the school, and incomparably by my wife who has not only done most of the work in the typing of both the preliminary and final drafts as well as the checking of references, but has shared in all the processes of "polishing" the book.

A final word should be said in gratitude to the trustees, administration, faculty, students and staff of Andover Newton Theological School. For many years I have had the exceptional privilege of serving my God and my Church surrounded by a keen, creative Christian fellowship.

NELS F. S. FERRÉ

Newton Centre, Mass.
July 1, 1949

SECTION I

THE ETERNAL PURPOSE AND THE HISTORIC PROCESS

Introduction

The relation between Christianity and society involves both the eternally ultimate and the immediately practical. It is necessary for both of these to be adequately understood in order for the relation between them to be rightly grasped. If we are to know whether, in how far, and in what way our actual situation can be changed for the better, we have to understand both what is true-no-matter-what and what is this actual situation.

In the two preceding parts of this analysis of *Reason and the Christian Faith* I have dealt with the nature of the Eternal Process which can best account for the origins of our world process (*Faith and Reason*) and the meaning and fulfillment of it (*Evil and the Christian Faith*). My present task is to show that Christianity gives us the right key to our practical problems. Our concern here, therefore, is neither with the origin nor with the end of our historic process, but, rather, precisely with present history as this challenges the Christian faith. The key to that challenge cannot, admittedly, be merely intellectual. It will also have to be motivational. It must, in other words, have practical power to effect change and to compel the will, as well as theoretical power to convince the mind.

Dean Walter G. Muelder of Boston University School of Theology has told how in his classes in social ethics it often happens that when the ultimate issues are being discussed the students clamor to get down to concrete problems; whereas when the practical problems are being dealt with, the students crave to know the ultimate reasons for these concrete policies being advocated. Any satisfactory solution of our actual problems will inevitably have to include, in

3

organic relation, adequate sanctions for concrete attitudes and actions as well as those attitudes and actions themselves.

In Christian faith the sanctions as well as the concrete attitudes and actions are understood in terms of Christian love or Agape. Agape is the nature of the Eternal Purpose, of God's holy will, which men must share if they are to enjoy right relations among themselves and the right use of this created world. Agape is God's spontaneous good will, in creation and redemption, which issues by its very nature in right relations, whether in attitudes or actions, whether in immediate enjoyment, reformation or redemption. The applicability of Agape to our concrete problems is the total thesis of this volume which is to be developed, illustrated and incidentally verified. I say incidentally verified because, obviously, what is more real cannot be proved by what is less real and what is more true cannot be proved by what is less true.

Most of our interest in the world is due to our own self-involvement in it. The sin of the refusal of God's Agape is mankind's deepest problem, socially as well as individually. Authentic Christian love, however powerful it may be when present, is truly rare. No analysis of our societal situation and no solution for it, therefore, can be at all adequate that does not readily and realistically acknowledge and deal with the range, depth and power of sin.

This basic fact of sin greatly complicates our problem. In one sense, since God's love is the nature of the Eternal Purpose which underlies the total historic process, this love must be organically applicable, directly or indirectly, to every part of that process, past, present and future. For that reason, it is possible in the first section of this book ideally to relate the Eternal Purpose to the historic process. This ideal relation is God's intention for the world. It is God's purpose for process which is even now open to our collective freedom.

Yet, in another sense, this intentional relation cannot now be inclusively direct because it is broken and distorted by sin. The only direct relation that is possible at all is, naturally, man's understanding, acknowledgment and acceptance, at least in intention, of God's will. The Church, as the genuine fellowship of believers and doers, is that order of society in which sin is broken through, at least in strong intention and some factual fulfillment, by the power of God through faith in Him. Yet actually our corporate churches, too, have sin as their greatest problem. They are dark distances from the genuine fellowship of believers and doers of God's will. For that reason it will be necessary for us to study the relation between God's will and the Church. Our second section will, accordingly, wrestle with this topic.

Assuming that by that time we shall have reached some definite understanding of the way in which the Eternal Purpose involves itself in the historic process, both directly and indirectly, our task will be to show concretely the general applicability of Agape to the actual realms of historic life and decision, especially to three selected areas: war and peace, property and education. The discussion of the Eternal Purpose and the historic process, in this third section, will, accordingly, be focused on the establishing of *clear Christian perspectives* on these concrete problems. What are the positive lines of solution for our social predicaments, is the question we must ask, both in theory and in practical power, and are they inherently Christian in nature?

Naturally, all that we can do finally is to indicate the orientation of Agape and from within this suggest broad directives for action. Detailed decisions will have to remain as complicated and directly existential as history itself. No system can ever contain life. Creative decisions cannot be thus cabined and confined. But life can and needs to use systematic analysis of its relation to the ultimate. Such analysis, however, is obliged to relate organically the eternally ultimate to the immediately practical. We turn, then, to the development of our thesis.

CHAPTER I

Christianity Is *More*
than Society

Society cannot be changed by its own power. It has not created itself. Neither has it created the environment by means of which it lives. Without God's sustaining it and its world, it cannot continue to live. Both as a fact and as an act, society is characterized better as becoming than as being, even though ultimately it is, of course, basically determined by the being of God.[1]

A Ptolemaic theology would have a God who is fundamentally related to our historic process. Its God would be good enough and strong enough, at best, to assure the realizability of human hopes and ideals. He would, to be sure, be *more* than society; but fundamentally he would amount to no more than the fulfilling dimension of human aspirations. A Copernican theology, on the other hand, holds God to be unimaginably beyond our historic process. It does not primarily relate God to the process, but relates the process to God. Few seers have observed this as piercingly as Fénelon, who saw that power often failed even men of constant prayer because what they worshiped was basically their ideas of God rather than God Himself.[2]

The Ptolemaic tendency is a strong temptation of theology and of personal experience alike. Because of its very subtlety it is all the harder to overcome. Since our experience has to come through

[1] Cf. *Evil and the Christian Faith*, chap. 2.
[2] Cf. *Christian Perfection*, C. F. Whiston, ed., p. 117, where Fénelon says that to relate God to us is to violate "the fundamental law of creation."

ourselves, the distorted perspective gives the impression that we are more real than God, that our experience is more true than its Source. In the same way, we tend to think that because we live in, and experience, this historic process, it is, therefore, more real than its Source. Herein, as we shall shortly see, lies one of our major problems for both an adequate authority and a sufficient motivation.

The dimension which is *more* than society, which in Christian theology always makes God rather than history central, is intrinsically different from any mere extension of man's understanding of God. Any mere extension makes the process to be changed more basic than the Power who alone can change it. Brunner has asked us to remember that man's refusal to be arbitrary *in this sense* is a grievous sin. An adequate interpretation of human knowledge points beyond itself for its truest perspective and fullest power.[3] But actually to break away in our consciousness from assuming the self and process to be central to the recognition of God as central is hard beyond belief. To do so is to pass from a Ptolemaic to a Copernican faith, from a man-centered to a God-centered faith, from a faith hindered to a faith helped by reason, from a faith hemmed in by reason to a reason released by faith. This is to pass from a false attempt at self-security to a genuine experience of God-security. It is to pass from the centrality in thought and life of the historic process to the centrality of the Eternal Purpose. It is to pass from centering our hopes falsely in mere society to the focusing of our faith in that which is *more* than society.

The question of this *more* than society, including the fullest knowledge of society and the highest legitimate hopes from it, is of deep significance for the total question of the relation of Christianity to society. On the one hand, the *more* cannot be a mere extension of our human scene without our being guilty, as Aristotle accused Plato, of simply adding another world to this one where its problems can be solved rather conveniently and without observable contradictions. We have had enough of ingenious rationalizations. On the other hand, the *more* cannot be organically irrelevant to this historic world.

The *more* must, in fact, in order to fulfill the conditions of adequate knowledge, have the capacity to explain this world as fully

[3] Cf. *Faith and Reason,* chap. 4.

as possible, reliably for truth and savingly for life, not only by the appeal to mere ideals, but also by the demonstrable actualization within the historic process of this *more* than society, observably transforming it, opening new vistas of insight, and making available new sources of power for its continued transformation. The more of our process we genuinely come to know, the more soundly we can predict that it will point beyond itself. The center of reference with respect to both ultimate knowledge and reality shifts, with the fuller knowledge and the truer analysis, from man's side of the equation to God's; from our historic process to the Eternal Purpose.

Christian faith, consequently, lives in a balance-in-tension, as Przywara would put it, between seeing and believing. For this faith to deny that the light of life, the truth and grace from the Father, has come, is to deny its own inner life. Christianity is centrally a religion of revelation. Man's reasoned interpretation of this faith is, for the most part, a response to that revelation and, within the full context of explanation, it is itself made possible by that revelation. Yet, on the other hand, to prescribe for this seeing any limiting objective and subjective scheme beyond error of mind or heart, is to deny man's actual situation as a tiny, erring creature. Even in the seeing of the revelation it is *man,* and not God, who does the seeing. In so far as man yields to the Holy Spirit's seeing and living in him, he is made capable of seeing the Infinite, God, and of having fellowship with Him. But he is not thereby delivered from his finitude in the sense that he sees as God sees. He sees rather as a man enabled by grace and faith to see Him.

The Ultimate is necessarily the Ground for explaining all else, but cannot itself be explained by anything else. Revelation cannot be revelation of the Ground of Being unless it remain essentially a mystery in depth and kind, however much light that mystery might then shed on the created world. Revelation is the eternal mystery to man of the eternally given. Human reason can reach up toward, but never reach revelation; it can neither be God nor see from God's point of view. It cannot change perspectives from the secondary to the primary. Revelation remains its own selfsame reason for being, namely, that it ever *is* the original light. No light can be thrown on revelation. Light can only break forth from it. Man can see only from its point of revealing in history and experience. God alone sees man's problems from the full perspective of truth and, therefore, from the point of right proportions. Revelation gives man, as he heeds it, true light adequate for life, but no reason singly or collectively can total up to the fullness of all light revealed and no pooling of perspectives can arrive at the proper proportions of final truth. Because of man's sinfulness and finitude, reason cannot contain revelation coherently within itself. Reason is "the whole man thinking," and man the creature can never change place with God the Creator. The seeing of reason should, accordingly, eventuate in the believing of faith. The constant and common mood of creaturely appropriation is some kind of balance-in-tension. Needful for our societal situation is the recognition in thought and deed, in actual whole-response, of the fact that man is created in the image of God, not God in the image of man.

Any adequate analysis of the relation between Christianity and society has to begin with this crucial fact, and all adequate Christian action must remain within this all-molding mood. We cannot be saved as a society unless we accept the mystery of the *more* than society which is the very Ground of our being and right thinking; for what society now is cannot offer us any genuine salvation in terms either of light or of power.

This *more* than society refers especially to our life beyond this life, to man's history beyond this earth. We have seen throughout our whole analysis of both the origins and ends of process the impossibility of accounting adequately for this historic process if it is treated as a self-sufficient and self-explanatory entity. Without faith in life after death and in a history, or histories, beyond earthly history, there can be no adequate perspective for explaining nor power for transforming our historic process. Hinduism, with its doctrines of *karma* (deed and consequence) and *samsara* (reincarnation), makes more sense of the total problem than does any earthbound naturalism. Christian faith involves what is *more* than society, especially in reference to our life beyond death.

Is it not equally obvious that any attempt on our part to spell out that which lies beyond our history and experience is simply our trying to extend our perspective indefinitely? The field beyond death has evidently been purposely limited from view for our good. Such limitation seems to be the function of death. We cannot see any details beyond death because this realm lies outside the focus of our light. Any attempt to do so seems to result in the distortion or dimming of the light which we now have. All that we can see is that the Eternal Purpose goes beyond our historic process and promises its fulfillment in His boundless time and inexhaustible manner beyond the edge of our temporary focus.

This analysis of the need for what is *more* than society leads us directly into the relation of the absolute to the relative. What is the reality and significance of the historical realm within the full Christian perspective? Some consider the notion of the absolute to be inconsistent with the reality of the historical. The absolute to them means the perfected or the completed; or it means unity without plurality; or it means the absence of any and all relations, of all that is in any way "relative"; or it means the changeless in the sense of the unhistorical or nonhistorical. Naturally, if we define the problem of the relation between the absolute and the relative in any such way, we are going to get into trouble, chiefly, however, because we have used some wrong approach. When we ask the wrong questions, we are likely to get unsatisfactory answers. No merely formal definition of the question, for that matter, will do. All depends upon the nature of the absolute, upon the kind of content, in fact, which determines its own forms. Partial perspectives always end in ultimate problems. Ultimate perspectives, on the contrary, when they are rightly used, clear up the clouded thinking which results from partial perspectives. So it is with this basic problem. We must look at it from the content of the Absolute, which is Agape.

To Christian faith, then, the absolute appears as Agape, whose very essence is creativity and redemption. The God who is Agape is not static but is rather the Creator and Redeemer, the Worker and Companion. God is not self-centered. While He ever *is*, and all things are because of Him, He is basically not for Himself, but is, rather, the outgoing love who shares His being and beauty. He is no mere unity, no oneness of form, whose being is polluted and lessened by participation in historic change. Hartshorne is quite right that God's nature is absolute-relative, an absolute completely concerned with the relative, intimately and inclusively related to it.[4] Shall we not say that Agape, which is the absolute, is intrinsically the kind of unity which is not only not inconsistent with plurality, but which, rather, involves by its very nature all the varieties of creative fellowship? Agape implies not the absence of relations, but the production and perfecting of relations.

With Agape as the absolute, the problem for Christian faith is not to find reality for history, but, oppositely, to find any concept of eternity which is not through and through historical in nature and suggestion. The "vision of God" as the content of eternity comes the closest to a nonhistorical goal which yet contains relations that we can picture. "Union with God" is obviously the denial of Agape by the losing of real relations. "Fellowship with God," on the other hand, has more historical content; while "the service of God" is, of course, almost completely like the warp and woof of historical existence.

The sovereignty of God as Agape, in the light of the world as we know it, involves, as far as we can see, the reality and the perfectibility of historic relations both on earth and beyond death. Without the former there is no reason for history, and without the second there is no outcome of history. Without the former there is no genuine explanation of evil, and without the latter no explanation is genuine. We find Agape as the absolute impellingly indicated by reason and the heart of full faith. Yet such faith involves our living within the tensions not only of incomplete but also of sinful history. To escape this tension we may try to deny the sovereignty of the Eternal Purpose, making it applicable only to its own self-contained being and to such qualities of experience as may be had in history, or even making it nothing but a logical abstraction from certain aspects of our own experience. Or we may try to escape this tension by the denial of the reality of history. From such a point of view there is no evil. Nature and history are figments of our imagination. Thus we land in the error of mortal mind of Christian Science or the *maya* of Hinduism and Buddhism. Christianity, however, believes in the all-inclusiveness and the full sovereignty of Agape. Such faith involves the reality and perfecti-

[4] Cf. *The Divine Relativity.*

bility of historic relations. History, as the sum total of human events under God, becomes the very arena of the activity of the Eternal Purpose.[5]

The Christian view would, therefore, find less trouble in showing the applicability of Agape to society than it would in writing, a finished eschatology. For Christian faith the stumbling block, in any case, is not history, but eternity. We shall shortly see that Agape constitutes a genuine ideal for society and a genuine basis for explaining history, but what is really hard to understand is the end of history and what can be really meaningful to us beyond our kind of historic struggle.[6] This, however, is not our present problem; for Christianity has an absolute which is known from history. It starts with history. Its knowledge roots in existence rather than in essence. Its absolute is an "existential ultimate."[7] Its essence is established from a historic event, a selectively actual occurrence. This was conclusively realized in history, at least in teaching and in dominant intention. Nowhere, of course, is history to be seen apart from its aspects of weakness, ignorance, or lack of complete, natural harmony with the full meaning and reality of eternity. But even so, the Eternal Purpose is arrived at by a historic event, an actual life, that represents beyond its own being the real potentiality of man in general, of history as a whole. Thus both the realization of ideal reality and its general realizability are historic categories, indicating eternity.

Christian faith thus never begins with essence; its universality springs out of solid particularity, such particularity as has the capacity universally to explain, to judge and to save. The category of finality in the Christian faith is an existential ultimate. Essence

[5] Edgar S. Brightman has made a daring attempt to solve this problem by his idea of a growing God, making historic relations real and perfectible without any absolute. But his analogy of growth is more convincing of history than of eternity. Eternal Isness as the Ground of change must be its own adequate cause as Self-being, and has nothing else whereby to be changed. The analogy from history is easy for the human mind to make, but fails to answer the crucially critical questions. When we have an adequate understanding of the full doctrine of creation, however, the need for the distinction between God's perfect will and a finite nature is obviated. Brightman has dealt better with the "Problem of God" than with the "Finding of God." Cf. *Faith and Reason*, chap. 4.

[6] For some suggestions compare *Evil and the Christian Faith*, p. 27 ff.

[7] Cf. *Faith and Reason*, p. 149 ff.

is throughout known by, and exists within, actual existences, whether divine or human. There are no essences apart from divine and human existences.

The significance of history in Christian faith, therefore, is elemental. Yet it also has more than a historical basis and perspective. The Christian faith bestows on history the ultimate power and purpose of eternity, for in history the Eternal Purpose is working out His plan. Historic urgency is finite; only eternal urgency is final. History and time are not absolute. They are the expressions and the tools of eternity. The urgency of faith within the Eternal Purpose is at the same time both more relaxed and more concerned than the urgency of fear or faith within finite meanings. T. S. Eliot suggestively writes that time is conquered only through time. Only through the historic process is the Eternal Purpose realized.

History is thus not absolute. Its freedom is neither irresponsible nor forced. It is, rather, weighted first toward self-freedom, or freedom from and over against God, in order that historic choice and life might be real; but through experience it becomes weighted more heavily toward God in order that His fellowship, whether through His goodness or His severity, may become real and historic reality find its full meaning within the Eternal Purpose.

Every choice is related to the absolute Agape; while no historic choice is absolute in purpose or power it nevertheless never escapes relating itself in some way to what is ultimate. In this way, the Christian faith combines the human and the more than human organically so that statements like these by Geraint Vaughan Jones, for instance, are equally true: "No analysis of history can be other than absurd which minimizes the 'human' element, for history is the sphere in which decisions are made, and it is men who make the decisions, though nature may set the problems";[8] and "the necessary ingredient of a revised prognosis of human destiny is not to be found in science, sociology, politics, or economics, but, however absurd and incredible it may sound to the 'educated' modern man, in theology. . . ."[9] Or we can say with Barth that Christ as the content of the Eternal Purpose for history "normalizes time, heals its

[8] *Democracy and Civilization,* p. 11.
[9] *Ibid.,* p. 15.

wounds, fulfills it and makes it real."[10] History is man's relative response, individually and collectively, to God's absolute purpose. "Man's attitude to God is the heart of his being."[11] Freedom from anxiety is organically connected with constant and serious choice. Heavenly essence hovers ever over human existence. Both condition any adequate moment of history. "He who has never meditated on the angels will never be a perfect metaphysician";[12] but neither will he who has not willed to do God's will in order to know the doctrine.

Much difficulty concerning the absolute comes from a lack of understanding of the reality and nature of freedom. Some think that if there is an absolute there can be no freedom. The vision of the absolute, to be sure, may lead to an anticipated attainment that prevents real attainment. Some absolutists dull and even deaden the seriousness of concrete and riskful choice by their paper solutions. Identification with the absolute in thought rather than in life kills the nerve of vital endeavor.

God as Agape, however, alone is ultimately and perfectly free. There can be only one infinite freedom. In order to effect fellowship in history, He has bestowed a measure of serious and responsible freedom on men; but this freedom is conditioned and controlled. When God shares His power He does not limit His freedom, but rather expresses it. The essential nature of Agape is to bestow freedom on the objects of His love. Such sharing of freedom limits God's control directly, but by so doing also expresses His nature directly. Since He directly and completely, without internal or external hindrance, wills to do this, He is not limited by so doing, but His freedom is thereby consistently and completely exercised. Since man, on the other hand, has received this freedom from God, it is genuine, through and through real, according to its measure. Historic freedom is thus real, serious and inescapable, both here in this life and in the life to come.

Yet this freedom is according to the capacities and bent of human nature *and no more*. It is real within a power proportionate

[10] *Kirchliche dogmatik, Dritter Band, Erster Teil*, p. 80: *"Er normalisiert die Zeit. Er heilt ihre Wunden. Er erfüllt, er verwirklicht sie."*
[11] Brunner, in *The Christian Understanding of Man*, p. 175.
[12] Maritain, *Degrees of Knowledge*, p. 272.

to God's purpose with us in the historic process; but all the while it is also within the total power of the perfect Eternal Purpose. It is as serious as our historic experience, for good or for ill. It may be far more real and far more serious in the world, or worlds, to come, because there, too, it will be according to God's purpose with us in our new circumstance. For this freedom of ours is ever within the hands of the inexhaustible resources of the sovereign God. He has not surrendered His power, but only delegated it. Thus within our personal and historic experience, while the choices that confront us are genuinely real with relation to the absolute, they are not, nevertheless, absolute choices. Only God can make such.

Our freedom of time is ever surrounded on all sides by God's freedom of eternity. Therefore it is that the long-suffering of God is not slackness, as some figure it, but is rather the right condition for our salvation. The patience of process is due to the depth of God's purpose with our freedom. Thus the relation of Agape as the absolute freedom to human or historic freedom is "symbiotic" as MacIver and Gallagher call it. But the symbiosis is not of qualitatively similar lives or kinds of freedom. One kind is infinite and eternal; the other kind is finite and for a temporary purpose. When the finite freedom finally accepts the infinite freedom, the problem of freedom is gone for conflict has turned into creative co-operation. Then metaphysical freedom, the mere freedom of choice, has eventuated in spiritual freedom, the fulfillment of man's deepest willing and seeing within the Eternal Purpose for him.

God knows what He is doing. Even the worst abuse of freedom is within the compass of His purpose. Our freedom is as great as it is in order that the fellowship in the end might be great in the same proportion. Thus *the significance of history is precisely freedom.*

The significance of freedom, however, is that it is from the Eternal Purpose and for the sake of effecting it. Our kind of freedom, it follows, will cease when the full historic process is over. The content of our freedom will no longer be mixed with evil. The Eternal Purpose and the historic process will be in line. At this point our kind of history, our kind of time, our content of freedom are done away. That this process be, is precisely the purpose of the absolute Agape. Yet it is even more His purpose that this process be completed.

Even if God, however, is fully free, both in creating and in the redeeming of the process, is not man, at least, caught within it, making somewhere necessary a final contradiction between the absolute God and finitely free man? "We are free," says Bergson, "when our acts spring from our whole personality."[13] Within the historic process this means that we are free when we freely and fully accept the whole will of God for us. Both ignorance and sin keep our personalities from being whole. And there is, indeed, a closer relation between ignorance and sin than we may think; for one who understood perfectly, in will, mind and emotion, God's way as being in every way the best for him, would not sin. Only the creature, who is not whole, sins; not God. Any human response, of course, is in one sense a "whole response" because the whole person is always involved in his making of choices. Yet this actual whole is not so whole as he could be. He is limited by ignorance, by evil desires and by immoral choices from within; and, therefore, he is kept from being a wholly integrated self, and, it follows, from being his fullest possible self. He is contracted from within and contradicted in being and power. A sick person is, in a sense, a "whole," but in a fuller sense he can yet be made whole. A whole-response can be "whole" only as it expresses its fullest possible nature with relation to the best possible circumstance for it. Otherwise it is limited from being whole either from within or by the external situation.

Even if the self, moreover, accepts his freedom according to the will of God for him he is then, nevertheless, free only in so far as he expresses his fullest possible nature. He is still not free within the historic process to choose the best possible circumstance. In other words, he is still limited from without, with a limitation that is contrary to his best finite nature at the time. This is exactly the reason that history is indispensably important to reality as we know it. No solution of this situation, therefore, is forthcoming until history *as a whole* is redeemed. Freedom is not individualistic, but through and through social. Freedom is not only for oneself, but for all others.

[13] *Time and Free Will*, p. 172.

The way in which Whitehead put it in conversation is that life has two different aspects which hang inextricably together: "It matters to me; and it has consequences to others." Only through freedom can freedom be attained. We are involved intrinsically with one another. History weaves us into one cloth with many colors and kinds of stitches, and history is itself woven fine into the fabric of eternity. Its net results are woven on the heavenly loom. Social responsibility is consequently the prerequisite for social freedom. Full social freedom, too, waits until the last bound person is delivered from bondage. Each person has an irreplaceably significant freedom. Then all persons can act according to their fullest possible nature, with relation to the best possible circumstance. In this way, the Eternal Purpose and the historic process belong insolubly together; in this way, the absolute Agape gives full reality and significance to history. What such experience can be like and how we human beings shall then feel and function is beyond our best thoughts, and almost beyond our desires, because rightly we feel now far more at home within the preparatory struggles and incompletions of historic process. Yet the meaning and task of history are the realization of full freedom in the fellowship within the Eternal Purpose.

Have we not, however, ignored the reality of evil without which our history would surely not be the kind of place that we now know? If the absolute is Agape, what reality and significance can evil have? How could evil have originated in the first place? Here there is a question no longer of that which is *more* than society, but of that which destroys society. Our answer has already been presented at length in *Evil and the Christian Faith*, but in this context the following reply will have to suffice.

While evil is actual, it is not real in the full metaphysical sense. Evil is a genuine part of experience within historic process, where it plays a genuine pedagogical part, but it is never a part of Eternal Being. Within the Eternal Purpose evil has positive, but not permanent, reality. Evil is a pedagogical part and condition of experience, but not a lasting part of it. It is a temporary means, and not an everlasting end. It is never substantive being; rather

it is always verbal being, the way a thing operates or people be-
have.

As far as our experience goes, evil consists of two basic aspects:
moral and natural evil. Moral evil consists of the false use of
our freedom. The term "evil" has an unfortunate natural conno-
tation, too, as though this kind of world should not have been
made. We tend to rebel against the conditions of created existence.
We wish that we had been created perfect, in the sense of free
moral agents and real fellows, without the genuine way in which
such freedom and fellowship can be had. The trick of truth and
of life is to affirm in thought and affection God's sovereign goodness over us now and thereby to surrender all fear-born anxiety
while also affirming that God has made us for perfection so that
we persist with divine determination to change things as they are
for the better. Evil, from one side, is both a concomitant and a
condition of our freedom, and from the other, it helps to exercise
effective control over that finite freedom.

The only evil which is possible and ever present within the
moral sphere is the persistence of a false freedom; and that we
can thus persist sufficiently long to become real individuals has
its genuine and necessary value and reality within the pedagogical
process of individuation and fellowship which constitutes the
meaning of history. By means of such over-againstness, do we
become free. By means of such freedom, do we come to accept and
to enjoy the fellowship which is the content of the Eternal Purpose.

Natural evil, again, is simply the precariousness of nature for
our sake in order that we might have the right kind of pedagogical environment. Nature is steady enough yet risky enough
to let us have responsibility without self-sufficiency. Predictability
is balanced by precariousness. And with us all things end. The
finality of human life is written not in black, but in red. Death
is certain for us all, but not life. Thus God gives us genuine
freedom, while still conditioning and controlling us within and
beyond this life. The setting of life is thus precisely of a kind to
effect fellowship and is, therefore, the gift of Agape. What is
called evil may be rightly so named by us, but God means it for
good. With Him all things in the end work out according to
His will.

If our ultimate problems of society must find their solution only in Agape, which is *more* than society, how can such absolute authority constitute adequate social authority? After all, as far as our human scene goes, regardless of ultimate truth, does not any absolute authority become a block to historic progress? Does it not, in fact, impede the expression of human freedom and creative choice? Does not any absolute create a hard, rigid, fanatical attitude?

The problem of authority is not an easy one to solve in practical life. How can any absolute, like Agape, be accepted as an ultimate standard *more* than society? First of all, we need an adequate authority; indeed, an absolute authority. Micklem is right in claiming that "a society that lacks a cohesive philosophy and regards all questions as open is on the way to dissolution."[14] Mere relativism will not do. We cannot say, furthermore, that authority should reside simply in the group itself. If we say that authority is merely an aspect of the enforcement of group behavior, we have an externalistic totalitarianism, at least in principle. The group is then free to do anything it pleases. It is itself under no law.

If we say, however, that while the authority belongs to the group as such, the individuals in it should be made capable of freely seeing and sharing the meaning of the group: at worst, we dodge the entire problem of the recalcitrant individual or group, and, at best, we arrive at nothing more than a cultural pluralism that will not serve as an intercultural or an intergroup standard. Such a cultural pluralism is merely an evasion of conflict in the sense of live and let live. It avoids the problem of our total involvement with one another. In the end, too, only the groups which have an adequate kind of authority over them will live and let live. Groups which have lost their ultimate direction are all the more restless with life. They tend to aggressive exploitation. "To live" should mean, rather, to be alive in order to help live, because we are all deeply interrelated and vitally involved with and among one another, to an extent, in fact, of which we are most of the time nearly totally unaware. An unauthoritative cultural pluralism is also an evasion of the question of the common truth and the

---

[14] *The Theology of Politics*, p. 143.

common good, as they refer both to a common human nature and to a common human environment, basically speaking. How, then, shall we avoid this evasion and yet have any kind of common authority that is not repressive and impeding?

We need, as we have already said, an authority that is absolute and that is, nevertheless, neither arbitrary nor artificial. We need an authority which is *more* than society to direct it into its fullest good, including the vast historic unknown, and which is yet also an intrinsic and elastic aspect of societal decisions and creative adventure. Agape, I have claimed, is this authority; but how can such an indefinite content as spontaneous love constitute an authority that is both fixed enough in meaning to give concrete light on specific problems, and yet, at the same time, elastic enough to allow for the free growth of an experimenting society?

If there were complete good will all around, of course, our problems would be reduced to technical intelligence, which would itself be free from all group pressures which tend to distort basic seeing. This is surely in itself a good deal of an answer, for this would realize the maximum attainable, desirable social condition, and beyond that we cannot go as human beings. Yet we do not stop there with our answer, but shall go on to show how something *more* than society is also introduced into the total situation, both new creative forces and new and better channels of communication. For such a state of general good will is unrealizable apart from its one true Source beyond society, and therefore, if Agape should be realized, new powers and light would be brought into the situation itself by the very contact with that Source. What I am saying is simply that this authority of Agape cannot be had apart from its inevitably accompanying motivation. In Agape, motivation and authority are inseparable.

As we now are, however, what can constitute an organ of authority *in history?* Christian faith has usually resorted to one of three kinds of historical authority: Bible, Church or Creeds. Can any of these serve as concrete contemporary translators of ultimate authority, the authority of Agape, into concrete history? Can any of these form the basis for present objective authority?

Anyone aware of the many strands of thought and of the many levels of conduct within the Bible can hardly maintain that the

Bible can constitute the historic standard of Agape. Surely if the Bible as such is made the final standard, we are left with a most ambiguous and questionable authority. One of the basic problems of modern culture is that the Christian churches in no small measure constitute a real lag both in thought and in morals on account of their being bound to a book. The Bible has, as a matter of fact, by means of its many strands, become a bulwark against the single eye of Agape which alone fills the whole body with light. Even the method of interpreting Scripture with Scripture is inadequate as an objective standard. The whole-pattern has often, yes, usually, tended to obscure the necessity of acknowledging lower and average reaches of Biblical material in contrast to the full revelation of the Most High in Jesus Christ as Agape.

In an era of insecurity there is likely to be a great cry of "back to the Bible," while what the world needs is to go forward to the Christian community based on Agape. Even Jesus becomes a retarding influence and a puzzling problem when he is made into an all-wise standard for all ages. If we are to believe some scholars who reduce Jesus mostly into a first century Jew, there is not only a question as to what he said but also about much that he did say. To make Jesus the standard rather than the Bible, is correct in so far as it is in him that Agape breaks forth in its fullest declaration, and, we think, enactment; and also because Agape as a standard is much more personal than a mere principle or idea. But we must also remember that it is because Jesus taught and lived Agape that he is the standard and that, therefore, he is himself under the constant standard of Agape. Only because our meanings come together in a Personal Purpose of Agape can Jesus be accepted as the strong Son of God, the first born among many brethren.

The same is also true of the Church. Only in so far as the Church, as a corporate historic existence, expresses Agape in teaching and life, can it constitute the absolute standard. But who can look at our actual churches without seeing how very far from this standard they are? Who, on the other hand, can honestly say that there is no Agape outside them? Was there none at all in Gandhi, for instance, or in Hosea? Naturally, the Church can express Agape more fully than the Bible because a fellowship can come closer to the living reality of what God is and wants than can a book. But actually it is far easier to get direction toward the Agape fellowship from the New Testament than from any actual church. Where high Agapaic preaching and living are maintained in a fellowship from faith to faith, how much of such preaching and living have been fed on the New Testament! Both the Bible and the Church, however, are none the less under the searching judgment of Agape. Neither of them constitutes a clear, unmixed historic standard of this absolute. Through neither does the absolute authority of God's own holy Agape become transparently and inerrantly present in contemporary human history.

Do the creeds, then, constitute the needed organ to transmit the Eternal Purpose authoritatively *into history?* Certainly not. They are usually concerned more with the central Christian events than with their meaning, thus making these events less than Christian in character. I, at least, know of no creed which offers the consistent and full interpretation of the central Christian events in terms of the Christian meaning. And I know of no creed, for that matter, regardless of its use of historic event, which unexceptionally expresses the main Christian meaning in relation to God, to all men and to the whole created world. All of historic Christianity from its founding until now is, therefore, under the judgment of the Eternal Purpose. This, too, is exactly the way it ought to be.

Absolute authority, then, cannot appear in absolute historic form without freezing history. History is characterized by change, by decision, by a measure of real freedom. Any authority for history, therefore, must be open; it must be embodied absolutely in content only, but never in form. We must be free to give our own creative forms to our own historic decisions. For this reason no theology or ethics can ever be at the same time mostly imitative and truly creative. While the source and reality of authority is absolute, the form in history must always be relative. As far as the medium for expressing it goes, this seems true even of any conceivably meaningful heavenly existence. Only such authority, absolute in content and relative in form, gives both a steady standard and a flexible freedom. There is no use, therefore, in complaining, as does, for instance, Jean-Paul Sartre, that the Christian faith gives no specific rules for concrete ethical choices; that it leaves us with only general principles. Daring faith applies, in freedom, its general insights to its specific choices.

No authority, furthermore, is truly binding on free choices except the authority of personal insight. As long as authority is merely externalistic and objectivistic, it has no legitimate power over mature responsibility. Objectively grounded authority can become personal and social authority only through insight into its right to rule. Absolute authority can have no high and adequate meaning for humanity as a whole until it is seen by the choosers that this authority is best for all concerned in the long run, and with respect to their full destiny. Absolute authority can similarly have no legitimate power over an individual until he has personally appropriated its significance for him in relation to the total situation. Authority is thus an aspect of the societal situation, but it can never be reduced to merely an aspect of it. Authority is that aspect of the societal situation which gives to it its deepest significance, truest relation and fullest reality. And no societal situation contains within itself that aspect. That comes from what is *more* than society. The Eternal Purpose and the historic process belong organically together.

The fraudulent truth seeks unquestioning submission. The imposter demands unthinking allegiance, making himself dominatingly central. The genuine Agape comes humbly for all, pointing to what is *more* than society, that in its light and power all may find for themselves what the truth is that can make us free while yet binding us freely into creative and co-operative community.

The whole truth of Agape can never produce fanaticism, for the more it is practiced, the more humility, openness and pedagogical patience are also practiced. But idols or false absolutes cause divided loyalties and make people do even dastardly deeds with good conscience. Bishop Berggrav in *Staten og mennesket* has profoundly explored the relation between ideology and camouflage and shown stirringly in what a subtle way ideology becomes camouflage, not only for the outside world but for the demonic forces in ourselves. Both to find security within and to escape the jagged edges of questioning conscience, we lose ourselves ever more passionately in the service of this partial truth and good. This ideology becomes our master, and explains how we can then act as we do with seemingly good conscience. We act, after all, not for ourselves, but for our master!

Similarly, when faith insists on absolute form in history, along with absolute content, this very faith becomes the effective and destructive ideology which constitutes our camouflage. No objective authority in history should become absolute in form. It is a matter of real importance to understand clearly the fact that God's Agape comes to us absolute *in content only,* not in historic expression nor in perfect personal form.

Yet the other side of the picture is equally important. To be inwardly compelling, authority must be definite. Faith cannot be strong while it wavers as to content. We rightly need definiteness of *content.* The abuse of this truth does not deny, but confirms its importance. Nothing hampers motivation more than confusion. Even though the form of full faith is relative, the content must be absolute. Relativity belongs not to the heart of faith, but only to the understanding and the expression of it. Religious faith always concerns our response to the absolute, the ultimate, "the unconditioned." Therefore religious authority must be definite as well as flexible; it must be *flexibly full.* When this note is lost, religion has lost its power because such religion is no longer authentic. People seem to be able to endure more than they dare to imagine, and for good causes, provided that they are sure that they are ultimately right. The thousands upon thousands of martyrs throughout the ages attest this truth. The cause itself cannot, therefore, be relative at heart. The cause cannot be indefinite or merely probable.

Agape is fully definite without being specific. It combines theoretical objectivity with existential openness. Its content is fixed, while its form is fluid. It describes general attitudes and relationships without strait-jacketing them. It requires completely good wills. But these wills, these dispositions, these attitudes, these intentions cannot be wholly good unless they also genuinely intend, and realistically set out to effect, right relations in the objective world. Inner attitude and outer consequence thus are joined organically. The I-thou relationshhip is obviously central to the

Christian faith. Yet in a world where there is complete involvement of life with life and of lives with nature, goodness itself is required from within its own nature to assume responsibility for right relations in the "it" world, as, for example, with regard to property. The personal order is primary, in God's plan, over the natural order. Definiteness in goodness is, therefore, definiteness in the primary category of human existence.

With regard to its application to the realm of external relations in history and in nature, however, there is need for flexibility. Agape answers both needs. There is enough definiteness in Agape to be completely compelling, by its intrinsic worth, by its fullest potential meeting of our basic needs, by its ultimacy as a category of inclusive explanation, but, at the same time, not so definite in detailed application as to preclude moral seriousness of choice and real freedom for creative adventure. Agape as absolute authority is thus at the same time a flexible aspect of fellowship and also a definite kind of inner relationship that gives steadiness and lift to choice by its being in source, standard and dynamic *more* than society. Agape, again, is flexibly full.

Dynamics is also all-important. Authority cannot be severed, except artificially, from motivation. The two belong organically together. If authority fails to move, either it is not authority, or it is prevented from moving by not being presented at a relevant level of thought and life. When the authority is absolute, it is all-inclusive and must, therefore, touch every individual and group at its most vital point of contact, if that point is actually reached. As Hocking rightly maintains: truth that does not work is not truth. Truth is a relation of appearance to reality. Whitehead calls it the conformation of appearance to reality. Where freedom obtains, truth is at least the *confrontation* of actuality with reality in meaningful terms. The eternally real relation, can, of course, be rejected for the temporarily unreal, which is the false choice by freedom of an evil actuality.

How, then, does Agape as absolute authority provide any commensurate motivation? It does so only by being allowed to work according to its own nature. God is the source of all Agape and therefore no motivation can be Agapaic that is not the working of

God in the world. The reality of Agape as motivation is the reality of God's life in ours. Jesus himself said that he in himself could do nothing. No one, surely, can be the original source of, or isolated possessor of, Agape. Only as we become its conductors into the world can Agape come with power. The divine motivation comes only through human weakness which becomes God's strength for the world. Only a certain kind of human weakness, of course, will do; the weakness of trust and humility where we become the bearer of power instead of its originators. This weakness is as rare as it is powerful. But when Jesus or Francis or Gandhi finds it, he displays unexplainable strength through it. The reason that we have so little motivation is that we refuse the authority which can really move us, trusting instead in our own wisdom or efforts. Or else we falsify the authority of human weakness before God into some kind of quietistic acquiescence, which is actually the withdrawing from responsibility for ourselves in relation to our problems. Sometimes we even try to force God through acquiescence! Agapaic motivation is the determined acceptance of the full truth and the full right for the world within the accepted weakness of our own efforts and within the accepted strength of God's purpose and power.

The Agapaic motivation is always a social reality that comes only through fellowship, first of all through fellowship with God and then with men. The Agapaic power, therefore, comes mostly through prayer. Laubach is surely right that prayer is the strongest force in the world. Prayer force is the inner core of ultimate reality, our relation with God in the eternal dimension. Men like Paul and Wesley moved the masses by the creative power of their insights, inspired by the Spirit, and by a personal presence which also sprang out of their prayer life. On the human level, as well, our fellowship must be genuinely Agapaic, centered in God's will for us all, and not in personal purposes and ambitions. Unfortunately the latter get easily mixed in with our prayer life, and by a subtle rationalization they then become almost invisible to ourselves. As à Kempis says, we love ourselves in our work. When our fellowship with God and men is genuine, however, and we become ever more widely opening channels for God's creative grace, then we receive new visions of insight, new affections for the common good, and the inner power to will them accompanied by the outer effectiveness to move others toward goals of common good.

Geraint Vaughan Jones claims that "power itself is a demonic force, and its potency for evil can only be removed when it is controlled by a community which has learned to derive its sovereignty from the Word of God, and when it is actuated by the living impulse of creative *agape*",[15] and that "the human order is bound to fail as long as it is separated from the divine order. . . . The Christian doctrine of man is the necessary precondition of human progress and of the rescue of politics from the grip of demonic forces."[16] Naturally we do not believe that power is itself demonic. All power is ultimately of God, as the New Testament claims, and no historic power is ever "of itself." Power is always in the service of some purpose, God's or man's, directly or indirectly. But power becomes demonic when it is perverted and misdirected by human purposes. We have in our possession a delegated degree of freedom. God's kind of power, Agape, does not destroy nor abuse this freedom.

His way with power, positively, is patient and constraining. Negatively, of course, it can come as a compelling and catastrophic invasion of our lives. God by our freedom is not limited to inaction. He controls and conditions this freedom both from within and from without. But He does not force faith. He does not compel love. He uses His power negatively only to invite us to look for fuller and better sources of security and satisfaction of His kind and way. In whatever manner God uses us, therefore, no power can be so positive, so great and so vital, in the long run, as when we let the Eternal Purpose flow through our historic wills to enlighten and to reconstruct the historic process.

The answer to motivation, therefore, is closeness to God. The authority of Agape is the authority of God and the motivation of Agape is the demonstration of the Spirit and of power. As far as

---

[15] *Op. cit.*, pp. 212-213. But compare Bishop Berggrav's definition of power: "Power is substitute. The real thing is authority. When there is immediate authority, it occurs to no one to use power. The standard of authority is: One word—and it happens. Only in case the authority is not grasped, does not take effect, does the *ultima ratio* become power." *Mennesket og staten*, p. 77.

[16] *Ibid.*, p. 213.

the ultimate relation of this power to process goes, most of this power of Agape is now being spent in pedagogical patience. It is letting itself be used humbly for individuation, for making real our freedom at this particular stage of man's history, within the large eternity of God's purpose. But as we are ready for the fuller, yet also freer, fellowship in Him, we can avail ourselves of this central power to recreate a disintegrating historic process and disillusioned lives.

Christianity is *more* than society not only with respect to freedom and to history, not only with respect to authority, whether individually or socially understood, and whether subjectively or objectively considered, but also with respect to the place for prophecy, whether of a spiritual, social or intellectual kind. Actual history is changed most significantly through the new moments of insight and of spiritual and moral appropriation which come from beyond itself. The genuinely historic new, in the sense that it is not a recurrence of previous patterns nor reducible to previous chains of causation, cannot be accounted for, obviously, from within society itself. It is the illumination of society. Thus, in so far as progress of any kind has genuine meaning, and signifies real newness beyond mere growth or improved arrangement of social patterns, this progress has its root in what is *more* than society. Inventors and mystics, geniuses and prophets have been discoverers of the hitherto unexplored realms which have been added to the domain of the historic. When once added, they are seen to belong organically to history, to the context of societal situations, but they were once beyond society and therefore are not dependent upon it in the way in which it is dependent upon them for the fuller meaning and means of its existence.

The fact seems to be that genius and prophecy have a most important place in human history. "It is through genius that the significant moments of history are born."[17] "The pioneer in morality is almost always the man who breaks with conventional conduct."[18]

The idea that religion advances by a process of gradual evolution does not seem true of the period of which we have historical knowl-

[17] Jones, *op. cit.,* p. 190.
[18] Dickie, *Revelation and Response*, p. 87.

edge. Advances can almost always be traced to the irruptive action of great personalities, for whom the field may indeed have been prepared by gradual process before their coming, but whose coming means a stormy crisis, whereby some portion of mankind is impelled along a new path in religion.[19]

Toynbee likewise concludes that the creative act comes always from some individual soul, that the action which is an act of creation is always performed by a soul which is in some sense a super-human genius; that the genius expresses himself, like every soul, through action upon his fellows; that in any society the creative personalities are in a minority.[20]

Man's history cannot be interpreted apart from creative newness. When that dries up, society decays. History must go forward, or eventually die as far as its present form of civilization goes. The creative newness which alone can make it go forward, in any authentic sense, comes into society through those who are open to what is *more* than society.

The fact is that man is mostly the recipient of the new. He is mainly its discoverer. The real source of creativity is God. With fine insight Whitehead named God "the principle of novelty." Creative novelty is a basic aspect of the life of God. God is the power for creativity and the lure for it. The new in history does not come from nowhere nor does it appear without a purpose for its coming. It does not come simply at man's beckoning. The new in history relates itself organically to what was there before, and, if it is positive in nature, it relates itself savingly to history because God is its source. In order to have intrinsically such capacity for organic connectedness with what went before, it must come from the same source. It already was related beyond history before it appeared in history to join that which also had come previously from beyond history. God is the source of both sameness and novelty and through Him both belong to each other.

New evil, which usually accompany creativity, are temporary negations of God's purpose. They are concomitant expression of maturation of responsible freedom. The reality of freedom and the full conditions needed to surround that reality in order to make

---

[19] Bevan, *Symbolism and Belief*, p. 55.
[20] *The Study of History*, Vol. VI, p. 175.

freedom vital are the reasons for the coming to be in history of such evil. Such evil, however, is only of a temporary character. It is adjectival and not substantive. Neither may the good, of course, stay in the same form in which it comes. But in so far as the new is of the essence of the Eternal Purpose, it will find both its patient preparation and eventual fulfillment in historic process in the fullness of time. The fullness of time is everywhere God's and man's patient preparation to elicit an individual or a small group who will accept, and be prepared to accept, the pregnant truth for that particular occasion, which at the same time embodies within it true universality for all occasions.

No fullness of time is ever consummated except as a creative new enters history at a particular time. God creates now and man participates in that creation. Something genuinely new, that is, is authentically born into history. Yet this which is *more* than society can be explained at least only in terms of its ultimate purpose and cause, which is God. The creative Agape of God, as Barth points out to us, loves what is *not* more than what is.[21] The measure of what is real and practicable for history is never past experience or systematically interpreted history up to any point of it, for God is the principle of novelty and the adequate ground for the better new. Agape has seldom become a real force in history because it has been obscured and circumscribed by our understanding of what can be done. Faith in God as Agape is the most realistic approach to history, in Him who can make all things new, but who awaits the dedication of our freedom to Him in faith. We might say that God is more interested in that which is in terms of that which it can become than in terms of what it now actually is.

Thus the message of living faith is a new heaven *and* a new earth. Many discussions of our actual human situation go astray because slowly and subtly any perspective that is *more* than society is lowered into the perspective of what now is actually our history. Only in line with some such background as that of our total investigation of this series and the purposeful opening stress of this volume can we have the light and can we find the power to explain and to change history in line with God's purpose for it and with us all.

21 Cf. *Kirchliche Dogmatik, Dritter Teil, Erster Band*, p. 103 ff.

Christianity as *more* than human society is also the dimension of completion for society. Our earthly history never solves our problems, for society is composed of individuals who die. Even if the world order could be drastically improved, most of its members would still not remain to share in it. To think of societal solutions in terms of historic process is, therefore, to indulge in collective illusions, to which we are very prone anyway. The Eternal Purpose makes use of the historic process, but only for a short stage. Both as meaning and as means, this earthly history is unbelievably limited in comparison with the largeness of the Eternal Purpose beyond any adequate comprehension. We can see only the least bit of the plot. Before our human life and beyond death lie periods of preparation and of completion. It certainly is true that we live "between the times."

Our *whole* history, however, both generationally and transgenerationally, is between the times. Our historic process finds new orientation, impetus and opportunity in the illimitable ages and conditions beyond this human stage. Here on earth we hardly begin to catch even the slightest meaning of the divine story. If we should try to explain meanings from within our earthly perspectives and from within our societal dimensions, we should be honest enough to admit basic frustration. It is a pitiful human weakness to try to seek adequate meaning and comfort within such inadequate limits and by means of such unsatisfying and often horrifying facts. Our very trying, however, is a witness to our nobler origin and to our more complete destiny. When we then see the nature of the Eternal Purpose and how that is even fragmentarily revealed and realized within this earthly life of ours, we grasp with fascination the truth that history is important mostly with relation to the level of completion which is beyond society and which is *more* than society.

Life beyond the grave is a prerequisite for any adequate social theory. Eternally we are made for the Eternal Purpose. In that perspective there is no option. Our only option is to delay our own true good and to keep the true good from others. Our creaturehood is from God who has made us for Himself. Historic importance is thus genuinely found within the Eternal Purpose, and only there. We can find our true selves and societal solutions only to whatever extent we realize that the whole historic process is made for the effecting, *by means of history,* the Eternal Purpose. The perspective of completion is not, nevertheless, the perspective of cessation from historic activity. Eternity consists of Purpose and of personal relations and, therefore, it is by nature akin to our historic activities. What is meant, rather, is that the kinds of evil and problems which characterize our human history here on earth, as a stage in our growth and decisions, will be solved mostly not in our earthly history, but beyond it, in God's place, condition and time. The Eternal Purpose is available to us right now. He works in the midst of our historic process; yet is He also mostly beyond it. *He works in it to complete it.*

Our lives, consequently, have need of both the vertical and the horizontal aspects of His presence in terms of both understanding and power. We need to know the presence of the Purpose now, but also to see that it has as yet been realized only in a very small part. We therefore have to work in its presence and power to realize it now, in our future history on earth, and in the worlds to come. "And so the endless striving *towards* God is internally cut across by the condition of endless striving *in the presence of* God."[22] Thus are combined, in the depths of satisfaction and creative longing, eternal meaning and historic action.

[22] Przywara, *Polarity,* p. 54.

CHAPTER II

Christianity Is *True* Society

Society as it now is, is obviously not the way it ought to be. Consequently the standard and power by which it could and should be changed need to be *more* than society. Yet this *more* than society, in order to be completely relevant and rescuing, should also contain within itself that which is *true* society. The Eternal Purpose should constitute the standard and power for *pure* process. If the Eternal Purpose is of such a nature as centrally to effect fellowship, it can accordingly be known within process only in so far as it constitutes, in vision and truth, *true* society.

Christianity must, therefore, be not only *more* than society to qualify as the content of the Eternal Purpose. It must at the same time give evidence of being *true* society as an adequate ideal, not only beyond society, judging it, but within society, guiding and empowering it. *True* society must be the reality within process which can be realized (realizability), which has been realized in part (realization), and which constitutes the criterion as to whether society is getting better or worse. Christianity, then, is under obligation not only to answer the questions of origins and the questions of fulfillment beyond our historic span, but also to reply to the problems raised by our concrete situation within this earthly history. *While it is basically more than society it must at the same time also be true society.* We must avoid as inadequate either naturalism or supernaturalism if taken apart from each other and as direct opposites. We must accept both as true only when taken rightly together.

This brings up a basic problem of their relationship. If the

Christian kind of community is conceived of as the supernaturally premade pattern for history, is not history, then, merely the unrolling of eternity? Though it may be more than the shadow of eternity in substance, is it actually so in activity? Is not the historic process in some way prefabricated by the Eternal Purpose? Is this, perchance, a sense in which we may say that the Kingdom of God cannot be built by man, but must be brought to it by God? Is history, after all, mostly actualized from some pre-existent Reality rather than realized by a free and adventurous creation? If this is so, have we not introduced the problem of pre-existence in a most acute form? Is the ideal fellowship for man subsistent from all eternity in heaven? In that case, why have we any false history? If there is an Eternal Purpose envisaging and actualizing the true community, in what sense is man truly free? Is not determinism the implied position of this kind of philosophy? If Christianity is basically *more* than society, how can *true* society possess responsible and creative freedom that is genuine and not merely apparent? To say that Christianity is *more* than society is one thing; to say, beyond this, that it is also intrinsically *true* society is quite another matter. Considering any concrete society that we have known or know, how can such a double claim be made plausibly for Christianity?

Before we go on, therefore, to describe and to discuss in what sense Christianity, as Agape fellowship, constitutes *pure* process and *true* society, we ought to take a close look at this problem of the relation of the more than society to *true* society. The whole question of ultimate reality is, of course, inevitably involved. Consider, then, that the essence of deity is always to have possibility exceed actuality. Formally speaking, infinity means the boundless capacity for finitude. No finite series of orders can ever exhaust infinity. But formal inexhaustibility in no way prevents limitation of content within infinity, because the infinite is no theoretical allness. Infinity (or deity) is defined by Agape. God as Agape is the nature of eternal self-being, the author of all creation, the sustainer of all finite processes, the final principle of explanation, the full personal pattern for judging, guiding and fulfilling history, both by the cleansing and redirecting of man's freedom and by the God-given growth of creation. Thus infinity is defined both by boundlessness and by its own content. The boundlessness of the infinite is the boundlessness of its nature and activity, of its own being, becoming and doing according to its own nature. It is, however, God as Agape who is infinite and who structuralizes all created content. The Eternal Purpose is the Kingdom of God which superarches all histories and all civilizations within history.

But not without man's real use of his freedom. Man's free choice, according to his measure, constitutes the reason for, and the meaning of, history. Since in deity possibility always exceeds actuality, man's freedom can be real without necessary disorder, while there can also be a total purpose without determinism. There never needs to be a merely prefabricated or predetermined history in any *concrete* sense. The Eternal Purpose is general enough to include man's creative freedom. History is not *actualized,* but *realized.* While man does not add new possibilities to God by his creative activity, he none the less affords God by his creative choices the opportunity to bring to bear on any genuinely creative human situation a new relationship, a new set of possibilities for that particular occasion. In this way history is both grounded in Eternal being and vision and also open to genuine historic risk and consequences, both for good and for evil. History is fully fixed to eternity, yet, at the same time, fruitfully free from specific directions. The reality of the eschatological dimension in no way belittles, but rather strengthens, the existential aspect of the ethical situation.

The heavenly city, therefore, is never a finished model for the earthly. No heavenly city, as a matter of fact, precedes any earthly city either *chronologically* or *logically.* The earthly city is an authentically new creation. Something genuinely new and eternally important takes place when a creative choice is made. Not only the universe, but all reality and all times are actually changed when a vibrant spirit beholds a new relationship of beauty, of freedom, of fellowship. All eternity is that far changed on earth, for eternity organically includes all positive temporal realms and all true histories. This life is consequently no mere recollection, and no ideal reconstruction of lost glory. Beethoven's Eighth Symphony, for instance, was never written in heaven. God did not write it before Beethoven lived. God wrote it along with Beethoven, and Beethoven wrote it along with God. In such works heaven and earth meet in joyous creation. In creative activity joy and beauty sanctify hard labor, even as the divine-human fellowship brings forth out of the womb of indefinite possibility the child of concrete wonder. What kind of ultimate reality, however, does this view of the relation between what is *more* than society and *true* society presuppose? Was God ever, and is He ever, and will He ever be a community of creative abundance? Has He always worked before He created this world and this history, and what can that possibly mean to us creatures of time? Is God's very nature to create, to have His goodness overflow, a living in His own excess? Is God sufficiently pleased with having man as His only advanced creature, a sharer of His own creative zest? Or is God always the artist, wrestling creatively with infinitely possible worlds, finding His life in producing them and in sharing with His productions their good and evil, their satisfactions and frustrations?

Perhaps we have an inkling from the deepest image in us that since possibilities always exceed actualities, there will never be any static finality, nor any rest from all creation, nor any complete fitting of all creative patterns to all actual worlds. The elimination of evil in any world that is ever to come, or is ever possible, is not the end of creative zest, nor the complete removal of the veil of individuality whereby lack of knowledge and skill gives us incentive ever to enrich our lives and to be of use. Perhaps perfect coherence is never a possibility among possibilities because that would involve the elimination of finite choice as creative participants in actual processes. If all finite choosers became so yielded to the infinite will and wisdom that they simply transmitted that will and wisdom, would they then be truly individuated? Would they not rather be mere puppets of the absolute?

How, then, before we go on to societal analysis, can we answer the question as to the relation between what is *more* than society to what is *true* society, without attempting to conceive the inconceivable? We have to combine God's responsible freedom of infinite possibilities governed by His central purpose, with our own responsible freedom, which makes a meaningful difference both within history and within the inclusive content of eternity.

Our best present view may be suggested by the following analysis. God as Agape is always creating. Each new creation adds to the richness whereby Infinity translates possibilities into actualities. This Process, beyond and through all concrete processes, is inexhaustible. Infinity is qualitatively of a different order from all finitudes. Different finite series are, of course, differently related to Infinity, and in this sense there are different contents within Infinity. There is, therefore, qualitative likeness *among* contents within Infinity, but between all finite processes and Infinity itself there is fixed an unbridgeable gulf. The Infinite can relate Himself differently to finitudes and can thus appear to any finite process as a new kind of relation (hence becoming), and actually be new as a *relation,* because the Infinite includes all relations not even only positively, but as the ground of all possibility for being and becoming. Infinite Agape expresses Himself by the free limiting of the power of His own being and by the participating in creative and redemptive activity within the several orders of imperfection. The beginning of any creation can never be a legitimate question because such a question is itself based on a false conceiving of the infinite in finite terms. Each new creation adds nothing eternally new to the ground of being; only to the mode of being; and these modes are infinitely open to newness.

In this sense, we repeat, no creation is ever new in its ground of being; only in the modes of its being. We are new as actualizations of possibilities. Creation *a nihilo* is then not arbitrary nonsense, but the eternal work of Him who by His presence with all creation turns possibilities into actualities; even man shares in creation *a nihilo* in so far as any free choice creates a new mode of being, even within eternity, but adds nothing to the ground of being. All societies are then eternally choosing, forever being perfected, but never reaching the infinite perfection which is qualitatively distinct eternally from all finite societies, including all *pure* process or *true* society.

While there was never a time before time, there probably have been innumerable times before the time of our cosmic epoch. Time is the medium of fellowship, both as *kronos* (duration) and as *kairos* (filled time). Every time is created by God. For Him there is no abstract duration, but time as *kronos* depends entirely upon His *kairos.* Thus rest and creation have no self-being, but refer entirely to God, except as they are part of, or aspects of, created epochs, in which case they become joint media between God and men. In that case history becomes God's creative concern concretely; and what happens in history matters to God. Freedom becomes significant both to God and to man. In the Eternal Purpose for this freedom for fellowship what is *more* than society is thus organically joined with what is *true* society, and, as we shall see in the next chapter, with the way in which both affect actual society.

Creative choice, then, is part of eternal being which becomes creatively differentiated by means of historic process. God cannot grow or become in the sense of adding to the ground of being. In that case, something would come out of nothing in a false sense, something which is without any adequate principle of concretion and actualization. Growth is the nature of God's work rather than of God. No growth is ever absolutely from God and to God. All growth is from God, with creation, and remains ever within the sphere of the finite. God's creative joy is not self-enjoyment in an isolated sense, nor mere external manipulation of the finite, but is along with creation, crowning it. Edgar Brightman once suggested that the truest symbol for God's creative work, as far as this temporal problem of beginnings is concerned, is that God is always halfway through eternity. He is never farther from the beginning nor nearer the end. Inexhaustible being is not easy for us to grasp, but we can conceive the idea that no matter how much is done there can be no end to the doing, and still what is being done is infinitely meaningful with respect to the Infinitely Good. Paul Minear, in order to sharpen the sense of importance, likes to say that God's work is always two minutes to twelve.

Both figures are needed in the sense that God's eternity includes inexhaustible opportunity with absolute importance. Creation may have no one necessary goal ever,[1] according to our analysis, but

---

[1] We must always distinguish between the singleness of the Eternal Purpose and the richness of its concrete content in historic activity. Thus Kierkegaard's assumption that plurality of choice is inconsistent with eternal seriousness is true in the one respect of the singleness of the Purpose, but not in the matter of the plurality of choices ever expressive of that Purpose. Cf. *The Gospel of Suffering*, p. 15. "There must be only one way to choose if the earnestness of eternity is to rest upon the choice. A choice, of which it is true that a man may just as well choose one as the other, does not have the eternal earnestness of the choice."

many goals, infinite goals offering to every creation eternal growth in freedom and fellowship within the vision, the service and the beatific enjoyment of God. In this sense the creative joy of God underlies our whole process, even while "the suffering which is but for a moment" cannot be compared with the perfection and the satisfactions of the results.

My concern at this point is to indicate that the ultimate relations of Agape to history, of Eternal Purpose to historic process, are not confined, on the one hand, to some prefabricated model in heaven which is actualized in time either by God's direct determination or, on the other hand, to man's trial and error within an open and basically neutral historic situation, but are, rather, a combination of sovereign direction and free, finite choices. In this way what is *more* than society adequately involves *true* society. This is the basic relation between superhistory and history. The main burden of the present chapter, however, is to see whether Agape is *pure* process or *true* society, and in what sense Agape can explain and include all else.

In conversation, Whitehead once defined God as "the unity within the universe which gives the sense of holiness and the sense of supreme guidance towards the best possible." Our hearts are restless, as Augustine maintained, until they find rest in God, for they are made for Him. Man needs to know that his social reality is rooted in the very depths of reality. He needs to find permanence of meaning, not only for himself as an isolated individual, but as a social being. Hinduism, for instance, finds that man himself is rooted in the absolute, that "thou art that." This is a vigorous insight which gives meaning to life.

The ideal society then, of course, would be part and parcel of the Eternal Purpose which gives meaning to the historic process. Then permanence of meaning would have been joined with the faith and urge to improve society in order that it might fit some eternal form appropriate to it. Apply this observation to Christianity, and Christian society, assuredly and *a fortiori,* becomes integrally conjoined with the judgment that "no human good of any kind is conformed to the relevant divine will, except as it is thus brought into connexion with that predominance of the God-consciousness in our soul which we owe to Christ."[2] Christianity has been continually restless because it has been not only, as Whitehead observed, a religion seeking a metaphysics, but also a religion seeking a social expression. While no society has been meaningless within the Christian vision, all societies have found a haunting restlessness for improvement within the vision and the power of the Kingdom of God. *True* society must be basically founded on the Eternal Purpose. *The fullest dimension for sociological inquiry is, therefore, the vertical.*

The most important relation of any society is the way in which it relates itself to truth. Whenever the Christian Church has been persecuted because of its insistence on putting first the Kingdom of God, even the worst persecution has left it stronger and tougher. Even the Communist cause, when it becomes infused with religious zeal, *the Cause,* is hard to fight with arms. Right or perverted—and generally it is a mixture of both—faith in the ultimate truth and rightness of a Cause is the root of its intransigence. What social theory needs today is to be founded not only on historic fact but also on Reality.

Perhaps one reason why *true* society needs basically the vertical dimension is that man tends easily to divisive pride. Reinhold Niebuhr has made almost a life emphasis of the fact that practically every social form of life founders on the fact of its refusing to admit sinful pride. Original and endemic sin is suppressed into the unconscious, covered up by a defensive-aggressive self-righteousness, a Pharisaic perfectionism which confuses and confounds social intercourse. Calvin goes back to Chrysostom's assertion that humility is "the foundation of philosophy." He then cites Augustine to the effect that humility is the first, the second, and the third rule of the Christian religion. The Christian faith in God as Agape, beyond all finite processes, makes human distinctions puny and unimportant, without destroying the eternal significance of history. The truth of "our common humanity," as Kierkegaard puts it in *The Gospel of Suffering,* at the same time levels all earthly distinctions that falsely separate by specious superiority while also binding all men together under God by the fact that the highest good possible to man, namely that of being man, is

[2] Schleiermacher, *The Christian Faith,* p. 730.

equally open to all comers. It is a good thing that "God is no respecter of persons," even while the hairs of our head are all numbered. Here is a humility which comes not from the recognition of our common vanity, but from the vision of the great Reality and Community to which we are all called, and of which we are all falling short.

Another main reason why social process needs to be rooted in the Eternal Purpose is the fact that man has a superhistoric sense of responsibility and guilt. Man transcends the temporal realm and seeks his peace within the eternal. The great prophets and seers who have given new vision and impetus to human history have often been lonely and forsaken within society, and have usually been persecuted, if not killed, by it. The truth which they saw was greater than a matter of social approval or of social judgment.

Man feels responsible, but is not clearly certain to whom, for what, and in what way. His responsibility is mixed in with his sense of the good that earth cannot give. He reaches on and out for more. What is life? What is this responsibility? What is this right?

Nor is this sense of responsibility an individual affair. David Swenson has said that "religion is a synthesis of cosmic gratitude and personal responsibility."[3] It is this and more; for personal responsibility includes, by the very nature of the cosmos and of man, social responsibility. Religion is a social affair. As Ritschl rightly declares, "All religions are social."[4] The blood of man's brother cries from the ground to heaven. Man's guilt before God when he comes to the altar usually concerns some other human being or group with whom he is not right before God. *True* society needs the vertical line to be the clearer if social relations are to become clearer and stronger in the right.

Christian fellowship naturally is founded in God. Only by the knowing and the serving Him does society find a universal basis for its ethics and that sharp sense of responsibility which marks a highly moral society. Christian fellowship consists of two concentric circles: one consists of those who in humble concern have seen and accepted the Agape fellowship and try by faith to make it real;

3 "On the Nature of Morality," an informal talk published privately by the Philosophical Department of the University of Minnesota, 1940.
4 *Justification and Reconciliation*, p. 27.

the other consists of those who are yet mostly bound to God, at least consciously, by creation and by general human needs. The first group by its humility and concern is closer to realizing the *true* society, to letting the Eternal Purpose effect *pure* process. But the very fact of their being so also draws them closer to all men, however little most men have themselves seen the more gladsome life or choose to believe that it can be real. Thus *true* society, in all stages of its becoming, is united by the Eternal Purpose, by what is *more* than society. *True* society has as its prerequisite the primacy of the vertical dimension, of the eternal God.

But the vertical dimension, which must ever be primary to *true* society, is not only a matter of permanence of meaning, or of cure for pride, or yet even of responsibility. A more basic need for society as well as for individuals is the need for a true and lifting faith. Man needs not only faith as authority and motivation, generally, as we have seen in the last chapter, but *faith in God for society.* Or society itself needs the faith that its meaning and being as society are part of God's eternal purpose and plan. Social living gets hard and the individual grows utterly weary of its evils—the stubbornness, blindness, foolishness and futility of most of its doings. Because of these, there is in society much "don't care-ism"; but, perhaps, even more "can't do-ism." People become defeatist, disillusioned and discouraged. Why should individuals, after all, inflict on themselves the frustrations of social responsibility and effort? Is not individual rightness before God enough? Perhaps God made society so frustrating in order that man's frustrations might lead him to Himself and to flee the external situation as such; which cannot save eternally anyway. What is the use of all social striving? Does not society remain basically as it is, and as it always was?

So men lose heart, and after the heart is lost, the head soon follows. In this way the nerve center of social endeavor is injured; the will to the good society is broken; the faith in God's purpose for society, which underlies the whole cause, is severely shaken. Only when they understand that God as Agape is the completely capable and trustworthy author of all creation and life who intends precisely to effect fellowship, do they see that the very meaning of history is *true* society.

To live and to work for *true* society on earth and beyond earth, in God's power and patience, becomes now our highest satisfaction in life. We suffer from no evasive optimism; we suffer from no corrosive pessimism; we countenance no escape into a merely personal Gospel. Faith, joy and gratitude become the incentives of our action. Our lives are turned toward God and tuned to His wave length of approval or disapproval. This vertical primacy is needed if *true* society, the Agape community, is to be vitally attempted by us.

From faith come hope and love. Human hope is a rare power when it is high enough and holy enough. Much hope is for personal or social power. Much hope is for personal or social success. Much hope is for personal or social having. All such hope has effect on human life. Hope is a good power often made evil by a bad content. The bad content sears the spirit from within, and from without comes either disappointment or dissatisfaction, except as man hopes on and finds a transcendent quality to life amidst its finite fleetingness. But hope that is based on faith in God's love for all transcends all human objectives and is ever fresh in power, success and having. For its power is of God, its success is of God, and its having is of God.

When hope holds that nothing can permanently stay God's effecting of society, its power is unconquerable. It knows that *true* society is of the essence of creation. It knows that *true* society is the object of God's redemptive purposes. True hope for society must result from man's learning the deeper hope through the fuller faith which depends upon the unfailing love.

Society, to become true, therefore, needs love. We often speak of individuals as needing love. We commonly speak of love as applying, at most, to limited group relations like the family. But love is the great need and great reality also for nations and for society as a whole, for love is society's basic relation to reality. Since God is basically Agape, He is the basic reality underlying society, and, therefore, society has a basic need of Him if it is to become its true self.

Society, most of all, therefore, needs to feel the love of God for itself *as society*. But few have the sense of the great love of God for mankind. Few feel the warmth of His love for each nation, for America and for Russia, for Palestine and for Switzerland. God is more real to us, particularly with regard to secular group life, on the level of justice and fear than on the level of love. Thus we tend to think of God as demanding justice from the nations, and not love. We tend to think that justice is the highest norm of togetherness within the nations as well as among the nations. But actually nothing is more close and real than the love of God for society, whether secular or sacred. This must be the basic message and the basic sense of the Christian, for this is the basic relation which *God actually sustains to society*.

The vertical dimension and its revolutionary influence on the horizontal plane is the main concern of this chapter to which we now turn. Without seeing *pure* process in the light of Permanent Purpose or *true* society in the light of the Eternal Fellowship, *pure* process or *true* society cannot be seen rightly at all. This involves basically the whole relation of Agape to Eros and to Philia as well as to other basic perspectives. Since too much writing is done without precise definitions, particularly in these realms of thought, I shall first try to define these kinds of love and then see what place they all have in the divine economy of things, particularly as they refer to true society on the horizontal plane.

Before we go on to see how Agape fulfills man's needs for community on the horizontal level, we had better define Agape in relation to Eros and Philia. Both of these terms refer to some actuality within God's created universe and can, therefore, never be in complete contradiction to the ultimate. At most they can be demonic, perverted goodness; they cannot be Satanic, totally evil. Only one Reality can be infinite in nature. Somehow, therefore, there must be a valid relationship of subsumption, in the light of which the false use of the created reality can be understood.

By Agape we mean outgoing concern, creatively and redemptively. Although Agape is God's love which was first conclusively taught by Jesus and illustrated by his life, Agape can be structurally described and identified by the kind of love which it is. Even though the livers of Agape may not be conscious of the structure of their lives, Agape always unites intrinsically attitude and action. In the great parable of Matthew 25, the people on the right hand of God finally were placed there because their attitude was so spontaneous, so deep-grained and so humble that they were not even conscious of having done any good which God could particularly commend and accept. As Alan Wehrli puts it: "Heavenly treasures catch up with us from behind." They cannot be aimed at. If they are, there is a split between attitude and action.

Agape is the basic structure of God's being and purpose. Agape is, accordingly, not eternal activism. Fellowship is a deeper category than doing. The fellowship itself is a fuller reality than the media by means of which it is made or expresses itself. Persons, as the primary realities, are the centers of attitude and action: in particular, persons who potentially or actually have Agape as their main attitudinal structure. We may think of it in the following way. The basic ultimate reality is Spirit. The form of that ultimate Spirit is personal. The content of that Spirit, its purpose and kind of character, is Agape. In the meantime, however, it is well to keep clearly in mind the fact that Agape is not centered in process as process, but in Reality. This self-sufficient Reality includes organically all the promptings, possibilities and actualities of process, but goes itself beyond process.

On God's level, Agape includes fully both creation and redemption. I feel that Bishop Nygren identifies Agape far too much with the level of redemption and not enough with the level of creation. He claims that Thomas Aquinas, for instance, has taken over the Greek creative love at the expense of the forgiving love, the personal love of God in Christ. Yet we must stress just as strongly God as Agape on the level of creation. The whole problem of the origin of evil and the full perspective on sin have been left out of Nygren's theology, as far as any real solution is concerned, because of his not having wrestled with the problems of creation in the perspective of an omnipotent God, a God of Agape who is the final source of all possibilities and creativities. God, the omnipotent Agape, has created precisely this kind of world, and the world, especially human community, must be squarely understood in the light of this central fact.[5]

[5] Cf. also D'Arcy, *The Mind and Heart of Love*, p. 71: "The point made here is that grace does not destroy all that is human; it perfects it and elevates it to a new dynamic, and the real problem is to work out how both nature and the super-

What we need is the Reality which is fully both creator and redeemer *precisely as Agape* and can, therefore, constitute the full meaning for our explaining, as well as our being judged and saved. This means bluntly that both Eros and Philia must be defined in relation both to the God who creates and to the God who redeems. It is inadequate simply to say that Eros and Philia fall short of Agape and are therefore not Christian. Agape means not selflessness, but self-fulness. Since Agape is the basic content of the creative ground and the purpose for every created self, no person can find his right and soul-satisfying form until he is shaped by the Spirit into his destined Agape nature. It is not a giving of self which is based on any negative ground, nor based on any masochistic psychology, nor yet again upon any indeterminate world where giving as such is good but finds no reward either on earth or in heaven. Agape is the accepting of the self in the total perspective and purpose of God, where to live is to lose one's life in the service of the fellowship, in order that God may effect the fellowship in which there is fullness of life both for the one who gives and for the one for whom it is given. Agape is the losing of the isolated self for the finding, eventually, of the God-embraced and socially accepted self within the *true* society for which we are made.

False approaches to Agape come in, which are so dangerous that they must be pointed to even in trying to define it. The new creature in Christ truly lives. Being a branch in the Vine, he does not wither up and die, but lives. No Christian is absorbed by God; that is defeatism, escapism, an only partially satisfying approach to the self, because it represents only part of the truth. Every Christian is found by God and made whole by Him. He finds not union, but communion.

Even as a white corpuscle he lives for society and may have to die for it physically; but such death is liberation from the body for the sake of finding God's fuller life. It is not a severance from the Body which gives life; only from the body which is always connected with dying. Selflessness is thus the false philosophy of Agape, on the one hand, even as an aggressive trying to gain the

---

natural life survive in their integrity in the Christian order." D'Arcy's criticism of Nygren's neglect of the order of creation, though not fully cognizant of Nygren's purpose of *diastase,* explicitly set forth, is yet often very much to the point.

fellowship is on the other. Some still try to take it by force. Agape is a gift, a rest, a relation to God in fellowship. It is not basically activism or a cause by means of which the self can be subdued or escaped. If Agape is to constitute the content of *true* society it cannot be either activism or self-negation. It must, rather, be based on God's eternal self-being, the Spirit, and as such, even on the horizontal level, it has a certain self-sufficiency of being. In Agape both the self and the community are found at their highest and truest in the full fellowship love for which God has created us and which He works to effect through history.[6] In this sense Agape alone constitutes the permanent basis of *pure* process or *true* society.

Whereas Agape is outgoing concern, creatively and redemptively, Eros, in its proper function, is *intaking concern, creatively and redemptively.* In its right function Eros must be good, since it is created by God. There may be Eros even in God. How else could it be created? Sin is the faithlessness and the rebellion of finite freedom against God. God cannot sin and has no need to have created it, only the possibility and the condition for its being. But Eros is, properly speaking, concern directed toward the self, *receptive concern.* Sin, however, is the perversion of Eros by finite freedom. Eros is necessary for all finite creatures, and that which God has made necessary by creation is not in itself evil or sin. Living is a matter of steady intake and outgo on every level of life. For that matter, the self cannot escape being psychologically central. No fellowship experiences the self from within; only the self does that. Perhaps even God does not know the self precisely as He knows Himself. Can it be that God has made us so real, and creation so genuine, that there are private areas where no public knowledge intrudes? The finite self, in any case, must need; and needing, it must seek. Self-seeking as such, therefore, is not wrong. All depends upon what and how the self seeks, and why he seeks, what, and how.

Intaking concern can be dedicated to man's highest co-operation with God and to his fullest redemptive living. The self can seek, under God and in the context of the full fellowship, to be his best

6 For a beautiful passage to this effect, cf. Demant, *Theology of Society,* p. 79.

self according to God's will and His purpose for the fellowship.[7] Then the seeking is still Eros, but its content is Agape. Then Eros and Agape meet in the full mutuality of fellowship. Perhaps Eros is God's guarantee of fellowship. Perhaps He has given us Eros in order to prevent absolute absorption, to make us real and free. "In the elimination of Eros man has been eliminated."[8] Eros, man's striving and seeking, is, at least, a beautiful and an indispensable part of God's creation. Properly understood and accepted, Eros is God's gracious gift to be appreciated and acted upon in terms of the fuller context of Agape.

The false use of Eros is practically the same as the abuse of Agape. In the false use of Agape, or pseudo-Agape, there is either selflessness or a forcing of fellowship. The false use of Eros may be the obvious putting oneself at the center of things in a rather natural, open way. Or Eros can be abused by not being accepted as a gift from God. The self then refuses to take responsibility for himself, remains immature and lacks the proper seriousness about his own life.

But the most common abuse of Eros, perhaps, is identifying oneself with a limited group or cause and then being selfish about that in terms of the interests of that "closed society." Thus many people will even die for their country, or work their fingers to the bone for some cause, all the while being selfish about it.

Eros exhibits itself when a fierce resistance is made to God's claim to have no ultimate loyalty except His will for the good of all. A common abuse of Eros is the identification of the self with some limited loyalty, family, friends, club or country, perhaps denomination, considering itself the catholic church or the "true" church of God. Eros is an instrument of individuation and group development, but is wrongly used when it arrests the development of the fuller loyalties and becomes a limited fixation.

---

[7] D'Arcy, op. cit., pp. 91, 92. "To neglect the universe and cultivate his own garden would be the gravest of sins for a being who lives in that universe. But really it is not the universe but God to whom man owes everything in whose order he has his place and work. Everything he has and is belongs to God, and therefore he must love God more than himself and love himself truly only as belonging to God. . . . We feel the coin of ourselves before we recognize that it belongs to the mint of God."

[8] Ibid., p. 71.

The third kind of love, Philia, is *mutual concern based on equality*. Philia is covenant love. It is conditional love depending upon what the other contracting partner does. It is not unconditional, like Agape. It is neither simply outgoing nor intaking love. It expects both to get and to give, both to give and to get. It is the kind of self-love and other-love which fulfills the law and the prophets, but which cannot constitute the heart of the Gospel. Philia is an attempt to balance Agape and Eros. It starts with the self and with others on the basis of justice, of equality. Nomos, law, or right relation, underlies it. "You like me and treat me right and I will do the same for you." Outgoing and intaking concern become balanced in Philia. There is no superior and no inferior, no senior and no junior partner. The relation is basically democratic. It contains no pedagogical relations and no paternalisms. Philia is extremely congenial to the natural man and to much of our present political, social and cultural background.

There is a real place for Philia in the divine economy. On the horizontal level, man's fellowship with his fellow man is genuine. When man truly meets man, the Other, as Hocking calls God, is humble enough not to intrude directly. There is a private meeting ground for man himself with other real men.

God has depersonalized certain areas of His will; out of His infinite possibilities He has called forth something which is not directly His own conscious self. He appears there not as mind and heart, but more as body. Shall we say that He becomes the impersonal means and media of fellowship through nature, in order that man may be free to make his own serious choices and to have his fellowship among his own kind without the direct relation of God, as far as that kind of fellowship goes? If God were always *a conscious* third of whom we ought to be conscious, there would never be any free human fellowship for itself. An important level of life would be missing in the universe. If whenever we meet other people we have to pray directly, or whenever we are visiting intimately with other people we have to appeal directly and consciously to God, continuously by means of a kind of co-consciousness, we are still in a pedagogical stage of the Spirit. People need to be and should be liked for themselves. They are real, as selves, and not even God comes in between selves in such fellowship.

Philia as a horizontal fellowship, based on mutuality of concern, has thus real importance. It guarantees the reality of selves and the actuality of creation. One reason, I feel, that Nygren does not go into Philia in his lengthy discussions in his great work, *Agape and Eros,* is that he has never done justice to the level of creation. Philia, however, should always be organically related to Agape and Eros in any full discussion of them. Eros as the principle of individuation is the opportunity for this kind of horizontal fellowship on the human level; Agape has bestowed this freedom on man purposefully that his fellowship might be real. Thus Agape, Eros and Philia set the stage for God's long and careful effecting of the fellowship, for all the wonders and complexities of the perspective of process, which must not be underestimated if God's work is to be rightly honored.

Man cannot live in any easy and natural Philia relationship with his fellow men, simply because he is a sinner and cannot raise himself by himself into a free and easy mutuality of concern. Man must be born again. From that creative minority of the reborn comes the best strength for co-operative living. Surely non-Christian civilizations have developed real degrees of creative and constructive community. That must be frankly and willingly acknowledged. But the full and free fellowship that Philia *can be* depends upon something beyond the natural man, who openly or covertly tends to seek, most of the time, his own well-being first of all. Philia cannot, in any case, constitute the *basis* of *true* society. The finite Eros must be governed and possessed by the infinite Agape in order for Philia to become full and free.

Philia is thus basically dependent upon Agape and is legitimate only as man's fellowship with man, his *horizontal* fellowship, when this presupposes and acknowledges Agape, in so far as this is known by man. Man's relation to God is ideally Eros in form and Agape in content. No human being is totally without God nor is he totally, therefore, lacking in outgoing concern. And this concern is not merely God's reflex action in him. It is his deepest nature. No man can be totally bad and live. Every man shares some of God's outgoing concern, the very content of His nature. Total evil is impossible for any creature. Man is a perverted, partially depraved creature; or to put the case in a truer perspective, man is an immature child, dominantly selfish, while at the same time, deep down in his being, refusing to be such and longing for his true, full fellowship self for which he was made. To say that man can have no Agape toward God is to deny the reality of creation and the reality of redemption. By the reality of the former, man is made in God's image, which can only be Agape, however much this image be covered up and rendered ineffective in much actual living; by the reality of the latter, man becomes at length a son in full fellowship with God, fully restored and matured in the family fellowship.

But one aspect of man's basic relation to God must ever be Eros, the intaking gratitude, obedience and love which belong to the finite. Man is a creature-son. He is both made and begotten. This Eros of his he cannot lose, even though he fill it with Agape. He is the receiver and not the original Reality and Source of Agape. All receive God's Agape through Eros as creature-sons, and become basically related to each other through Philia as creature-brothers.

Man can be understood most deeply only as the creature and child of God. Man is the glory of all creation, the sharer of God's own nature. Though of earth earthy, formed from the dust and long in the making, he is also God's child by the very inbreathing into him by God Himself, of His own Spirit. Man is both made and begotten. I have thought of the image of God, in times past, in terms of reason, of responsibility, of the gregarious drive to fellowship, of man's capacity to transcend time, of freedom to make his own deliberate choices and thus to determine his own destiny. But none of these reaches into the full image of God. God, the eternal, personal Spirit, is love, and no other essence can be ascribed to His image than love itself. Man is made by love, in love, for love. This image may be woefully immature, distorted, perverted, partially destroyed and lost, but in so far as man is man, his deepest being, in terms of need and meaning, is nothing but love. No doctrine of society can ever be adequate which conceives of man in terms less or other than this deepest fact in man.

What, then, does a man need, as an individual, to have his deepest nature satisfied? He needs to be himself. God wants man to become a genuine self. He started to form him far back in his animal heritage, and has worked over him with extreme tenderness, austerity and patience. No man is satisfied and secure, or deeply happy, who has refused at the depths of his life to mature into selfhood, refusing responsibility to God.

Each person, furthermore, must learn to accept and to love himself genuinely. Self-love is wrong only when it is a caring for the self as the only one or as the most important one in life. True "socialization" can be had only in terms of God's eternal purpose for each individual and for us all. This involves the breaking through of this self with all its habits, attitudes, conventions and points of view. The self, to become "socialized," must become adjusted to God's purpose for *true* society, an act and a process which involve the destruction or elimination of this kind of Eros and the redirection of it in terms of God's will for all.

Thus true self-love is the love of the self within God's will, and within His purpose for the establishing of the full fellowship, wherein the self rejoices in its own afflictions, as did Paul the Apostle, when such sufferings turned out for the furtherance of the Gospel, for the hallowing of God's name and the helping of humanity. True self-love is the finding of the meaning and joy of the self within the great eternal Purpose of God where all things work together for good, for each and for all. Tillich is right, indeed, when he writes:

> He who is able to love himself is able to love others also; he who has learned to overcome self-contempt has overcome his contempt for others. But the depth of our separation lies in just the fact that we are not capable of a great and merciful divine love towards ourselves.[9]

Rabbi Liebman, of blessed memory, never tired of stressing the same point. Depth psychology is now continually pounding home this same truth.

A great mistake that has been made both by much of historic Christian theology, including the greatest of its theologians, and by much modern psychology, is that self-love has often been made a natural possibility. Many have written that we must start with self-love, learning to accept ourselves, and then extend this love to others. This cannot be done. Starting with self-love, one ends with

[9] *The Shaking of the Foundations*, p. 158.

self-love. We naturally do not love ourselves in a full and constructive way. It is true that *naturally* we have a will to die and a will to self-punishment. It is true that much cruelty to others is simply a form of punishing ourselves. No one can find true self-love until he is redeemed from false self-love. No one can accept his full self until he has learned to hate his partial self, his narrow self which is over against others and God. The fellowship self, however, must be the work of God who alone creates fellowship in order that no one might ever be able to live unto himself.

This word "creativity" is one which must not be lightly used. Man needs not only to be himself and to make responsible choices. He must feel that his life means something to himself in terms of creative participation and production. Self-being, to be meaningful, must invest itself in creative concern. God who is love is by and in that very fact Creator. He creates worlds and fellowships. His nature overflows, not like a fountain by natural necessity, but by the free choice of His nature. God receives pleasure from creative adventure; His is the joy of doing, of constructing, of molding, of causing to be.

One of the problems of our present world is that mass production gives little chance for creative living. The worker, in Christian thought, is always man the creator, the co-creator with God. No societal situation can be horizontally right that is not open to authentic opportunity for creative zest. Christian society makes such creative expression an integral demand of its essence.[10] Christianity becomes concerned with working conditions and with the kinds of work which are performed. Impossible working conditions that choke creative impulses should be remedied. Artificial and perverted kinds of work, as Robert Calhoun well stresses in *God and the Day's Work,* must be weighed and decisions made concerning them. We cannot, to be sure, abandon mass production and return to the Middle Ages for the sake of allowing people once again to be independent or semi-independent workers in leagues, but we must, rather, so order our new technological advance as to shorten working hours and redirect man's opportunity

[10] Cf. Einar Billing, *Our Calling,* a translation from the Swedish by Conrad Bergendoff.

for general creativity. Christianity, when genuine, takes essential account of man's need to create.

The Bible, especially the New Testament, has been criticized for making little or no room for play. Richard Cabot included play as one of man's four basic needs. Man needs to work, to play, to love and to worship. Obviously worship is the very center of the Christian life, the vertical direction in which the whole horizontal takes its meaning and power. We have stressed repeatedly that Christianity must be *more* than society if it is to be *true* society. Work, moreover, issues from man's need to create outside himself, whether in terms of need, convenience or beauty. Love, again, is the heart and meaning of both worship and work, for love is the heart of God and of the fellowship. Love is man's basic nature and need. But what of play?

Play is mostly a matter either of growing up or of exercising fellowship. Instrumentally, play is the way in which each child imitates the adult world and solves its problems in terms of pretense. Play, instrumentally, is also catharsis, a purifying of our own emotions and intentions, by the vicarious acting out on an artificial plane of what we feel or will. As such, play contains the pedagogical value of picturing to ourselves externally what we ponder and brood over within. Such play-acting and play-watching are still mostly a matter of immaturity, of externalizing through pretense our problems or our feelings. Much writing about play falsely interprets it as merely pedagogically idealistic. A good deal of play is, rather, the expression of our evil drives and desires, enacted for us by others, not only to get rid of them but to cherish and enjoy them. Here vengeance is taken, or evil acts committed, with which we can identify ourselves in pretense, and still escape the onus of actually performing the deed in the world of consequences. How much vicarious satisfaction in sinning is not derived weekly by the American people from the motion pictures? How many American housewives commit adultery vicariously via light periodicals? Play has been so often in the hands of commercial interests, or in the hands of limited group interests, that for the Christian faith to endorse play outright is consequently dangerous. Perhaps the wisdom of the Bible in not developing the lighter side of life has been sounder than its critics!

But surely play has its positive sides which ought to be accepted. Play is either creative pedagogically, whether in childhood of years or of emotional development at any age, and as such is part and parcel not only of the Christian acceptance but also of its *demand* for creative living generally; or else play is merely a medium of fellowship, such as a friendly game of tennis, whereby people find an active and interesting way of community expression. Such play Christianity obviously, by its very nature, endorses and advocates. But play generally it cannot endorse without knowing the drives which motivate it and the kinds of desire which are satisfied by it. As far as the Bible goes, perhaps the Biblical times were too serious to allow for the inclusion of the good aspects of play. Or did the Bible fail us in this respect? We cannot afford to be defensively apologetic about the New Testament, for instance, or about any other earthly message. No historic word contains and confines the full, absolute orbit of every sphere of man's life. The Bible is a prophetic book, concerned mostly with man's relation to God and with what he can do to be saved. Few prophets have had time for the well-balanced life, of art and of sports, or seriousness and of fun, at least as far as their public leadership and work are concerned. Concentration on "the full balance," including the whole gamut of fun and play, often leads to a scattered life and may be the excuse for keeping one from the full focus of commitment. Nevertheless, in so far as play is creative or a medium of fellowship it surely must be warmly included within the Christian fulfillment of the deepest needs of the individual life.

Now, fellowship is often frustrated because the self is afraid. How can an individual remain himself, free and creative, and yet have real fellowship with others, without fear and without aggressiveness, and in this respect, too, satisfy his deepest needs and cravings? A completely outgoing fellowship concern, centered in God and empowered by Him, delivers the self from defensive fears, suspicions, inhibitions and self-consciousness and sets him free for fellowship. His self is centered in the making and bettering of the fellowship according to the will of God for him and for all. This breaks down the barriers between people, particularly since the deepest in them is God's image, the divine Agape. Here a level of contact is touched which goes far beyond and below ordinary reasoning, experience and convention. People know in their depth self, unexplainably, that something new and something different is present; more is always accomplished *at the depth* than we can imagine.

Because Jesus was crucified, the man through whom Agape first became conclusively illustrated in deed and word, we have fallen into the habit of saying that if perfect love were to appear today we would immediately kill its bearer. We are not ready for it, we claim, and we will not have it. This may or may not be true; and the whole story of why Jesus was killed, besides, is not as simple as that. We, too, make defensive myths and rationalize the past. The record, for instance, does not show Jesus as extending much sympathy and understanding to his enemies, the Pharisees. Jesus was, perhaps, killed as much because of his human weakness as because of his divine strength.[11] It is, in any case, false to make a facile ratio that the more loved a person is the more he is *automatically* hated everywhere. The depth of people is, still and always, drawn to the depth of their own being, the image of God in them. It is for Him they long, and are restless, and often wistful because they have no clear face in which to see Him. At most, the reaction to love is ambivalent, a deep conflict within. We had better stop taking for granted the automatic rejection of the good by people generally.

Instead, true love, humble, wise and simple, breaks down defensive barriers and creates communication. Fellowship depends upon communication. We are pretty much bottled up within ourselves. Martin Buber in *Between Man and Man* has ably illustrated how most of what passes for communication is really directed at the self. How many speeches and actions, how many exclamations and even exhortations never hit the target of anyone else because the speaker is basically wrapped up in himself, in his own purposes and in his own thoughts. There can be more communication of reality, as Martin Buber maintains, between two strangers passing on the street than between so-called friends who are enjoying themselves in each other's company and by means of each other's com-

[11] Cf. II Cor. 13:4.

pany. When two open spirits met at a level deeper than words, where there is true yielding to the other, and where real interest is taken in the other, there is real communication. Christian love means exactly this openness to others and this complete concern and involvement in them which makes possible effective and meaningful communication.

There is a deep longing in us all to be understood and to make ourselves understood. At our depths, we long to love and to be loved. We are made in the inner heaven of heavens for each other by One who understands, better than anyone else, all that we are and want to be. We are the sons of One who yearns to make Himself known to us, but will not when such self-revelation would kill our real freedom and selfhood. Kierkegaard's illustration, in the *Philosophical Fragments*, of the prince who dared not reveal his identity to the poor maid whom he loved, lest his self-revelation kill the beloved, is an interesting pursuit of this thought. God may not be able to show His real self to any extent because we are too far away from fully understanding and accepting Him. *We* need not worry, however, that too much love is let into history by us for people to endure! No human measure, no incarnate love, if genuine, and therefore perfectly patient and wise, can be too great for our needs. Rather, we die as civilizations because there is so little of it.

When the power and depth of God's love become actualized in us, to any genuine extent, barriers are broken down, first in us and then also in many others, which makes for real communication and, therefore, for the effecting of genuine community.

Creative fellowship, at its highest, goes beyond mere communication: in the mystic's baring of the soul in the joys of interweaving community of lives; in creative fellowship, cemented as well as expressed by the sharing in co-operative tasks, the fulfilling of common loyalties, and the undertaking of shared redemptive tasks. Pure society, on earth surely, comes both from what Berdyaev calls "solitude and society," and from what he calls "communion and communication," meaning by the former, direct fellowship, and by the latter, the indirect fellowship which comes from the creative sharing, within the indirections of culture, of the common purposes which characterize historic experience. John Dewey has been a close student of this experience and has shown how history and culture continually overlap and intermingle. Agape, by stressing the purpose for the created order, and God's pedagogical use of it, namely, the preserving intact of our degree of freedom, never idealizes *pure* process or *true* society, but sees it, in history, as the joint relation between man and nature, and all under God, where neither history nor nature can be right except according to the purpose of God and by means of His direction and power.

Thus, finally, we come back to the thought that though Agape is the clue to *true* society on the horizontal level, a clue which we must follow more concretely in the third or "applied" section of this volume; nevertheless, once again we must remind ourselves that there can be no pure society except in faith. Faith is the response of man's depth to God's depth. Faith is the releasing of the image of God in man from its bondage to man's sin, fearfulness and pride, and the joining of it to its Source. Faith is not over and against love, but in and by love. Faith is the acceptance, in increasing reality, by the whole self of the whole reality which God wants to make real in history. Faith is the yielding of the entire self to God's will for freedom and faithfulness in fellowship. Faith is the inviting of God's power and promises to make real in actual life the *true* society which He longs to create. Formally speaking, faith is simply active and transforming trust. But the content of faith is structural in man, because he is made in the image of God, with Agape as the basis of his being and meaning. No true society can be real without a faith which is adequate in both form and content, in both strength and direction.

True society depends upon what is more than society. What is *more* than society directly intends *true* society. What we actually face now, however, is concrete society with all its mixtures of good and evil; exactly how shall those who have creative concern within God's power relate themselves, in principle and in power, to this actual society which we know? That must be the inquiry of our next chapter.

CHAPTER III

Christianity Is Completely
for Society

In the preceding chapters we have shown how Christianity is *more* than society; that it is, in fact, the Eternal Purpose for the world which makes it at the same time *true* society. In this chapter we shall deal with the general principles which relate this *true* society to actual society. Some modern theologians affirm that Christianity has no such principles at all, but must, rather, obediently answer its Lord in concrete situations, directly and with ever new freshness of insight and daring. Others, on the opposite side, reduce Christian ethics to a matter of mere rational choices, founded upon the most inclusive good. Both sides are guilty of man's basic fallacy, a false either-or. For there are such revelational norms as are implicit in the holy Gospel of God's Agape and the involvements of the full fellowship love.

That a maximum opportunity be given to each individual and to each group for freedom and faithfulness in fellowship is such a norm. That each person and group be given the maximum chance for creative living is another. That all be done in faith and love is a third. That God's honor be placed first, an honor which, all the same, unreservedly involves helping humanity, is still another, and naturally the one of primary importance. These revelational norms, in order to become concretely effective have, nevertheless, to be related to the actual thoughts and practices of society. In attempting this relation it is soon discovered that these revelational norms have no exact and unequivocal bearing on the traditional norms, that is, on the actual practices which are considered by any society to be standard for its behavior.

This being so, some stand by the rules, whether revelational or rational, or both, and then tend to underestimate the problems connected with their concrete application. The ground for most actual choices of social action cannot be established and defended by rational rules or in terms of precise moral motivations. The people who have decided for revelational or rational rules, or perhaps both, usually cling to these and to the idea that they can be applied. This often results in a brittleness of spirit which lays them open to the accusation of being perfectionists and Pharisaical at the expense of realism and humility. They are inclined, too, to derive most of their satisfaction from conformity with the norms, regardless of their present efficacy, and are likely, therefore, to minimize the difficulty of concrete choice within the dynamics of the societal situation.

Because of the failures of those who have tried this revelational or rational approach, the supporters of the opposite view want to be concretely effective in the actual situation, even though this may involve constant and outright compromise. They see that there is no possibility of establishing smooth pedagogical norms and, therefore, they prefer to be rid of all revelational or rational norms. Some of them believe that revelation has no rational relevance. It cannot be reduced to any system of thought or to any code for action, but is ever the concrete event of a life. Revelational truth to them is acted truth; it is existential. Logic to them becomes, not inference from general rules, but the concrete implication of the revelation for present obedience in unique, nonrepeatable circumstances. These revelationists or fideists start with the superrational nature of revelation and reject "principles" as the importation of Greek thought into the Hebrew-Christian tradition. Others start with the societal situation, are empirical, and feel that they must work out from situation to situation what is the concrete will of God; but as empiricists they, too, will have little or nothing to do with "principles" and rules that are universally binding. They believe that such an approach deadens and stultifies, besides falsifying, the moral life.

Thus we have a constant controversy between these two approaches. Actually both sides contain both right and wrong. There are revelational norms. The Gospel is truth. The whole-truth of action, of "acted truth," should include truth for the mind as well, norms for action. These norms have rational relevance and should be applied as carefully as they can be to the fullest possible analysis of all the concrete facts involved in any actual situation. But whatever pedagogical norms for action are thereby produced, can, at most, be suggestive. They can never be concretely mandatory on the Christian conscience, or prescribe concrete action as the only Christian approach, to be universally accepted.

The opportunity for moral choices is God-given. Much of life consists in the making of serious and subtle choices in confused circumstances where there are no exact slide rules. Life exists for the sake of our growth through these decisions. Our whole indirect relation to God through nature and history is precisely for this reason. To attempt, therefore, to establish all-encompassing rules for moral conduct in any sphere of life is to attempt falsely to freeze history. It is to try to take a short cut to heaven. It is to declare God's creation to be needless. Neither revelation nor reason shines so precisely on concrete life that exact principles or rules for action can ever be more than a mistake and a hindrance.

While this is true, it is equally true, on the other hand, that there are definite revelational norms and that these have a certain rational relevance—precisely in order, too, that we might grow in insight and maturity. These revelational norms have rational relevance as a general context of meaning and as a general attitude or approach without which there could be no growth in responsibility. The ensuing discussion will be particularly relevant to those who cannot find satisfaction either in a rigid rational approach to revelational ethics or in an arbitrary discarding of all rational relevance in terms of some "pure," irrational existentialism.

The first general rule for the construction of a Christian blueprint regarding the proper relation between Christianity and society is that while the Christian faith is through and through world-transcending, this world-transcendence is also altogether *for* society. There can be no question about the fact that full Christianity is other-worldly.[1] This world is to be seen as but a small segment of what is *more* than society, as a world that has been created by it and is now guided and governed by it. The Christian faith is triumphantly supernatural. Its context of meaning sees this history as the inverted parentheses within God's full meaning, as the inverted parentheses within eternity. This kind of true world-transcendence is, nevertheless, suspect because much world-transcendence is escapist. It is the flight from reality into fantasy. Much other-worldliness is an attempt to avoid the responsibilities and disappointments of this life for the sake of inner security and stability. But all such other-worldliness can be branded as essentially unchristian inasmuch as it is not completely for the world.

Christian world-transcendence makes what is *more* than society primary; after that it emphasizes, in teaching and living, the *true* society that goes beyond this world; then, finally, with that point of view as central, it looks squarely at this history, the meaning of which is the production of *true* society. In this way the Christian faith is world-transcending, but its world-transcendence is through and through *for* society.

This point of view is central to the relation between Christianity and society. We have been going through a period when other-worldliness has been scoffed at as utopian and escapist, as the subtle endorsement of the *status quo* for the benefit of the rich and for making the poor content with being suppressed. Many people have actually not dared to think or to speak of other-worldliness lest they be thought economic conservatives, merely rationalizing their situation. As a consequence, we have become the victims of a shallow and almost impotent this-worldly theology. Social ethics has become "realistic" and "practical." Now, however, the reaction is setting in, and our fear-filled times also tend to abet a new understanding and acceptance of other-worldliness. Such a change is good, of course, to the extent that world-transcendence is the key and power of Christian ethics. But we need that this other-worldliness, with all its scope and meaning, be still completely concerned with the problems of this world: concerned, to be sure, not as

[1] Cf. the excellent discussion by S. C. Neill, "The Church's Failure to Be Christian," in *Man's Disorder and God's Design*, Vol. II, p. 72 ff.

though this world were all, but concerned, rather, because all of this world is related to the Eternal Purpose and can find meaning and reality only in its terms.

Such other-worldliness can, of course, be abused. But our transcendent concern for this world must also take that into account and try to avoid such abuse as can be avoided in this life. For when the truth of Christian world-transcendence is rightly seen, believed and lived, a new power and reality from beyond this life will touch the rich, making their present securities and privileges of less importance, and will also touch the poor, giving them a blessedness of life that no raise in wages can ever offer. Our first task consequently, is to find that full world-transcendence which not only will give lift and meaning to life, far beyond the vicissitudes and troubles of this life, including death; but which is, at the same time, so completely *for* this world that, when it is genuine, it can never become the excuse for reactionary social programs but, rather, the constant and dynamic impetus toward a new and better world.

Ritschl wrote that "to subordinate the ethical to the idea of the cosmical is always characteristic of a heathen view of the world."[2] But the point is not to subordinate the ethical to the cosmic, but to root the ethical completely in the cosmic. To divorce them is to court trouble. What we need is not to get rid of the metaphysical for the sake of the moral, but to discover for ourselves that true metaphysics finds the cosmic to be through and through moral. Much conservative theological thought has underestimated the cutting edge of the ethical;[3] much liberal theological thought has been, in opposition to such conservatism, concerned with values and with action, but has failed to find their eternal anchorage beyond the confines of history. Luther finely advised that "Christians should be aware of their citizenship in a better country, that they may rightly adapt themselves to this world."[4]

Calvin, also, took the point of view that "the faithful should accustom themselves to such a contempt of the present life, as may not generate either hatred of life, or ingratitude towards God. For

[2] *Op. cit.,* p. 25.

[3] Cf. Baeck, "Judaism and the Church," in *The Pharisees and Other Essays,* and Henry, *The Uneasy Conscience of Fundamentalism.*

[4] "Sermon Third Sunday after Easter," cited by Kerr, *A Compend of Luther's Theology,* p. 118.

this life, though it is replete with innumerable miseries, is yet deservedly reckoned among the Divine blessings which must not be despised."[5] Here again we have a staunch world-transcendence that is not contrary to responsibility in this life, a point which Calvin stressed strongly. Calvinism has been of creative importance for the advance of responsible and creative civilization.[6] But it is to be questioned whether Calvin and much of Calvinism has ever had a world-transcendence that is, *through and through, for* society.

Christian world-transcendence, though going beyond society in this world immeasurably, yet makes society completely the object, *directly,* of God's creative concern. God the majestic, the towering beyond man's imagination, is none the less directly concerned with, and is even a participant in, human society and in all the conditions and relations which are important to society. Even for social theory there is a real suggestion in Barth's observation that the New Testament use of the Old Testament "nevertheless" is "therefore."[7] As Geraint Vaughan Jones indicates, the Christian's "politics are inseparable from his theology. The problem of Homo Sapiens is ultimately that of Homo Credens."[8] There can be no cleft of concern between the ultimate and the immediate. The only open place between them is man's free will, which exists within a mixture of ignorance and weakness in order to provide a place for the chooser to find for himself what is good. But this need for freedom is filled within the solid Christian front, wherein its world-transcendence is all the way through *for* society.

This world-transcendence which is *for* society is so in three different ways. Christian world-transcendence comprises, according to proper circumstance, world-affirmation, world-renunciation, and world-transformation. All three must, of course, be *for* society.

That world-transcendence is for society means, in the first place, that we must appreciate and accept this world as the creation of God. This acceptance of the world as it is, as the creation of God,

[5] *Institutes of the Christian Religion,* Book III, IX, 3.
[6] Cf. Dakin, *Calvinism,* Chapter 13.
[7] *Kirchliche Dogmatik, Dritter Band, Erster Teil,* p. 435.
[8] *Op. cit.,* p. 201.

we call world-affirmation. This world-affirmation, too, is *for* society.

We have no right to revolt against creation as though it should never have been. As Buber significantly maintains: "Creation is not a hurdle on the road to God; it is the road itself."[9] We have no right to be practical atheists by trying to argue away the actual situation, to soften the austerity of God, or to shorten the length of our freedom or of God's control. Christian world-affirmation is thoroughly *for* society in that it finds the poise and the rest which God has intended for us by the quiet accepting of His work in creation and of His way with history.

This means that we can accept the beauties of nature with joy and peace. This means that we can be relaxed in God's care and not feel that we ought to be up and doing all the time lest the world go to pieces. This means that we can honor God by our contemplating and enjoying His handiwork. Some people, even confessing Christians, get so bogged down in their own problems or in the troubles of the world that they can never really rest in God. They cannot be still to know that He is God. They feel a false self-seriousness, as though everything depended upon them. They are driven and driven by a restless guilt-feeling which makes them try and try to atone for their sins by hard work to save the world. They become nervous "do-gooders" who mostly interfere with the freedom of others and who fail to find the good part which shall not be taken from them.

A Christian world-affirmation recognizes the seriousness and beauty of man's freedom. Such freedom is through and through *for* society. It, therefore, has pedagogical patience. Agape identifies itself with others and takes their point of view. From that point of view we understand that God's free handiwork of fellowship would be short cut and frustrated if the world should be forced into goodness. It is easy for us to try to take the Kingdom by violence. We often pray and fight and feel that if we could only be completely consecrated, completely surrendered, a whole new world would have to come pell-mell. But even God who is perfect does not, even by His being perfect, change the world.

[9] *Between Man and Man*, p. 52.

Should our dedication, then, limit other men's freedom to find fellowship for themselves?

But, we then say to ourselves, God is not directly in history. He has given unto us the task, we say, to let His grace for redemptive change be channeled into history. Therefore He depends upon us. Our surrender *in history* is what He is waiting for all the time. Should we forget, however, that the freedom of each and every one is real, and that no matter how much one or many are radically transformed so as to be clean and wide channels for God's grace, nevertheless, God respects the freedom of each and all and the place in the development where they are? No redemptive urgency can be anything but anxiety, we must remember, which lacks the full world-affirmation which is thankful to God for the world as it is, wherever it is good and beautiful, and thankful for the freedom, both for individuals and for groups, which allows them to go through the experiences which they must in order to find for themselves the meaning and the truth of God's way with them for fellowship.

Some, however, would say that complete world-affirmation has no meaning and is even morally destructive. Life, they claim, is always a matter of selection. To love everything equally is to decide on nothing and, therefore, is actually not to love at all. Knight, for instance, has written that

> completely undiscriminating love is clearly without significance for action, and it is doubtful whether it is defensible as right, or is possible, or even intellectually conceivable. Human love is certainly discriminating and selective. For man, or God, to love equally and in the same way everything which exists or will exist seems to be practically identical with loving nothing. . . . Both [loving and hating] eliminate selective choice and responsible action and destroy the moral life.[10]

Certainly it seems that if love were unselective, marriage, for instance, would be impossible and complete promiscuity would reign; nor would there be any property barriers, but all things would be held in common, regardless of circumstance. No wonder that an outstanding economist has spent much time and effort in

[10] *The Economic Order and Religion,* pp. 34-35.

combatting the growth of the theology of Agape, especially with regard to its social and economic implications! But does a world-affirmation that is completely *for* society necessarily mean the destruction of discrimination and the abolishing of selection? Is not Agape, rather, the very principle of discrimination and the basis of constructive selection? Does the fact that we love all men generally mean that we love no one in particular, and that since our locus of affection is naturally limited, we cannot, therefore, truly love anyone?

Those whom we love we must love wisely according to circumstance. Agape is the identifying of oneself with the other person and the becoming involved in his problems. The more fully he is loved, the more he is made into a real individual and consequently seen from within his own reality and needs. Each person is unique, occupies a unique place, and plays a unique role in life. As such he is loved selectively and discriminatingly for himself, but in this love there is no invidious comparison and no destructive over-againstness. Agape never lives within the motivations of a "closed society," of any "in-group." The larger fellowship is not hurt or frustrated by this kind of discriminatory love or by this kind of selective cherishing; but the truer and fuller this love is, the more the whole fellowship is thereby enriched and made whole.

In economics, for example, there must surely be a real place, as we shall see in the third section, for over-againstness, in the sense of popular pricing and creative inventiveness. Surely Agape does not level down into sameness, but enriches both nature and history with endless variety. There is nothing wrong about difference as such. Surely marriage is "over against" in a practical and holy sense. But if marriage becomes a false freezing of history, a defensive or aggressive over-againstness, it frustrates the larger fellowship. Or if jealousy within marriage, for instance, distorts the selective relation so as to limit the interests of the partner to the marriage relation, thus preventing freeing fellowship outside it, then marriage does prevent fullness of life. "Godly jealousy," as Paul put it, is good because it is intensive, discriminating concern for the good of the erring person within the total context of full fellowship love. That certain aspects of life be limited, whether sex or property, is for the good of the whole; such limitation is evil only if such discrimination becomes destructive of the larger concerns and responsibilities whereby the full fellowship love, or love "in general," is effected. Complete world-affirmation means, rather, the personalizing of love into a personally selective and effective fellowship which enriches and fulfills the whole. In this sense, the world-affirmation of Agape is completely *for* society.

But Christian world-transcendence is not only world-affirming in the sense that it is invariably, undiscriminatingly *for* society as a positive approval of all that it does and a positive participation in all of its actions. Christian world-transcendence, as the occasion warrants, is also world-renouncing. But such world-renunciation, too, must be altogether *for* society. There has been a good deal of world-affirmation that has been nothing more than acquiescence. It has been a cheap tolerance, a refusal to pay the redemptive cost of differing. A false liberalism has lacked a policy of nonconformity. It has lacked a principle of exclusion. Its love was often nothing but a vague, easygoing inclusion of everything. Such an attitude caused no tension. Such a position caused no hard feelings. Such sentimentalism required no prophetic decisions. Somehow, if everyone was kindly and rather reasonable, everything would turn out for the best. As Professor Dillistone has said in *Revelation and Evangelism*, this easygoing tolerance had much to say about speaking in love, but it forgot to mention that it was the truth that had to be spoken. That truth, too, is not always easy or pleasant. It often involves taking a stand, being counted, and taking the consequences in patience.

When Agape motivates the world-renunciation that is completely *for* society, there can be no brittle self-righteousness based on an illegitimate identification with the absolute. There have been many absolutisms, whether of institution, or of book, or of creed, which have been fanatically destructive. They have excluded all others and treated them, in the depths of their consciousness at least, as heathen and heretics. But Agape is ever humble, "is never puffed up," and identifies itself with the world which is being judged.

The world-renunciation of Agape is never opposed to its world-affirmation. What is denied is, rather, a certain sinful course of

CHRISTIANITY IS COMPLETELY FOR SOCIETY

action which lacks faith and love and which is impure in its motivation as a personal or fellowship action. Thus it is for the sake of all the persons involved in war, for instance, that a Christian may refuse to participate in it. World-renunciation is, accordingly, not monastic for the sake of personal counsels of perfection. Unless in motive and method world-renunciation is completely *for* the world, it is not Christian. In that case it is not the child and creation of Agape which is ceaseless and constructive concern *for* society. This concern may be channeled more toward "the brethren." In this sense, it may have a true selective basis. But if the love, even of the brethren, becomes an obstacle to the loving of those without, the fellowship is no longer Christian. Christian fellowship is the fellowship of the concerned for all men and for all the relationships which are necessary to men's living together. It is concern for the total man, all men, and the total situation in which men live individually and together.

World-renunciation, if completely *for* society, is a powerful weapon against evil. It safeguards the reality and inward purity of the fellowship, not defensively, but with regard to its true being in God and with regard to its most effective being *for* society. Unless the Christian and the Christian fellowship know where, when and how to say no, they will have little influence in actual life. World-renunciation also acts as the world's conscience. The function of conscience is to say "no" to questionable and dangerous courses of action in common life. Similarly should the Christian fellowship say "no." As a matter of fact, we live in an age when man is largely a political and social creature, rather than an individual.

Even the churches do mostly what society in general does. We are driven along by the world in general, never thinking seriously of differing with it *in action*. The early Christian church differed first of all from the world by its actions. Often it might seem to us to have been overscrupulous and nonconformist, but its actions sprang out of an integral man, as Maritain would say.[11] The early Christians were made whole in the depths of their lives, and, therefore, thought, speech and action agreed. They were new creatures in Christ and simply lived their new creaturehood.

11 Cf. his excellent discussion in *True Humanism*.

World-renunciation can be most effective in evil areas of life only if it is completely *for* society, humble and wise, expressing itself, of course, in concrete conduct, and not only in thought or speech. In the long run, life must be taught by life, especially by what Professor Dillistone calls "the pattern" of revelation which was a kind of life in Christ and is a kind of life in the Church.[12] Principles have their place in the divine economy, and they are not to be underestimated, but they never have existential relevance so long as they remain merely rational rules. When, however, they become life, they no longer are letters which kill, but become part of the Spirit which gives life. Thus we stress that Christian world-transcendence is altogether *for* society whether as world-affirmation or as world-renunciation, because its whole concern is with the effecting and the perfecting of the full fellowship of love for which all are made.

Not only, furthermore, are world-affirmation and world-renunciation *for* society; so, more than any other relation, is world-transformation. The primary relation of world-transcendence to society is, beyond doubt, world-transformation. By world-transformation we do not mean the mere change of externals. Our position is no advocating of a social gospelism which would reduce our problems to environmentalism and leave untouched the heart of man's problem, his inner self, his relation to God. By world-transformation we mean, first and foremost, the conversion of the human soul and the effecting, through faith and grace, of the kind of fellowship for which the world has been made. In the Christian perspective, personal realities and relations are always primary. But we mean also, after that, the transformation of all the conditions of creation which are affected by, and do themselves affect, the individual and the fellowship. We consequently include all of men's social means and media, such as economics and political questions.

Why do we make world-transformation the primary relation of world-transcendence to the world? We do this because the most important category of time for us is the future. We are not mostly what we have been; nor are we mostly what we actually are now;

[12] Cf. his *The Word of God and the People of God*.

we are mostly what we shall become. Becoming is the most important category, by far, for persons and for conditions in process, a process which is not an end in itself, but is actually on the way somewhere, a process that is realizing God's eternal purpose for us. As a consequence, our potentiality is far more important than our actual being. Where our self and our fellowship are pointing is more important than the precise place where we are. The transformation that must take place with us and with our process is what really matters. The way in which we are changed is what is crucial. In this sense, the kind of world-transcendence which is *for* society is not primarily *for* society as it is, but, rather, primarily *for* society as it might become. That Christianity is revolutionary is no radical babble and no homiletical hyperbole. It is a sane and sober fact without which Christianity has lost its very essence, at least as far as its relation to our process is concerned.

That Christian Agape is dominantly world-transforming in its relation to society means also that "having" is not a basic social category. All having is for the sake of becoming. The reason that it is harder for a rich man to enter the Kingdom of God than for a camel to go through a needle's eye is that the rich man tends to cling to what he has, and to maintain the present situation in being. Yet it is precisely such a living for the present that is death. The spirit that lives truly and vitally lives for the future. Those whose main approach to life and main attitude about it is having, want as little change as possible, unless perchance to get more for themselves. As a matter of fact, the very topic of change usually irks them. "Why do people have to stir up things? Why can't they leave well enough alone?" are statements which represent their outlook on life. Those who hunger and thirst, whether physically or spiritually, long for a change, and in so doing are that far blessed. All having must be means toward transformation, whether of the individual soul or of society.

Whenever having becomes a primary category and present enjoyment becomes the most desired end, then the meaning of the historic process is prostituted and the basic nature of man is warped. But when having becomes freely used for the becoming of the full fellowship, in concern, wisdom and patience, then having is good. Then God can "make all grace abound" unto us that we "always having all sufficiency in all things, may abound to every good work."[13]

World-transformation as a basic category not only throws light on the category of having, in relation to both being and becoming, but it also throws light on the category of doing. There has been much talk to the effect that religion is what a man does. The upshot of this thought is that talk is cheap and that only that for which a man genuinely lives represents his real faith. In so far as such an opinion refers to religion as whole-response, it naturally is a true observation. But what the thought usually amounts to is that it makes little difference what a person believes or actually worships provided that he does the right thing. In that case, one basic element of whole-response has taken over the dominance and we are left with an ineffective activism. On the other hand, there has recently been a tremendous reaction to this point of view and a loud wail against all "activism." Some have gone so far as to renounce world-transformation altogether as a Christian category. Man's response to God's grace has, in many instances, been left out of the equation of salvation, and in other cases that response has been scaled down to a meek acceptance of forgiveness and has not been given its full creative due with regard to the total activity of man in all his areas of created and historic life. What, then, is the place for doing in relation to world-transformation?

Doing is a basic category. A man may not be what he does, but he does very largely what he is. That means simply that outward action is not the basic form of action, but man's total doing is represented by the relation of his being to his becoming. The saints who have moved the world may not actually have performed so many externally sacrificial deeds as many others, or have done so many meritorious deeds as some "do-gooders," but they have done something so profound by the relation of their being and becoming to their external act that the world has become transformed through them.

Perhaps we may profit by a summarization of this whole question of the relation of world-transcendence to world-affirmation, world-

13 II Cor. 9:8.

renunciation and world-transformation. The primary relation between them is world-transformation. The most important thing about the process is that it points forward and the direction in which it points. That is the center of our first volume, *Faith and Reason*. That process points to the effecting of a Christian fellowship of Agape in the light of which evil finds its meaning, and in the power and wisdom of which it finds its solution, is the center of the second volume, *Evil and the Christian Faith*. That Agape which is *more* than society is also *true* society, but that this *true* society lies ahead of us, and is the very key to the solution of our practical, present problems, is the center of this third volume. The world-transcendence of Agape is, consequently, at the same time intrinsically world-transforming.

All of us are caught in the total situation and, as far as external features go, must share in its evils. That these externals be, however, is for our good and, therefore, the Christian accepts all, and thanks God without qualifications and reservations. All the good, he enjoys and uses with thanksgiving. The beautiful he appreciates and accepts into his life. There is thus a rest and a peace in the Christian life which come from a total world-affirmation. But such rest means *in no wise* that he, therefore, also accepts the world as it is as good, but, rather, that he works with all his might to transform the world toward what it ought to be. In this way his world-affirmation keeps his world-transformation from being a nervous and ineffective activism. From the present good he gets healing, strength and growth, the better to work for the coming of God's new and better world. From his understanding of why the world is the way it is he also escapes merely trying to redo the externals while leaving untouched the deeper causes of the world's suffering. He knows that no world-transformation can be more than superficial that does not start and continue with man's relation to God as He revealed Himself in the Agape-pattern of Jesus' life.

World-affirmation also serves another purpose. This Christian stress maintains the primacy of the fellowship relation. The present is not only an instrumental mode of being. It also contains reality. When a man meets his God in faith and love, eternity is always present. The fellowship relation is thus understood and accepted for what it is. We receive an earnest of the Spirit. We receive some substance of "things hoped for." To accept this reality with thanksgiving and become rich and "abounding" through it is precisely what we ought to do. To accept it in such a way that we become satisfied and build our dwellings on the Mount of Transfiguration is, however, to pervert the reality of present fellowship. The world-transcendence of Agape, therefore, needs both world-affirmation and world-transformation, and needs them together in constant interaction—joint-being and joint-becoming.

Similarly, world-renunciation in the deepest perspective possible exists justifiably only as a mode of world-transformation. Only because we can more fully help the world to become what it ought to be, can we refuse to participate in such actions as separate men from men and thus far harm the fellowship. Only because our participation in the long run is the fuller and more powerful do we have a right to remain a remnant and carry on what J. Burnet Easton has called "the strategy of the remnant."[14] When the world, either by not knowing or by not caring, steers away from the right course, we must humbly stay on it not for the sake of withdrawing from the world that is missing the course, but for the sake of keeping the course which the world will want, sooner or later, to find and follow.

World-renunciation is also for the sake of keeping the fellowship intact. This is a real need always. This constitutes the proper place of being in becoming. The keeping of the fellowship is in essence the maintaining of present being. In order for there to be becoming there must first be some being. That being has, to be sure, no full reality in itself within our process of becoming. The fuller truth of it is, rather, its becoming in relation to eternal Being. But for the fellowship to become there must *always* be the present being. To deny the reality and importance of present being is to deny the reality and importance of God's creation. He wants to grow the fellowship, not to manufacture puppets. But the fuller truth, we stress again, is the becoming of the full fellowship, rather than of the remnant; and, therefore, the fuller reason for world-renunciation is again world-transformation.

This summary is brief, but it should serve to call attention to the many relations among world-transcendence and world-affirma-

14 *Theology Today*, July, 1948.

tion, world-renunciation and world-transformation. The primary eternal mode is, of course, world-transcendence, but this world-transcendence is itself *for* the world. The primary historic mode is world-transformation and obviously that is *for* the world. But this primacy of world-transformation does not exclude, but organically includes, both world-affirmation and world-renunciation. Both abet the primary reality of the becoming of the fellowship and our living for the constant change of it in accordance with God's will. Then we find the deeper reality in social living which is, at the same time and dominantly, *for* society as it needs to *become* in order to find its most effective living.

Not only history, moreover, but also nature is *for* society. The Eternal Purpose is the key to the right and full interpretation of nature. Nature individuates us by making us learn for ourselves, through our choices in it and in connection with it, what is good and what is evil. Nature keeps society from being in a continuous, open relation with God. His face it could not endure, in its dazzling brilliance, and still consider important the relative choices which are necessary for growth. God, as Kean has suggested in *The Meaning of Existence,* sets the stage of nature for history to play on. God's concealing of Himself is, then, for the sake of the effecting of His fuller purpose. He does not conceal Himself because He is eternally qualitatively different from us in a totally unbridgeable or infinite sense. Such a claim would make meaningless and of no effect the revelation in Jesus Christ through which God is seen to be a loving Father and we to be joint heirs with Christ. He does not conceal Himself for the sake of guarding His own glory or for the sake of keeping Himself important. He conceals Himself behind nature precisely in order that we might not see His will directly, but that we might instead learn it gradually and, in the learning, become real individuals and a real society. His direct revelation in Christ can be seen only directly through the Spirit, in which case the face behind nature becomes clearer and the purpose of nature more graspable.

Nature provides enough challenge to initiative to make individuation genuine. We become ourselves as individuals and as a society by our struggle with it. Nature provides enough dependability for us to develop dependability. Prediction is necessary to production, and our steadiness of endeavor depends upon the right relation between prediction and production. Nature, besides, provides enough difference of interests to enrich the content of the fellowship. Nature, moreover, provides enough uncertainty to keep us from self-sufficiency and self-security, except as we sin and shut our eyes and hearts to its lessons.

And finally comes death, the merciful deliverer from all permanent self-certainty and self-satisfaction in human terms. Thus society is led, as it will, to find the meaning and strength for *true* society only in what is *more* than society. Thus even nature is the proper medium for the growth of Christian community, beginning here and pointing beyond itself to some nature different from what we can imagine, where God will once again continue and perhaps discontinue His fellowship work with us. The Eternal Purpose which has planned and caused nature to be, will go on, but the way in which that Purpose will work may be far different from what we can know in terms of the part of the scale of experience now audible to us.

Especially must we keep in mind what a socializing factor suffering is. Since we devoted our whole last volume to this question, it would be duplication to discuss it in detail here. Nevertheless, the reader cannot feel the fullness of Christian solution unless he recall how we need to be delivered from self-sufficiency and self-security by means of self-despair, in whatever form that letting go of our clinging to self comes. Such self-despair opens the door to the release of the imprisoned and isolated self, if he will but walk through it.

But the most socializing kind of suffering is not the physical. The most socializing kind is the suffering for eternity. All of us are made for heaven. Our lives reach indescribably beyond this little life. We transcend time in thought, purpose and interest. Here we have but a foretaste of life. Without life beyond this life there is no full accounting for any of our basic problems and no meaning to our fullest seeing. This is true mostly in our depth suffering for eternity. The absolute, both in conscience and in hope, keeps up its persistent depth-work. We long to be other and different from what we are, and our longing is not simply in human terms. Something else and deeper works there, too. This leaves us dissatisfied, always unsatisfied. One hundred thousand people a year in our country alone may try to commit suicide. The number staggers us. Much mental instability is, of course, the immediate cause; much adversity and grief are also to blame; but in all people there is a body of death, a longing to be rid of the load, to be through with the burden.

In a broader and deeper perspective we would deny that "innocence and ill desert are inconsistent ideas."[15] The innocent suffers with, from and for the guilty, but he suffers redemptively and *for* society. In *our time* there is no complete equivalence between virtue and reward. In eternity all partake of the result of fellowship to which each one will have contributed his sufferings according to God's measure for us, which *may* mean that the most innocent suffer the most! Suffering is for society as a means of socialization.

If, however, the external world as a whole is in accordance with its deserts in general, should we try to change anything at all in that realm? Is not, then, the Hindu doctrine of *varnasramadharma*, for instance, a truer analysis? This doctrine holds that since society is as it is because of our deeds, our *karma,* the wise man does not interfere with it, but, rather, tries to live according to his station in life. Ethics, says this doctrine, is a relative matter, according to the basic balance of good and evil in the scale of life. May not Knight actually also be right, then, in charging that "idealistic reformers are perhaps a greater menace than the outright criminal"?[16] Does not the wise man recognize things for what they are, start to change himself, and then share humbly and patiently his experience with those individuals who want to learn? People, say these wise men, have to be changed from within, and there they can be changed only by example, by being led, not by being forced by law or by external pressures to conform to the good which they themselves do not recognize as such. Perhaps the Hindus have amassed a profound wisdom over the ages which we had better heed. Why cannot we accept their wisdom?

In the first place, as we said above, we do not think that justice,

15 Butler, "On the Nature of Virtue," in *Analogy,* Vol. I, p. 401.
16 *Op. cit.,* p. 125.

either of gifts or of work, is on the basis of invidious comparison or of an invidious equalitarianism. Christian justice is, rather, creative and reclamatory. Happiness here in this life is not the chief end of man nor the chief reason for his being here. Far from it, indeed! We cannot be materialistic or hedonistic from our point of view, or expect our problems to be solved within the earthly span of existence.

But Christianity believes that no one is where he is solely because of his own deeds and their consequences, but also, to an immeasurable extent, because of the deeds and consequences which operate interactingly in the history of society as a whole. One aspect of his situation is a man's own work, but rewards may come to him socially which have little to do with his own investments of ability or of application. Someone happens to own or buy land where oil is found or a city is begun to be built, and he profits, in that case, by "happenstance" or by social decisions. Neither his virtue nor his ability may have determined a great deal of his external circumstance, whether it be position, possession or power.

The Hindu, of course, believes that "the happenstance" was due to *karma*, which was accumulated in some previous existence; but for that we have no warrant except the idea that things in this life do not seem to follow the law of just deserts, and that, therefore, there must have been a previous life to account for this obvious discrepancy. Actually, historically, that is the way, of course, in which the doctrine developed, from *karma* to reincarnation, from a demand for justice in this life, to a previous life to account for there not being such justice. Purpose can, to be sure, be interpreted retroactively as well as prospectively in order to have us account for all the facts. But there is no need for this at all when the full sphere and operation of God's justice is glimpsed.

The full meaning of Agape is precisely that the end of life is not justice but a full fellowship beyond justice, where invidious comparison does not obtain. In this light, the present inequalities of social living are, in fact, the very conditions for the growing of such a fellowship, where the rich, for instance will not be hardhearted and proud and the poor will not be bitter and envious. Christianity is not a religion of justice; such a religion is built on law and on comparison. Christianity is the religion of complete concern for all, that each and all may find full development and richness of life. The Christian view of justice is *for* society; it is ever creative, redemptive and outgoing.

This statement regarding Christianity's being beyond justice, however, is on the level of present being, not on the fuller level of becoming. This attitude, which is characteristic of much New Testament ethics, is on the level where world-transcendence meets world-affirmation. This proper condition for fellowship can be accepted as such, for what it is, but it cannot rightly constitute the excuse for a lack of concern for the fullest possible well-being of all the members in the fellowship. The Bible must not be the tool of reaction or a self-justification for our lack of redemptive concern. The Bible must be the road to truth, not a hindrance to it. The higher and truer view of the Bible is that much of its explicit ethics, namely, that of a humble and resigned acceptance of the *status quo,* as in the case of Paul's Epistle to Philemon, is not its highest ethics. Its highest ethics can be only the full implications and involvements of Agape, the Word become flesh for our sake and for the redemption of the whole world.

The fullest implications and involvements of Agape, the center of the Biblical revelation, are world-transformation. "That there be equality" in the fuller sense of providing the maximum well-being for all, out of common concern and sharing, is also a Biblical verse. We must not lower the Bible to the teaching of mere passivity, a complete acceptance of things as they are externally. We must find its driving center—that God's will be done on earth as it is in heaven, with regard to all areas of life. The task of Agape is precisely to work for others in *all* their needs. The needs of others exist also for our sakes that Agape may have an object and find reality in us. Not to work for others in all their needs is to deny in life the central nature of Agape, God's complete concern for all in all ways.

The fellowship is effected precisely by the members' working for one another, and the conditions of the world are as they are, not only as the consequence of individual sinning and ignorance, but also as the opportunity for the growing of the fellowship as a whole. The need *of* others and *for* others is our own inescapable need. Paul says, "I seek not yours, but you." In a differing perspective, however, we can say that we seek not only you but yours for your sake! Agape without the fruits of the Spirit is a sham profession. Agape can never be individually other-worldly; it must always, by its other-worldliness, be socially this-worldly.

In the next place, Agape cannot accept *varnasramadharma,* or any conservative social theory that stresses the spiritual side as all-important, because to do so is to forget the level of creation. We repeat that Agape is not radical in the sense that it says that the world should not be this way at all. Those may be right, consequently, who say that more urgency is had when we do not believe that God has anything to do with evil except a striving to create new and better values out of the social situation. Such a theology, or even the denial of God entirely, may give a real urgency to social endeavor, but it is the urgency of fear or the urgency of vain hope. At best it is the theology of the bootstraps. Agape has the utmost urgency available, the full purpose and reality of God's love, in so far as we truly understand and accept this for our lives. But this urgency cannot be limited to the spiritual realm precisely because it knows the level of creation and the truth of world-affirmation. This realm of creation has its semi-independent being, for the sake of our fellowship's becoming real, and that does not change automatically when the spirit changes. The physical craving for dope or for liquor does not cease with a change of spirit. The man who has cut off his finger in a religious frenzy of an ignorant kind does not grow it back when his spirit is enlightened and changed. Institutions and external conditions in history can become temptation and often a hindrance to good intention. People who have surrendered denominational ties as a partial view and a partial creed may tend to rise above that view or that creed in spirit; but unless the view and the creed are broken through in the very fabric of the institution, they are going to bedevil even many good intenders and the children who are being indoctrinated by them.

The great problem connected with the Bible is that since it contains so many levels of insight and so much reactionary and low-grade material, much low-grade living perpetuates its deplorable ideology under the protection of the Bible. And the Bible is in nature; it works through objectified experience and thought. We can touch it with our hands and put it away with our fingers.

Spiritual attainment needs the aid of the highest objectifications in nature, whether in books or in institutions, and it is simply untrue, therefore, to claim that to change the spirit is automatically to change the whole situation. That is the opposite heresy of saying that to change the external environment is thereby to change the spirit which is formed in its terms.

Only by the correct relation of spirit, mind and body can we get real world-transformation. We need a new Church of the Spirit, built on ever higher grounds of God's love and the faith which makes this real. But even the Church must remember that it is spirit, mind *and* body and, therefore, it must attend well not only to its spiritual life, but to its educational opportunities and the economic and social side of its nature. The educational aspects of life, similarly, cannot get along without proper care for both their spiritual superstructure and motivation and for their organizational efficiency. The spirit, the mind and the body affect one another. God has made them constantly to interact. To cure the intention is not to enlighten the mind automatically; to enlighten the mind is not automatically to cure the body. All go together in ever blending interactions. Creation has its own degree of reality and its proper function to play in the divine economy and in human history. That is precisely the reason that we cannot reduce everything to the spiritual, and to good example; and that is a strong reason indeed for our needing to change society in all areas of life with all the means and methods which are appropriate to its several areas.

This placing of all blame on the internal situation or on the spiritual condition, even though it is unquestionably primary, is thus false to the full Christian understanding of life. Life is spirit, mind and body interacting continuously, all of which must be attended to and wisely satisfied, as separate aspects of life and all together. But this view is false not only because of neglect. It suffers from more than a serious omission. It is often the result of either spiritual pride or of spiritual evasion. When the spirit is blamed directly or given direct credit, then a person and a group are also accordingly where they are because they deserve to be there. This idea gives an extraordinary opportunity for spiritual pride, and is, indeed, the outcome in many instances of such pride. Those who hold it often belong to the successful group. They are those who have. Instead of feeling gratitude and special responsibility because they are fortunate enough to have been born with certain ability and within certain circumstances or received certain helps or good fortune on the way of life, they take all the credit to themselves, either for belonging to a certain fortunate group or for being self-made.

If we know anything at all sociologically, it is that social and personal factors interact inextricably in personal and social situations. Modern juvenile delinquency, for instance, often in stunning circumstances, cannot be accounted for apart from the kind of civilization in which we bring up our children. The civilization and the circumstance, on the other hand, do not produce equal effects in all. Yet the old idea that goodness and prosperity go together is hard to root out of the general consciousness, particularly of the prosperous, and of those who ape their thought-forms and ways of life.

On the other hand, there are those who simply evade the problem and, accordingly, rationalize their situation differently. They claim that the spiritual has a distinct realm and has no relevance for the material and social world. That the spiritual can be only spiritually understood, in that case, becomes a thought that does not appeal as it should to the surrender of the whole spirit in order that we might not rationalize but truly understand in the divine perspective; but becomes, rather, the idea that the spiritual has nothing to do with the natural world and is to keep itself uncontaminated by it. Therefore, we hear of "pure spirituality." Pure spirituality, evidently, means the living within the spirit and for the things of the spirit, and having no care for the things which are impure or less than spiritual. In this way we have religion as a special sphere of life, with all other things in their sphere outside its direct relevance. Thus "business is business" and "religion and politics do not mix." People sweat and argue over fine points of faith, over Biblical interpretations, while such questions as war and property are important only to "the worldly." These are secular problems. We have those who conform to the world and those who do not conform; but both agree that the spiritual is a realm apart from the worldly. Thus the challenge of all that is high in religion to all of life is lost. We have ɔrld-conformity or world-nonconformity, but no great and deep doctrine of world-transformation which is all the way *for* society.

To a great extent this position is a spiritual evasion of the social issues. Life is hard. We need security with regard to God, to death and to sudden misfortune. We carry a kind of special insurance for these areas of life and are willing to pay for it in terms of money and activity. But life out in the actual world is very complicated and runs according to low standards of ethics. To introduce religion there would be costly and confusing.

All that we need to say in this connection, however, is that to limit the Gospel either to our individual relation to God or to our direct relation to our neighbor in the spirit, and not also in the body, in the institution, and in organized social and political life is to deny the full Christian Gospel of creation and redemption.

We have, then, come to the end of the first section of this volume. Our concern here has been to deal with the general relation between Christianity and society. We have tried to point out three things: that Christianity is *more* than society; that it is *true* society; and that it is completely *for* society.

Before we can go on to the third section, that will analyze some concrete social problems in the light of our theological perspective and try to offer some practical points with regard to them, we have to turn to the relation between the Church and society. We suggested in our general introduction that some social theories suffered from reducing all perspectives to the level of the world, while others distinguished so sharply between the life of the redeemed and the secular life that they refused to produce any social theory. What we are now setting out to do is to introduce a double relation between Christianity and society, one indirect and the other direct. Whether or not what we have to say is going to be as helpful as we should like it to be, depends a great deal upon the adequacy of our analysis of this coming middle section.

THE CHURCH AND THE WORLD

Introduction

In the first section we dealt with the ultimate principles which govern Christian social action. In the third section we shall try to apply these more concretely to our social problems. In this, the second, we shall elucidate the indirect relation between the Church and society. As we have seen, quietism is a denial of the Christian faith. But direct participation in social action, on the other hand, is not enough. There is, as we shall find in this section, a distinctive dimension of Christian social action. This dimension does not refer only to ends and to motivation; it refers also to means and to methods, particularly as these are involved in the ends and motives. In general, we are now to discuss the Church and the world. The main distinction which we are to draw is that the former is governed by the Holy Spirit while the latter is under the sway of the Spirit of God.

CHAPTER IV

The Church as the Incarnation of the Holy Spirit

Since the Holy Spirit and the Spirit of God have often, with good reason, been used as synonymous terms, and since we are now to build a whole analysis on the distinction between them, we have to be most careful about our definitions. Once the distinction has become clearly seen and understandingly appropriated, it opens many doors. Especially true is this of our present subject: the relation between the Church and social action. A whole new approach springs forth out of this distinction, one for which I have sought long and carefully.

What is this distinction? The Spirit of God is God's nature and activity on all levels below Agape, whether in instruction, judgment or forgiveness. The Holy Spirit is God's nature and activity on the level of Agape. The distinction is definitely functional, not metaphysical in nature. God's nature is here understood operationally. God is ever the same in Himself. His own inner essence is selfsame, unchangeable. The Spirit of God and the Holy Spirit are the same Spirit. But God is not undifferentiated being. He operates differently in different media and circumstances according to the way He is understood and accepted. He has different *hypostases,* as the Greeks called it. They meant by *hypostasis* an essential, inner qualification of being, not different persons in terms of independently real and operative personalities.

Similarly, we have to think of the Spirit of God and of the Holy Spirit as selfsame in essence, while yet functionally different, not only in appearance, due to our ignorance, but actually, for a pre-liminary purpose. The Spirit of God is the pedagogical face and hands of the Holy Spirit. Though ultimately the same, or meta-physically identical, they are, nevertheless, functionally or opera-tionally different. Upon the validity of this analysis hangs a great deal of the adequacy of our social analysis. For this reason we must look at it more carefully.

The Spirit of God is God as He operates on the level of creation. If we use the words "lower level" for the work of the Spirit of God, this does not mean that God is here less than Himself in Himself, or that this level is "lower" than that of redemption which comes in cleansing contact with sin.[1] What can be lower? Lower, for our purposes, with respect to God, simply means pre-liminary in the sense of a stage of appearance, not necessarily chronologically, for the stage of creation is most probably never done away within human history. The Spirit of God is most widely used as the upward thrust of the creating Spirit, in so far as He co-operates with all creation, or concurs with it. Not all that happens in creation is, of course, due to the Spirit of God as a direct agent. To hold such a position would be to accept some kind of uncritical pantheism or personalism which would rule out the actuality of creation as having a semi-independent existence, with chains of custom and forces which are not directly due to any immediate activity of God. The more impersonal the operation is, the less the Spirit of God is present. The more personal the opera-tion is, the more the Spirit of God is present; unless His works have been fulfilled and He is consequently yielding to the opera-tion of the Holy Spirit. The Spirit of God, then, is primarily present in human history. It is present from behind as need, as the creative thrust of individuality, as the push of progress—not in so far as any of these is simply the outworking of natural forces, but in so far as these become the basis through decision and-or growth for God's concurrence with creation and history. The Spirit of God "broods over the void," but is not the void. The

---

[1] Principal Micklem has warned me, in a personal letter, that I must use the word "lower" carefully in connection with God. This point is well taken. One of the most profound cautions against my approach which I have ever read is also to be found in Gregory of Nyssa's *Against Eunomius* and *On the Holy Spirit*.

Spirit of God directs history on the basis of need, but is not the nature that causes that need nor the need itself.

There is a relativity of God as He operates, not as He ultimately is in Himself. He never is "for Himself."[2] God as He operates in a tree, sustainingly, though He is not that tree, is different from God as He operates in a horse, though He is not that horse. In either case the work is so instrumental or preliminary that it is difficult to know whether the term "Spirit of God" should be used at all in connection with it. God as He operates in a gunman is different from God as He operates in a saint. God as He operates in John the Baptist is different from God as He operates in the Son of Man. He who is least in the Kingdom of the Holy Spirit, the realm of the new creaturehood in Christ, is greater than the greatest born of woman under the old dispensation of the Spirit of God.

Either Eros or Agape operates dominantly in any human decision or whole-response. The whole realm of Eros is the realm of the Spirit of God. So is the realm of Nomos, or law. The realm of Agape is the realm of the Holy Spirit. The realm of Eros is the realm of individuation and of group growth. The realm of Agape is the realm of fellowship and the full community in Christ which transcends all barriers. These realms are qualitatively different in the sense that they are constituted by different directions, depending upon qualitatively different decisions. They differ basically with regard to whether the motivation *in content* is out from the self or toward the self. In the individual they differ in the fact that the Spirit of God is the pull toward the self, with whatever high load of ideals and prestations, while the Holy Spirit is the pull always from God as He is in Christ toward the full fellowship. One individuates; the other unites. In history one is the push of progress, God's use of our technological development and other expressions arising from man's need in its interrelation with nature and history; the other is the pull of purpose, God's gracious filling full of the fellowship from within the promptings and power of His own self as revealed selectively in history, primarily through Christ Jesus.

We cannot distinguish sharply, to be sure, between the levels

[2] Cf. Charles Hartshorne, *The Divine Relativity*.

of redemption and creation, connecting the Holy Spirit with the former and the Spirit of God with the latter. There are, obviously, preparatory stages of redemption of high validity even within the realm of the Spirit of God. This is true both of the Old Testament, which Tillich calls the direct preparation for the Gospel, and the pagan religions, which he calls the indirect preparation. When my distinction between the Spirit of God and the Holy Spirit was submitted to F. W. Dillistone, he was certain that it should not be equated outright, for instance, with what he calls, in *The Holy Spirit and the Life of Today,* "the dialectic between creation and redemption." This is true. For we are here drawing a different dialectic from the mere distinction between the level of creation and the level of redemption. We are drawing a distinction between all that is preparatory to the Agape fellowship, whether in creation or in redemption, and the full Agape fellowship itself, which is the cleansing and creating gift of the Holy Spirit. We are, in short, drawing the distinction between Eros and Agape throughout all history, though the former level is co-extensive with nearly all of human history, as an explicit dominant actuality, whereas the latter was selectively revealed as central in cosmos and conduct, for faith and life, in the teachings and life of Jesus, the Christ.

Because our whole understanding of history and of Christian social action hinges on this distinction, it is well to remind ourselves again that, at bottom, the Holy Spirit and the Spirit of God are one and the same. They are one and the same metaphysically; they are not different, actually, below their functional manifestations. Modelism is wrong as a metaphysics, but has a necessary functional truth. We must, furthermore, see clearly that as far as human history or human personality goes, the question is not of one or the other—of the Spirit of God or the Holy Spirit—being present. They are both always present in some interaction, though one or the other is dominant, as a set of the self or of the group; though even so, one or the other may gain temporary possession of concrete acts or attitudes over and against the generally dominant set of the self. Here is a dynamic view of the self, of a constantly struggling self, being basically possessed by one or the other, but having enough freedom to invite the other, or rather let the other gain dominance, either as discrete acts, or as the revolution or conversion of the self, one way or the other.

The natural self is never totally bad, devoid of the image of God. That image exists as its continuous essentiality; its abiding potentiality in depth-fact and depth-relation. The regenerated self is never devoid of the natural man, his body of death, unless he be so sanctified that he leaves human history as we know it, at least in motivation and continuous relation with God. Even Jesus did not do that, but had his terrific experience of the Spirit of God in Gethsemane and on the Cross; therefore, although it is not, naturally, under any circumstances, our wish to judge what God can and may do, we think that such total freedom from the natural man is at most an abstract possibility. Even so, the outcome in such a case would find Eros completely in the service of Agape; the Spirit of God and the Holy Spirit would be at one, even functionally, in that one place, or the Spirit of God would be subjected to the perfect service through which He and those He serves win perfect freedom, the freedom that is the fullness of God's fellowship.

For the most part, however, in all human beings, both the Spirit of God and the Holy Spirit are interactingly present, though one or the other is basically dominant. Albeit the Holy Spirit was not understood and received for what He is until after the coming of Jesus as the Christ and the establishing of the saving fellowship, nevertheless, He has always been subliminally present, lighting every man that comes into the world. He has been present as man's essential nature, even though pedagogically and preliminarily man was, until His coming, as most people are now, under the reign of the Spirit of God. Agape has always been present in the depth-dimension of human history, and also in some manifestation, but never until the fullness of time as clarified history open to personal appropriation.

Granting that this distinction will help to clarify the relation between the Church and the world, is it Christian? Either Christianity is truth or it is a falsehood. This distinction roots in the very nature of historic occurrence, as we know it from within the Christian experience and see it by means of its most inclusive light. The truth of Christianity is centrally Christ as the Agape of God revealed and made effective for an ignorant, needy and sinful world. This living truth of a personal event is the rock of revelation. That, and only that, is the criterion of Christianity.[3] This criterion must be applied to all the facts, giving them their meaning and context. Obviously most of history and experience, however, falls so short of God's own Agape that what has to be seen is its place in the pedagogical purpose of God. The selectively highest point in history has to illumine the general content of knowledge for the sake of fitting the whole together according to the historically selective Purpose, which ultimately governs and directs all.

The fact is that most of mankind's activities are on a lower level, qualitatively, than Agape, and that, nevertheless, God is not absent from them. He participates, rather, throughout the whole length and breadth of historic occurrence. The Christian distinction is not between God as present in the history of salvation in the definite sense of the Christian fellowship and present nowhere else; but, rather, between God as present in a special sense in the Christian fellowship, in what the Germans call *Heilsgeschichte,* and generally present in all history, though in a different way. In one case we have God acting with a clear face, in revealed history; in the other case, He is hid by a veil, in concealed history. Yet there is, all the same, preliminary revelation in the concealed history. This revelation is not only a dimly apprehended and confused history. It is God acting on a different level for the sake of preparing the higher. Thus God actually commands that there be done, on this level, such acts as are according to the highest stage of development at that point, and accepts such obedience, though a later revelation would make this same kind of action unacceptable to Him. The God who thus acts on the level of need and individuation is the Spirit of God. Though the Holy Spirit and the Spirit of God are one and the same in themselves, nevertheless, they operate differently, according to the Eternal Purpose in creation and redemption, and as conditioned by the concrete *kairos,* or

---

[3] Can we forget that Augustine made love, God's love to man and man's to man, the center and criterion of the right interpretation of the Bible? Or can we fail to see how free Luther was with the Bible as a whole? As a matter of fact, "the Spirit of the Reformation is diametrically opposed to the authoritative interpretation of the Bible." (Cf. Grant, *The Bible in the Church,* p. 109 *et al.*) Thus it must always be in a creative age when the Spirit is at work with power.

kind of time which is present. Though metaphysically the same, they are different operational actualities.

Suppose we grant that Christianity has for its final criterion the living truth of God's Agape, making the facing of the facts as they are with it a Christian procedure, can this distinction nevertheless be called Biblical? Obviously, the distinction is not verbally exhaustive as between the Old and the New Testament. One needs only consult a good concordance! Yet by so doing, the fact that the distinction is overwhelming is also established. The Old Testament uses the Spirit of God preponderantly while the New Testament is particularly partial to the term Holy Spirit. This is at least a suggestive situation. Thus Denio in his excellent studies of the Holy Spirit writes that "in the New Testament the proper name of the Spirit of God is Holy Spirit."[4] Similarly Conner, writing about the work of the Holy Spirit, says that "the Spirit has no mission except in relation to Christ and his saving work."[5] "When Jesus, the embodiment of truth, came into the world, the Holy Spirit came in a new way in his life; and when the gospel had become an accomplished fact in history, then the Holy Spirit came in his fulness and power. But before the Holy Spirit could fully empower the preacher of the gospel, there must be a gospel to preach."[6] Rees also brings out some of the distinction which we are trying to make when he writes that "one notable limitation of the sphere assigned to the Holy Spirit in the New Testament, as compared to Hebrew and Jewish literature, is that it is nowhere described as the agent of creation or as a cosmic principle. It does not act upon external nature, and it stands in no causal relation to the physical universe. . . . The Holy Spirit acts only upon humanity. . . . The Christian Church realized the fact of the Spirit first as a living, present, over-powering, unique, and exalted experience."[7] A New Testament scholar similarly writes: "We know that the Holy Spirit does not operate fully nor is rightly apprehended as such until Jesus is glorified in death and ascension."[8]

[4] *The Supreme Leader*, p. 8.
[5] *Revelation and God*, p. 300.
[6] *Ibid.*, p. 301.
[7] *The Holy Spirit*, pp. 84-85.
[8] G. Johnston, "The Doctrine of the Holy Spirit in the New Testament," in *Scottish Journal of Theology*, Vol. I, No. 1, p. 51.

The Holy Spirit is a Christian doctrine connected with Agape's becoming central in cosmos and conduct in Christ. He refers to the relation between the persons of the Trinity and between God and the Church. We have to use some term to indicate that God actually can act and acts differently when He is truly understood and appropriated or accepted. Both Augustine and Aquinas, two towering theologians of Christian history, "identified the Holy Spirit with Divine Love,"[9] the greatest gift of God, the chief principle of relation to men. The Holy Spirit is God operating in the revealed and effective Agape of His own nature after the fullness of time in that fellowship which will receive Him and live by His grace and power. Between this new creaturehood in Christ and the world as a whole there is a distinctively discontinuous relation which is determinative for Christianity, along with the general continuous dimension between them.

The New Testament is the result of an earthquake. When the Incarnation took place, which Whitehead in a personal conversation once called "the supreme moral moment of the world," a new basic reality and basic motif was introduced into history that played havoc with all previous ways of thinking. In so far as the New Testament fully reflects the reality of Agape, it is authoritative for the Christian faith. In so far as this distinction between the Holy Spirit and the Spirit of God is true in the full Christian perspective, that is to say, with regard to Christ, it is Biblical and written for the world as the Word that saves. We cannot again become guilty of the Pharisaism and Scribism that stood for tying all present life to the book rules and realities of the past. Against this we must ever say in the same Spirit as the One through whom Jesus spoke: "It has been said of old . . . but I say unto you."

Particularly today we must believe and show that God in Christ makes all things new, and we must live "in the freedom wherewith Christ has set us free." This freedom is the reality of Agape, the eternal "must," fulfilling man's deepest nature in freedom, but doing so with every pedagogical patience and humility. This living truth of a personal event, we repeat, is the rock of revelation, a living rock that follows with the children of God as they march from the bondage of sin and ignorance through the wilder-

9 Rees, *op. cit.,* p. 174.

ness of history. Apart from this rock of revelation there is no Biblical bedrock. When the Bible becomes thus livingly used, fresh light is shed both on it and from it. In this sense, "a true understanding of Christ becomes interpretative of *all* the ways of God."[10] Jesus' "whole personality was so possessed and controlled by the Spirit that his work was the work of God."[11] When we speak through the Holy Spirit who "gives Christians knowledge of the truth"[12] we, too, speak from the same God for the world, and our truth is one with the truth of the Bible.

But if we draw this distinction between the Spirit of God and the Holy Spirit, what can be the relation between the Spirit and the Son? Has not our doctrine of the Holy Spirit somehow changed the whole relationship? Or have we done to the Holy Spirit what early theology is said to have done to the doctrine of the Son? Have we bifurcated the Spirit, given Him, like the Son, a double nature? While the fuller discussion of this must, of course, wait for our volume on God, even here we ought at least to indicate the fuller background of this thought.

God is one and entire. Basically He is Spirit. Spirit unites meaning and mystery. He is both "nearer than breathing" and beyond human comprehension. Without an adequate stress on Spirit, God becomes somehow reduced to His relationship to earthly existence and history. Spirit simply cannot be grasped by us, but the Spirit can grasp us and search all things, "even the depths of God."

This Spirit has revealed Himself conclusively in Christ Jesus as love. "God is love." Love is a conscious Person, a free Purposer, an acting Creator. All this is Spirit. The Spirit of God, however, is God acting as what Luther called "the hidden God." He is the same, but His "circumstantial will," as Leslie Weatherhead called it, operates differently from His own open will. The God of wrath and the God of love are one and the same, inseverably. There is no split in God's nature. But God has to assume the shape of the avenger to the disobedient and to those who are fearful from selfishness.

10 Edwin Lewis, *The Philosophy of the Christian Revelation*, p. 4.
11 Conner, *op. cit.*, p. 298.
12 Denio, *op. cit.*, p. 40.

A metaphysical dualism had a Devil to play this role, but had no ultimately sovereign God, and no full unity of discourse wherewith to explain experience. If as Edgar M. Carlson says, Luther had only an empirical or existential dualism, the objective powers and the devil could be subordinated to the sovereign God of love.[13] His powers could then be that of Job's adversary and he could still appear among the sons of God in the heavenly executive sessions. There might be such a creature as the devil and such creatures as demons, *under God,* who have delegated authority to tempt and to plague men, for the sake of their growth and salvation. That, too, would help to explain experience without losing the unity of discourse and the sovereignty of God. But a far more noble and awe-inspiring conception is that of God Himself, working for us in both creation and in redemption, in both the pushes and pulls of history, in both the wrath and the open love. His condescension and humility for our sake to produce the fellowship is then complete. If we accept this point of view, however, have we not made unnecessary not only the doctrine of a personal devil, but also of the Son? Are not, then, the Spirit of God and the Holy Spirit enough to explain the main relations of God to history and experience?

The answer to this is "no," for the Spirit is always relational. Spirit is not undifferentiated. God is transcendent and immanent. Such a functional division of His nature is co-extensive with creation, with this or with any other creation; for that matter, with all conceivable creations. God the transcendent is the Father. God the immanent is the Son. Both are Spirit. Both are Agape. Both are personal. Perfect Spirit is the relation between them, the Holy Spirit. All are conscious and personal. Personality is not a matter of complete disjunction either of form or of content of nature. Consciousness centers in functional differentiations of Spirit. The Holy Trinity is God in three persons, three functional centers of consciousness, the transcendent, the immanent and the relational. The Son is the Word which was in the beginning with God, and

---

[13] *The Re-Interpretation of Luther,* p. 57. "It is not a metaphysical dualism which is concerned with the origin of evil, or even with its ultimate issue, except as this is involved in the experience of faith. It may more properly be described as an empirical dualism" etc.

was God, and through whom all things were made, but the Spirit brooded, even then, over the void, for where the Son is, there is the Spirit also. "The Lord is the Spirit." But the Son as the cosmic Christ was not disclosed until the Incarnation, the first full enactment and teaching of the Agape, not apart from the weaknesses of the flesh, but dominantly through them, or in spite of them.

The Son is then more than the historic personality of Jesus. The Son is the second person of the Trinity, the immanent God, who lights every man who comes into the world. But such lighting is only through the Spirit. Before the Incarnation the relational reality is the Spirit of God, including all the Godward functions of the level of creation which fall short of the divine Agape. After the Incarnation, where the Son is revealed afresh and appropriated through the Spirit, the relational reality is the Holy Spirit. The cosmic Christ is thus always with creation and shares the weaknesses of the flesh. It is only after the revelatory event in Jesus that the cosmic Christ is understood as the personal Savior of those who believe and obey, who accept the love of God, effectively revealed and empowering to newness of life in Christ Jesus. The Spirit speaks of Christ and Christ is God's. And all are one, and all are Agape.

This view of the Spirit of God gives basis to a general revelation and an all-pervasive activity of God, outside the redemptive fellowship itself, which goes beyond the doctrine of natural theology. Here we have no static view of natural revelation, no static natural law, and no static orders of creation. Here we do not have a pantheism where all things are the direct outworking of God's sovereignty, a view which even a great Christian and theologian like Luther came close to holding.[14] Neither have we a deism where we can see the watchmaker only from the operation of the watch. Here we have a reality of creation as a semi-independent realm, but one in which God works, concurring with all of it, or creating new situations and forces. This is existentialism in the sense of the immediate and spontaneous which has characterized a great tradition in Christian thought. Consider, for example, the *Proceedings of the American Catholic Philosophical Association* in 1946, under the topic, "The Philosophy of Being," where

14 Cf. *The Bondage of the Will.*

Thomas Aquinas is upheld as the great existentialist. Modern books on Luther stress this aspect in him, and how strong, indeed, it was! Upon reading a great work on Luther's doctrine of vocation, I was constantly impressed with this fact.[15] His whole distinction between law and command centers on this truth of immediacy, spontaneity and *creative newness*. Did Calvin, again, restrict to conversion and sanctification "the Spirit, that internal Teacher, by whose energy alone our hearts are penetrated"?[16] What we have here in the idea of the Spirit of God, in any case, is the reality of God's order in creation, but a flexible structure, a steady rather than a static light, a continuity open to further light and to the refocusing of the beam.

The Spirit of God, then, is the underlying reality which activates the preparatory work for the Christian fellowship in both creation and history. This preparatory work is not merely chronological in the sense of B.C. It is also the constant background of historic Christian experience and operates all too strongly in all actual Christian churches and most probably in all Christian individuals. The Spirit of God urges to individuation in order to make our freedom real. The pedagogical use of individualism is not sinful. Our choice to accept consciously, and within our depth-self, egocentric living is the sinful part of the process. Not individuation, however strong and falsely pursued, but spiritual egocentricity is sin. The Spirit of God never urges sin, yet becomes the constant occasion for sin.

There is a real place for the activity of God in history on the sub-Agapaic level, which is obviously most of it up to now, while God is yet, of course, in Himself the same. Here is a condescension which is as deep as the Cross, for here God assumes the form that is needed to reach us before the fullness of time. Here God is willing to be thought the avenger to be feared, while all the time He is really the Father to be loved. Here He is willing to command the hard things that are needed, willing because He loves us enough to assume His foreign nature in order to prepare us for the fullness of time when His glory can shine in the face of Jesus Christ as one full of grace and truth. This incognito of God explains the power

15 Wingren, *Luthers lära om kallelsen*.
16 Institutes IV, xiv, 9.

of religion even on its lower levels. The Kingdom of God consists "not in talk but in power," even when the power is that of preparation for its fuller coming.

Miller in *Christian Truth in History* has pointed out that secular rulers in crises will appeal to people's religion, and that there is power in religion beyond their concern for secular interests. What, he asks, is this extra power of religion which can be used to back up secular aims, if, deep down, it is not the power of truth, however distorted? Alan Richardson has also observed how "ideology disguises itself under the forms of religious faith,"[17] even though true faith is not ideological in essence. Somehow there is in this an intimate relation of secular thought and interests to religious truth and power. Yet they cannot be directly connected with religion because creation is both partially, yet also truly, independent of God's direct activity. The Spirit of God is the kind of concurrence which individuates and makes freedom real, without separating it from the concurrence of God.

As Geraint Vaughan Jones has shown us, the pagan world rose to *caritas generis humanis,* this love of humankind which was based on natural law rather than on Christian experience.[18] With it man could organize society and perform almost endlessly constructive deeds, yet without arriving at the creative power of Agape for genuine fellowship. The same writer has well phrased this thought:

> The modern disparagement of humanism fashionable in contemporary Protestant theology seems to be equivalent to a refusal to see that even the secular order must live by a standard of values which are not biological, and are therefore ultimately of spiritual origin. We do know that the particularly *human* characteristic *is* the sense of responsibility and obligation; the moral law in ourselves, the feeling for the rightness or wrongness of institutions, the very fact of law itself, bear witness to something which distinguishes man from sub-rational creation. . . . It [the humanist conception of man] is incomplete because it rejects the New Testament virtue of *agapé* (love), which is the very source of spiritual creativeness of the highest order; and *agapé* is the fruit of the spirit (Galatians v, 22). It is, in a word, the Kingdom of God (Romans xiv, 17).[19]

[17] *Christian Apologetics,* p. 82.
[18] *Op. cit.,* p. 198.
[19] *Ibid.,* p. 207.

Without approving the whole citation in detail, I feel, nevertheless, that the heart of this affirmation is solidly sound. The standards and values of the whole order of creation are not due to a dead natural law, neither are they merely positive in nature, but they are due to the dynamic concurrence of the Spirit of God with the whole order of creation. They are flexibly the command of God for concrete situations, yet not without a general recurrence of experience in the broad sense which is due to the created constancy both of the environment and of human nature. Neither natural law nor merely God's direct activity is enough to do justice to a Christian theism which takes seriously both the actuality of creation and the presence of God with all His creation. Such is the work of the Spirit of God in preparation for the coming of the Incarnation and the Holy Spirit, and as the constant background for both on the level of creation.

Having indicated something of what we mean by the Spirit of God, we turn to the relation between the Spirit and the Church. The Church is the fellowship of believers constituted by the revealing and redemptive activity of the Holy Spirit. The Church, even as Jesus Christ, has two natures, one human and one divine, but the constitutive nature of the Church is the divine. The Church is the extension of the life and teachings of Jesus, his death and everlasting victory over death, not merely as the perpetuation of a human consciousness or the historic transmission of a personal influence. The Church is primarily the direct activity of God in history, working openly in the fellowship through the revelation and empowerment which took place in the Incarnation. The Reality which became known in Jesus is still present making itself live and be known through the Church. In this sense it is the "fullness of him that filleth all in all,"[20] the very body of Christ.

Christ is the head of the Church. This Christ operates in history as the Holy Spirit. He is here not as the invasive event that created the fellowship through the discontinuous event of the Incarnation, but as the relational presence of the immanent God, as revealed and accepted. He is present as the Person of the Trinity that relates the triune God to the Church. "Christ in you" is "the hope of

[20] Eph. 1:23.

glory," but the Christ who is seeable and receivable only through the Holy Spirit. Only in the Spirit and according to the law of the Spirit, which is "joy and peace," are we sons and "joint heirs with Christ." Only in the Spirit can we walk "even as he walked." Only in the Spirit can we say, "Abba, Father."

We need this stress on the Holy Spirit, or the Spirit of Christ, as the reality and power of the Church. "The Holy Spirit is the life of the Church, the organizing energy within the Church. . . . While not identical with the Church, the Holy Spirit by his presence gives it an organic existence."[21] "The Holy Spirit is the soul of the Church. He forms a church consciousness."[22] "The Holy Spirit is the heart of the Church, for from him are the issues of the life of the Church."[23] "Christianity without the Spirit is not Christianity. It may be an ecclesiastical organization, but organization is not life. . . . What Christendom needs is . . . to become a worldwide brotherhood created by the Spirit of Christ. . . . It is unity—unity of spirit created by the Spirit."[24] Athanasius, we recall, wrote that Christ "assumed humanity that we might become God."[25] This is the high note of the Church, which is blasphemy if taken without the presence and power of the Spirit, but which is the Kingdom of God's sovereign love and power, where the entire process is initiated and carried on under the tutelage and in the reality of the Holy Spirit. Only thus can the Church constitute the "pillar and ground of truth." Only thus can the Church be considered glorious, as "without spot and wrinkle and any such thing," as "holy and without blemish." We need this New Testament doctrine of the Church.[26]

The Church is the only Incarnation of the Holy Spirit, or the Spirit of Christ, directly in human history. The fact that the Church is constituted by the Holy Spirit and owes to Him its deepest reality does not mean that the Church thereby loses its

---

[21] Denio, op. cit., p. 189.

[22] Ibid., p. 192.

[23] Ibid., p. 193.

[24] Conner, op. cit., p. 286.

[25] The Incarnation, p. 93 (Centenary Press).

[26] F. W. Dillistone has carefully examined many of the passages referring to the Church in his The Word of God and the People of God, and we commend this work for further study, as well as his book, The Holy Spirit and the Life of Today.

distinctive existence as a redeemed humanity and as a humanity being redeemed. We speak not of union or of absorption, but of communion and intermingling. The most important fact about any Christian is that Christ lives his life; yet lives he, too, in Christ. To live in fellowship and by means of it is not to lose individuality, but to empower and to enrich it. The Holy Spirit is present in history through the Church and is its deepest reality, but is not the Church. The eternal Christ is not limited to the historic personality of Jesus, nor the Holy Spirit to the historic fellowship of the Church.

Before we leave this subject, we ought to include the relation between the Holy Spirit and the Word. With regard to this question we shall say that the traditional formulation of the problem as one between the Holy Spirit and the Bible is unfortunate. "The Lord is the Spirit," and "the Word became flesh." The Lord is now the Word through the Spirit. In an address, Henry Joel Cadbury pointed out that in the New Testament the Word always refers to a Person, never to a book. The Bible is not the Word, but is the record about, and the witness to, the Word of God, which was in the beginning with God and was God.

Calvin made the correspondence between the Word as the Bible and the Spirit the criterion of Christian faith. But his stress on the "internal testimony of the Spirit" was so strong that had he known the scope of historical criticism now available, he would surely have had an even freer view of the written word than he did, though, even so, neither Luther nor he was a strict literalist.[27] A richer and more creative meaning, and less fixed, should now be given to his many statements to the effect that "the testimony of the Spirit is superior to all reason. For God alone is sufficient witness of himself in his own word, so also the word will never gain credit in the hearts of men, till it be confirmed by the internal testimony of the Spirit."[28] The nature and activity of that Spirit alone, which is God's high and holy love, as enacted in Christ, can rightly interpret the Bible, can rightly constitute the present Word of God.

The Puritans and the Dissenters later argued "whether the

---

[27] Cf. Lilley, *Religion and Revelation,* for a good account of this fact.
[28] *Institutes,* I, vii.

Word is to be tried by the Spirit or the Spirit by the Word. Logically, the controversy is preceded by the question whether the Spirit which was in those who wrote the Scriptures *can* be in contemporaries; and if so, whether, or how far, in the same mode."[29] The whole perspective shifts, however, when it is understood that the Word is Jesus Christ, God's enacted love in human history, His own self incarnate, rather than the external record. To limit the Spirit to the Bible is to deny His present efficacy, whether in prayer, preaching, sacrament, or the Christian community, by chaining Him to a closed canon. All Scripture is to be tested by the Lord who is the Spirit. He is the principle of authority, who builds up and does not cast down. This principle of truth and power gives us a basis of selection, discrimination, unity, cohesiveness, and organization of the Biblical material. Without it the Bible can be harmful; with it the Bible becomes a steadying light for weary travelers.[30]

Someone will say that this is subjectivism. So it is, in a real sense. Kierkegaard is surely right that subjectivism is truth in so far as the spirit is always a subject, never an object. The personal, the spiritual, is ever subjective. Personal relations are primary not only in the spiritual life, but also in reality and truth. This we have tried to show elsewhere, and how the right interpretation of the spiritual-personal category alone can show us Him who can explain, judge, and save all relations including the objective or the impersonal.[31] Heim is surely right, therefore, that "real speech can take place between two persons only when they are in action, when they meet each other on the plane of the Present."[32] *Revelation cannot be both past and primary.* The past can constitute the occasion, the needed condition, but not the exclusive condition, for that revelation. Though seldom unmediated, the Spirit is always immediate, and cannot be limited by us to any past.

This subjectivism does not mean, however, that the Spirit lacks structure nor that it lacks historic fixedness. In Jesus Christ we see the kind of community with God and among men, which alone

---

[29] Nuttall, *The Holy Spirit,* p. 28.
[30] Cf. *Pillars of Faith,* chap. 4.
[31] *Reason and the Christian Faith,* Vols. I and II, particularly *Faith and Reason.*
[32] *God Transcendent,* p. 170. Cf. also Buber, *Between Man and Man.*

can fulfill our deepest needs, as individual and society, and give the proper meaning to the natural world. The Bible is the definite blueprint, the steady and strong strand of history, which gives form and perpetuity to this meaning as far as historic mediation is needed in a fellowship of "righteousness from faith to faith." Otto Piper is, therefore, right in calling for an objective faith anchored in the objective revelation of God.[33] The Bible gives structure to the Spirit through its witness to the Christ-deed and the Christian community. These, and these only, are the objective standards, in themselves acts on the part of subjects, and always dependent, at that, on their subjective reception by the work of the Holy Spirit in Christian experience. They are, however, needfully witnessed to, or continuously declared by, the right use of the Bible.

In one sense, of course, the Holy Spirit is as objective as Christ and the Church, because He is not we, but He is first of all over against our actual selves. Then follows an interpenetration of spirits, as we live in, by and for Him, just as there was the interpenetration between our spirits and the Spirit of God before that. Unless we are recipients of the Holy Spirit, moreover, "Christ in us," we are not genuine recipients of the saving mystery and power of the Gospel.

The Holy Spirit whether in Himself or as the Spirit of God, is the principle and power of historic novelty. He is the source of creativity. Thought and language fail to fathom reality beyond the now in its mysterious depths. Whitehead rightly maintains that not "ignorance but the ignorance of ignorance is the death of knowledge," and that the measure of a man's intellectual competence is his sense of mystery. Bevan maintains that the human mind revolts against descriptions of heaven that stop short of the boundless, that lack "the suggestive 'halo of poetry.' "[34] "Newness belongs to the very essence of revelation," writes E. F. Scott, and comes with more than intellectual assent, with living power.[35] The Holy Spirit is truly "the gift of understanding which comes to

---

[33] *Theology Today*, Spring, 1947.
[34] *Op. cit.*, p. 294.
[35] *The New Testament Idea of Revelation*, p. 233.

raise us from our poverty."[36] Within His richness of feeling and thought are generated new creative and constructive actions, combining, when genuinely His, "ardor and accuracy," to use Hugh Vernon White's phrase, to remake both our inner lives and our social living.

Such creativity involves, naturally, much change both in approach and in action. "A fruit tree will bear no fruit unless it be occasionally pruned, and progress is impossible without a painful disturbance of cherished and accepted customs, institutions and beliefs. . . . The world is looking for guidance, but the guide is one who has the courage to discard what is obsolete and the insight to create what is new. It is looking for the guidance of the Constructive Revolutionary."[37] That is it! The relation between the Spirit and the Word is that the Lord is the Spirit whose Word is "quick and powerful, sharper than any two-edged sword, and piercing even to the dividing asunder of soul and spirit . . . and is a discerner of the thoughts and intents of the heart."[38]

Naturally, in identifying the Church so closely with the Spirit and the Word, we are not forgetting the other nature of the Church. The Church has definitely its human side, not only in actuality, but intrinsically as part of its very nature within our created order. The Church is not only spirit and body, but spirit and flesh in the fuller Scriptural meaning of that term. "Flesh," in that fuller sense, means a dynamic opposition to the Spirit. But perhaps we had better analyze this relation in this way:

First of all, the Church is spirit as apart from Spirit. Every human being is spirit over against Spirit. The fact that the Holy Spirit indwells the Church does not cancel or negate its human spirit, its *Gemeindegeist,* but cleanses, illumines and empowers it. The Holy Spirit is God's side of the Church and is, to be sure, incomparably the most important. The Spirit of God also works with all zest in the Church, maintaining the urge to freedom and to initiative, and causing creative energies to spring forth. Both of these are from God and of God. But besides both of these is the spirit of the group which has a reality beyond the reality of each

---

[36] Gilson, *Philosophy of St. Bonaventure,* p. 111.
[37] Streeter, ed. (in his own chapter), *The Spirit,* p. 360 and p. 367.
[38] Heb. 4:12.

individual. There is such a thing as a social reality. Later we shall see that this stress on group spirit does not minimize personal reality, for although no individual is responsible for the total community, he is responsible for the kind of community that he does choose. The Church is always a corporate reality, however, beyond that of all its members *as such*.

The Spirit of God relates Himself both to an individual as such and to the urges of groups on the sub-Agapaic level, but the Holy Spirit never relates Himself to an individual as such nor to any group except to the Church, in so far as it is truly itself, in honest acceptance of the meaning and power of God's Agape in Christ, and in so far as it is, therefore, continually *for* the world. This discussion is now sufficient to indicate something of the meaning and reality of the Church when we come to discuss its relation to social action. But the discussion of a few subsidiary questions will further clarify our position and help to avoid easy misunderstandings.

We have not underestimated the shortcomings and sinfulness of the Church as a sociological institution. Surely we have not said that all of its members are dominantly drawn by Agape rather than driven by need or by fear. The history of the Church or a present survey of its attitudes ought to convince us how far the Church as an institution falls short of being a redemptive fellowship. This failure simply means that the actual Church is in no large measure to be equated with the true Church. We avoid the terms "invisible" and "visible" for the reason that the true Church, when it is true, is very visible. Even though God alone can fully judge as to who are its real members, nevertheless, we can judge well enough by the fruits and the lack of fruits that the Church is far from being God's light on the hill and salt for corruption. Darkness and corruption are rampant within its borders. Yet within that very visible Church, there is a true Church, a leaven within the lump, not only for the world, but even for the institution itself. There are green twigs in the tree of historic continuity; none apart from it; but the continuity is not in terms of physical transmission or hierarchical structures, but in the reality of the Holy Spirit incarnated in the fellowship. The real apostolic succession is the centrality of Agape "from faith to faith." Though a later volume is to develop this thought, in this connection we want to stress, and to stress again, that in the Church we are not placing a perfectionist society over against a sinful one, but, rather, a fellowship of forgiveness and the fruits of the Spirit over against a community that both longs for this fellowship, at the depths of its striving, and yet also keeps rejecting it for numerous reasons; sin within the Church being just as much of a reason, perhaps, as sin in the community outside the Church.

All of history is for the sake of effecting the fellowship. All of history, therefore, receives its meaning from the Church, which Bulgakov calls "the ground and goal of creation." In one sense, therefore, all of history is the history of the Church. History means community, whether potentially, falsely, partially, or actually. This is true also of "secular" history. This larger and preparatory relation we may call, with Tillich, the Church in "expectation." It is "the latent" Church. This Church in expectation, seeking but not knowing, or knowing and yet not wanting to know and to do, is under the sway of the Spirit of God, positively and negatively. When the Church "in reception" works together with the Church "in expectation," or even when the two work at cross purposes, even in opposition unto death, there is a common reality which combines them. The potential Church, because it is just that, both longs for and dreads the actualized Church.

The Church *in expectation* is mostly a church of seeking. It is a Church of questing and of questioning. It combines the not yet of knowledge with the not yet of will. Where there has been more knowledge there is more of a not yet of will. Where little knowledge has been given, the potential church cherishes a large not yet of understanding. The Church *in reception* is a church where there is what Hocking calls "clarified anticipation." The revealing event of the Christ-deed has made clear the pattern of the fellowship which is the Eternal Purpose for the historic process. The event has come with power as well as light and some have accepted both the light and the power in a real measure. Christ in Jesus was clarified anticipation of what is to be. Christ in the Church continues that clarification. Personal appropriation is the meaning of the contemporaneous Christ. It is the continued incarnation of the Spirit of Christ or of the Holy Spirit.

The Church in reception is always a matter of some having or it is not the Church. If there is no having, there is no clarified anticipation. Yet since the Church as an actual fellowship is mostly under the dominance of the Spirit of God, as far as actual attainment is concerned, the Church is more a matter of hoping than of having. The Church is Christian in some having and in much hoping, but below such having and hoping, it is not Christian. Therefore the anticipation is fragmentary and the clarification obscured. The more the Church has this fellowship, the clearer becomes the pattern of the Eternal Purpose. For the most part the pattern becomes clear in the apostles, not in the professional ministry as such, but in the actual ministry of those who have learned what it means not to count their life as dear unto themselves that they may discharge their ministry and proclaim the Gospel of the grace of God. Through them the Church in reception most vitally meets the Church in expectation. There the Church finds the fulfillment of seeking, in a peculiar measure, and most forcefully becomes the Church as "clarified anticipation."

The Church as the Incarnation of the Holy Spirit is thus both true human society and the heavenly society. It is *true* society because it is *more* than society. It is that *more* than society which is the expression and representation of the *More* than society. The Church is the Kingdom of God on earth, the procession of the Holy Spirit from the Father through the Son into history.[39] Just as the Holy Spirit, or the Spirit of Christ, is in a person who is not perfect, yet Himself remains perfect, so the Holy Spirit exists within an imperfect society and is yet Himself perfect, besides perfecting in being and judgment all those who accept Him, to whatever extent He is understood and authentically appropriated. Where the Spirit truly rules, there is perfection. Just as there can be a little gold in the body without arthritis' being cured, and still the gold be gold, so the Holy Spirit can be present without full, or even a dominant, cleansing of a person or of the Church. As the dose of gold is increased, if cure is to be had that way, however, the body is gradually cured of its ill. Even so, as the Holy Spirit is allowed to give more light and more power, the person or the

---

[39] Cf. *The Christian Fellowship,* chap. 5, "The Kingdom of God and the Christian Church."

Church is cleansed and empowered for the works of love and the fruits of the Spirit.

Thus the heavenly society is already present in history, the Kingdom is here even now, within the Church; yet the Church also, because of its large allegiance to the Spirit of God rather than to the Holy Spirit, far more represents the Kingdom than it embodies it. Allegiance to the Spirit of God in the Church over against the Holy Spirit often means the preference, in conscious or depth-conscious choice, of partial values which obstruct and destroy the fuller values. In other words, such allegiance includes sin.

All sin is mixed with finitude and with some value sought, however distorted. This does not mean that man's will is totally good and only mistaken in his choices. It means, rather, that no man is totally evil, Satanic through and through, but, being a "man in contradiction," as Brunner calls him, his sinning consists in his deliberate choice, in his depth self, of personal satisfactions and preferences over against what his fullest self knows are God's commands and promises. But though the Church because of this allegiance to the sub-Agapaic life far more represents than embodies the Kingdom, nevertheless in so far as Jesus Christ is there as the true head and in so far as the Incarnation of the Holy Spirit is actually taking place, even to that extent the heavenly society is present, which alone constitutes true human society.

When we have said this, however, and maintained that the Church is a supernatural reality embodying the true human society, we must be very careful, as we draw this chapter to a close, that we do not leave the impression that the Church, even at its best, is a finished pattern of any kind whatsoever. All creation, at all times and in all circumstances, is a relative matter and no perfection within creation can ever be a closed perfection.

At the same time, we must maintain that the Church is revealed history, the exemplified purpose for process, containing within it, by God's grace, the perfection of its heavenly society, and also that it is only an earnest of what is to be. Only a real sense of mystery leaves the spirit free to breathe the air of the Spirit. Much stress on mystery denies revelation and cuts the nerve of faith, hope and love. Much stress on revelation denies mystery and reduces God to human dimensions. A joyous faith accepts the Christ and the

Church as the meaning of the Eternal Purpose for our historic process, and yet feels itself buried, as in an ocean, by the eternal Reality and possibilities of God for creative newness. Thus even the Church in reception is in expectation, not only as the background and constant accompaniment of its life here on earth, but in expectation of the endless growth and discontinuous dimensions that are possible with God. A cramped religion is a crippled religion. The race is to the swift who see truly in part, but who also stretch ever forward toward the higher calling in Christ Jesus. Thus the true human society is the heavenly society in origin and in present being, but not a concluded heavenly society. Rather, it is one that is ever open to the constantly unfolding fullness of God.

We have thus at least indicated the nature and function of the Church as the incarnation of the Holy Spirit. The Church is the only place in history where God's Agape breaks through with saving power. Where this relationship to God in Christ exists, there is the Church. The Holy Spirit is the living Christ, or Agape, or God fully revealed and appropriated, though obviously always by a relative understander and accepter. The Holy Spirit is the God-side of the Church. The Holy Spirit is the relational love of God, conditioned through the life and teachings of Jesus and the living communion with the Christ, which He keeps incarnating through the Christian community. Only after Agape was revealed as central in cosmos and conduct through God's Christ-deed in Jesus, and in his filial obedience, did the Holy Spirit come into history. Pentecost is the illumination and empowerment through tongues of fire of this central truth of the Eternal Purpose for the historic process.

The Father is present with the Son in history through the Holy Spirit in the Church. This stress is wrong when the Father is reduced to historic dimensions, when His participation in history imperils His complete creation of it and control over it. Then co-existence and co-passion are dangerous errors. Hocking has rightly pointed out how the Son without the Father, as a distinct dimension, loses His power of transcendence, His power to save beyond the world. But to think that the Father is not with the Son in the Spirit, whether in creation or redemption, is to court a split God, a real division in the Godhead. We have stressed the Church as the Incarnation of the Holy Spirit because this is its distinctive dimension, but not the exclusion of its relation to the full Trinity. It is God Himself who urges us to freedom. It is He who has given us this longing for self-being that we might become real fellows for fellowship. It is He, who in His grace and wisdom pushes in us by our creative drives and makes us place ourselves over against others in order that our freedom might be real. "Personality growth proceeds through the constructive handling of conflict, not through the absence of conflict."[40] God has weighted us toward the self that we might never be mere puppets and He keeps enlarging the scope and scale of our freedom so that, even when we are "full of the Spirit," we can be led out into the wilderness to be tempted by the devil. The devil is the adversary who wants us to seek to have independent power to get along physically, by turning stones into bread; to be free of physical danger, by throwing ourselves down the precipice; to win power over the world, simply by worshiping its demonic powers: but all these temptations are part and parcel of the human scene. They are the experiences which we all must have of over-againstness, if we are to find the freedom of "not my will but thy will be done."

The order of creation is not ultimately opposed to God, but is in the service of God. To the fearful it must ever be under the control of the devil. To him it must ever be impious to attribute the trials of life to God. God to him is the god of the pure good, conceived in terms of finished ends. To the maturer Christian the God of creation is none other than the God of the Cross and of the Crown. All creation is cursed for man's sake, not out of arbitrary anger or out of weakness, nor because it is out of the control of God, but out of the love and wisdom of God, for the sake of the preparation of our redemption. Even the world is subject to redemption and, in the end, all will be subjected to Christ, and Christ to God.

For our social theory this fact is going to be crucial. We are now shortly to try to point out more concretely how neither the separatist-quietist, nor the social gospel method were genuine Christian alternatives. We are going to see, in the next chapter, what constitutes the distinctive Christian dimension of social action

[40] Hiltner, *Pastoral Counseling*, p. 75.

and how in that dimension both the direct and indirect approaches are organically joined, without ever being merged or confused. For this dimension, the relation between the Spirit and the Church is decisive.

Personal reality and responsibility are not canceled out, but consecrated, by this belonging to the community. Every human being must belong to some community, and that community has a social reality over and above the reality of its individual members. The self takes on a new dimension of purpose and power, of meaning and reality, in so far as he is truly a member organically of a group. Thus the group has reality in and through its members, and with regard to its kind of function, in relation to reality and truth.

Fellowship is "bound together" by purpose, as one of my students remarked, and differs from mere friendship by means of that purpose which causes the group to function in a particular way. There is what Walter Muelder calls "a communitarian" reality. The Church is the reality of a community normatively related and regulated by the Holy Spirit, but which is as yet largely in the preparatory stage, wherein it must be related to and regulated by the Spirit of God. Nevertheless, the Church is the dimension of divine discontinuity, not only on the level of redemption, but with respect to the eternal dimension of God's central purpose with creation, which dominantly transcends it and yet alone gives to it meaning and direction. The importance of this fact for social theory may already be glimpsed. Particularly is this true when we remember that the Church in expectation is also organically related to the Church in reception.

Even as God ever exceeds any actuality by His endless possibilities, even so there is no end to Christian growth in community. Thus a Christian is staggered both by what he sees and by what he cannot see. His certainty of the adequacy of the Christian community as true society is grounded in God Himself, who cannot be unfaithful, and his fear and trembling is grounded in his own littleness wherein all having is, at best, only an earnest of hoping; and all believing, at its truest, is merely the title deed to the fuller faith; and all loving, at its fullest, is merely the sense of ever being loved beyond any loving that we can ourselves do.

CHAPTER V

The Distinctive Dimension
of Christian Social Action

The task of this chapter is to point out in what respect Christian social action is different from social action in general. If it were not different, we should not talk about Christian social action; we should merely speak of Christians engaging in social action—if they should. What is it, then, which constitutes the distinctive dimension of Christian social action?

By "dimension" we mean a particular relationship in which one participates. There are different dimensions to life, as, for instance, the physical, the social and the spiritual. The person is the same, but he participates in different relationships. A dimension, in our use of the term, is thus comparable to a status. The person has a status of a citizen or of an alien. That same person can also have the status of a white man or of a Negro. In either situation he is treated according to his standing with relation to the rules or requirements, real or arbitrary, of each situation. Perhaps the word "locus" will serve our purpose, meaning the place which satisfies given conditions. The Latin word *locus* is often used to indicate what we mean by a dimension. Consider, for example, the expression, *in loco civile,* the relationships of a man as a citizen, or, more generally, in theology, his relationships with regard to earthly rather than to spiritual affairs.

A perspective, as differentiated from a dimension, refers mostly to seeing. Naturally, a perspective does not have to depend merely upon a subjective situation. It can mean, of course, merely that a thing appears different depending upon whether it is seen from afar or from a short distance, whether it is seen on the level or from above or below, etc. The word can also be used, however, to indicate a new relationship in which the same thing is seen so as to give it a different appearance. If a large building is erected behind an ordinary house, that house becomes seen in a different perspective. A partial perspective on the problem of evil, such as hedonism, is, of course, a way of seeing. But when the same problem is seen in the larger relationships which organically include and involve the place and function of hedonism, not only is the problem seen from a fuller angle, but the actual involvements or relationships are also different.

The word "dimension" may be a better word here, though dimension often connotes too much "up and down," levels of being or seeing, or a measurable magnitude of some kind or another, rather than a relationship. But even so, dimension certainly also means a new context of meaning, as, for instance, the difference of dimension which occurs when a certain kind of rectangle is first seen without depth and then seen in a new dimension. This idea of context of meaning has some affinity with what we mean by dimension, but does not exhaust it, for dimension in our sense stands for actual difference of relationship. The German word *Einstellung* expresses what we want, if it is thought of as the being placed into an actual involvement, rather than the perspectival identification with a situation. A "stage" of being could be used, like "the stage of the law," or "the stage of perfection"; but the difficulty with this is that, in this case, the developmental point of view is too strongly stressed, and also the successive aspects of experience rather than the actual relationship which characterizes the dimension.

We might say that in one dimension a person is a father; in another, a professional man; in another, a club member. Our conception of dimension, however, is not merely loosely related to a person or to a group as the uniting factor, but there is also a determining intrinsic relationship among the dimensions, without their being thereby either merely developmental or determined, either with regard to a central point of reference or reality or from within the participants who are characterized by these dimensions.

Determinism and freedom are symbiotic relations, for example, containing both immediate flexibility and ultimate order.

In order to arrive at the distinctive dimensions of Christian social action we must first look at all the dimensions pertinent to our subject, which characterize human life under God. The first dimension to be considered is the personal. We recall that in the last volume, *Evil and the Christian Faith,* we found that the personal-spiritual was the only adequate perspective from which to view the problem of evil. Only in that dimension of existence can there be an actual solution of the problem. This centrality of the personal-spiritual dimension is equally true with respect to our understanding of Christian social action, or to our grasp of the Christian answer to our practical problems of present life. Here we are naming this category *the personal dimension* rather than the personal-spiritual. This does not mean, however, that we now give a less important place to the spirit. On the contrary, when the ultimate is thought of in relation to itself, the spirit is always the primary category. The category of categories is the Spirit. Next in importance is the spirit, man's central relation to God. God is Spirit. Man essentially is spirit, created spirit, to be sure, but definitely and determinatively, spirit. The deepest reality and highest dignity of man is the fact that he is spirit, made by and for Spirit. The fellowship of God with man is in and through the Spirit, whether the Spirit of God or the Holy Spirit; and, as we have seen, both are in some way involved in this fellowship.

But spirit stands for depth-reality beyond full searching out. It bloweth where it listeth. The ways of the spirit can be known only in the spirit. Spiritual things are only spiritually discerned. When they are known on the level of communicable knowledge, they are known through symbols or thoughts which refer to the reality, but which can never either contain it or adequately convey it. Symbols and words point to the reality and can communicate to others the content intended, in so far as there has been a common background of experience. But as John Dewey well says: an experience "is had immediately." There is a qualitative uniqueness about all such having of experience that can never be transmitted to another person. Life in one real sense is an aloneness, a solitariness as far as overt communication goes. Nicolai Hartmann is therefore right that whereas consciousness separates, spirit unites. The basic individuation of experience is personality. Personality is the center of consciousness and, therefore, of knowledge. Whitehead is surely right that consciousness is the crown of experience seldom attained, that we have made too much of consciousness and not enough of the deeper levels of life. The language of the Bible is depth-language, and, therefore, when it is real it comes with power, whereas the language of mere knowledge often leaves untouched the deeper reaches of the self. Knowledge tempts to pride, whereas love builds the person up, because knowledge is connected with the separatist aspects of personality, his conscious experience which individuates. That is the reason that in ecumenical gatherings the discussion of doctrine often leads to estrangement whereas worship unites. Any real unity must first come in the spirit because it partakes of the harmony of truth and of the reality of the Spirit. In finding this truth and reality, however, knowledge has its secondary or instrumental part,[1] but knowledge, then, is the not yet knowing anything in the sense of adequate knowing, but still a being mostly known by God on the deeper level of the Spirit.

In stressing the primacy of the personal dimension, or the personal category, then, we have not meant to slight the spiritual dimension. Our discussion of this reality *in terms of knowledge,* however, must be centrally carried out *in terms of personality.* All other categories are partial perspectives or shallower dimensions. This fact does not preclude the other fact that personality is no matter of merely external relations. Persons are not individual in the sense in which billiard balls are individual. Even there we know that there is an organismic relationship obtaining throughout the whole world, making any disjunct and total individuality only a matter of appearance. Perhaps the billiard balls are less individuals than are persons. But we mean such an illustration to refer to the realm of appearance.

Personalities, in any case, are not individual even in the sense of totally disjunct consciousnesses. They may appear so, perhaps, to

[1] Cf. Hazelton's excellent chapter, "Faith's Need of Understanding," in *Renewing the Mind.*

the persons themselves and to others. But actually we need not depend upon recent research into telepathy to know how the origin, content and function of consciousness are social in nature. Consider the works of such men as Whitehead, Boodin, Smuts and Mead, to mention only a few. Social psychology is not a small branch of psychology specializing in certain select fields of experience; social psychology, rightly understood, lies at the bottom of all psychology. The individual treated apart from his total context of society is a methodological abstraction, even as he is a functional abstraction. There is, to be sure, a private knowledge and a qualitatively unique aspect of experience which cannot be subject to common knowledge. Introspection would be the only possible approach, and the result would be highly personal in nature. The individual, therefore, is real as a center of consciousness, of experience, of choice, or of satisfaction, but he is never real apart from his social background in origin and function. Knowledge is basically a social act.[2]

We cannot, therefore, accept any personalism in which the discreteness of the individual is strongly stressed, except for hortatory purposes. The common misunderstanding of the doctrine of the Trinity may even be due to this fallacy of the eye, this external abstracting of individuality, this clear fencing of one consciousness from another. In the realm of the spirit, the unity of the self with society and with God is far more deep than in terms of individual personalities, not necessarily in purpose, nor according to the ordinary categories of consciousness, but according to the depths of God which unite in the Eternal Purpose all the realms of life, beyond the temporary and surface division of our perception and acting out of personality.

The primacy of the personal perspective, then, is not over against the spiritual perspective, but is merely the stressing of the centrality for knowledge and conscious action of personal relations. After all, fellowship consists of individuated consciousnesses, of personalities. In this sense, God is the ground of consciousness beyond all personality, beyond all individuality as one more personality, as Tillich stresses over and over again; but God is the ground of being, the ground of consciousness, the ground of history, pre-

2 Cf. *The Christian Fellowship*, chap. 1.

cisely as the Spirit who has personal form, as the original, self-existent, all-including, purposing consciousness who is the Creator and Redeemer of all. The interpenetrating power of Spirit does not preclude real separateness.

But neither must we refuse to recognize the actuality, or the temporary reality, of creation in order to stress the primacy of the personal category. The fact that personal categories are the most inclusive and relevant for social theory does not mean that they exhaust reality. Spirit goes beyond personality as the all-inclusive reality which holds together all actual and all possible worlds; so that God's personality becomes a matter of true distinctness from all creation, and yet does not become a limitation or a fencing off from creation. Spirit, then, includes all, even creation, but includes all by means of differentiations, such as distinctness of the personal and distinctness of the impersonal realms. Creation is possible only on account of that which is not "objectified," to use the terminology of Berdyaev. The objectified, however, is not apart from spirit, but open to the concurrence of spirit. The material and the immaterial, the personal and the impersonal—all are open categories. They are penetrable and manageable by Him who made them. This, too, is important for social theory, as we shall see, for much of our approach has been in terms of physical vision, of space-thinking, rather than of spiritual understanding. Much social effort has been mostly externalistic in terms of legislation, the forcing of the good, the compelling of the Kingdom of God. Other effort has been purely internal, by means of conversion and regeneration within the circle of the elect, without any mighty realization that there is a Reality which unites the inside and the outside without confusing them, a fact which makes necessary the two-edged sword of the Spirit.

Why, then, do we emphasize the primacy of the personal category for social action? In the first place, community consists of people. Spirit underlies community, and nature is its necessary historic medium, but the community itself is made up of people. Only by making these persons the center of attention can we make a new kind of community in conformity with Christian truth. Persons are more than law or duty, for instance. Their final judgments, if at all according to the nature and not strongly warped, go back to personal categories. Externals mean so much to us, for instance, because we want the approval of people. Children try to satisfy their parents, to please, to belong, to be accepted. Our earthly parents are only symbols and temporary substitutes for God, whom we all should like to please though we dread having to do so, too, even though it is good for us. We may be like my son who, when his parents, home from a long trip, set him to mowing the lawn, said, "Gee, I hate to do it, but I love to have to!"

In the same way the personal category is primary because the satisfying of the law cannot take the place of satisfying the deeper needs of the person. A husband may help his wife wash the dishes and fulfill every domestic requirement, if his financial situation is of one kind, or if his purse can stand it he may buy her gifts and provide expensive entertainment, and still not give her the one thing her heart really craves: deep, understanding love and appreciation as a person. Men can try and try to please God by doing more and more, as they are driven on by guilt complexes, and still only weary the patience of God, who cares little for burnt offerings and sacrifices, whether of gift or of work. In this sense, the personal category is primary. In this sense, the prophetic protest against externals and the demand for spirit worship are ever needed.

In Christian theology this truth is very important. God's primary relation to man in fellowship is person-to-person. God is not satisfied with merely station-to-station calls. The relation of God to man is through the Spirit, but the Spirit is the relational aspect of God, the co-consciousness of God with men. The fellowship itself, however, is between God and men and between men and men. The fellowship is composed of persons. The objective Christ is the objective Mediator; the subjective Spirit is the subjective Mediator. Between the objective God, transcendent or immanent, must be the subjective God, and between all human community there must be present the subjective Other, whether of the Spirit of God or of the Holy Spirit. God's relation to man is always mostly in personal terms. Thus the main fact is not whether God is related to man on the basis of holiness, as Thomas Aquinas held, or on the basis of sin, as Nygren holds, but that God is always related to man primarily on the basis of personality, in and through the Spirit. Thus God is related to every man as Father whether the child is wayward or at home. God loves all men perfectly at all times. He loves them not as stones or as trees, but as men, as creatures capable of responding to that love. Whether, then, holiness and law are primary in the realm of the Spirit of God while love is primary in the realm of the Holy Spirit is a secondary question, functionally important, but dependent upon a prior reality and standard.

The primacy of the personal dimension makes it clear also, for instance, that the Cross of Jesus is not a primary category, eternally belonging, as it does, to the realm of means, but not being an intrinsic part of the eternal fellowship itself. The Cross is intrinsic to the effecting of the Eternal Purpose, but is not the Eternal Purpose. The Cross belongs in the dimension of law, of the satisfaction of the law, juridically and dynamically, and of the creation of a new kind of righteousness beyond the law, but fulfilling it. The Cross is thus a means to the full fellowship. God's basic relation to man is always that of Personality to personality through the Spirit. The personal dimension is thus always primary and central in relation to all other dimensions. But to produce the right personal dimension, namely, Agape fellowship, several dimensions are necessary. To these we now turn.

The first of these is the dimension of the natural man. We may follow theological usage and call this dimension man *in loco naturale.* Certainly it is obvious that no social theory can be at all adequate that does not consider the nature of the ultimate and the nature of man. In any social theory that calls itself Christian, God and man are surely pivotal points. The social process and its relationships cannot be fathomed apart from the main actors involved in that process. What is the given nature of man? First of all, in answer to this, we must remember that no natures are given apart from society. Human nature is partially a product from the past and partially a product of the present. Human nature may root back into animal drives and also depend upon its reach upward toward the sun of God's purpose for it, but it has a level and reality of its own. Human nature cannot be reduced to environmental stimuli and responses on the part of purely plastic organisms. Human nature has self-being. It contributes sameness amidst difference. What, then, is this sameness?

Human nature is constituted by its capacity for purposive fellowship. Purpose involves "free ideas," in the sense in which we use the term.[3] Purpose, moreover, presupposes choice and thus some degree of meaningful freedom. Purpose for fellowship requires the capacity for self-transcendence. Such self-transcendence depends upon reason, the sense of meaning, the notion of time, the importance of responsibility. Fellowship needs not only freedom, but the lure and longing for togetherness. Fellowship depends upon a capacity for love which is not founded on mere mutual interest but on mutuality of concern. Nor can this concern, to be purposive, be merely social in nature. It must go beyond the immediate needs and problem-solvings of organically related groups, in the biologically instrumental sense. This concern must unite the group through its being related to, and serving, something beyond itself. Purposive fellowship is grounded in a goal toward which the fellowship moves and which holds it together.

In other words, purposive fellowship points to the universal Transcendence which is God and to the transcendent goal which is the Eternal Purpose. Unity, cohesiveness and vitality of purpose come only from this transcendence of meaning which to move man must fully recede into mystery. Such transcendence combines creative zest with steadiness of light and lifts fellowship into living purposiveness. Purposive fellowship, in other words, presupposes the capacity for religion. Community is never its fullest and freest when it is severed, through false understanding or even through social zeal, from its religious roots and its religious outlook and drive. Human nature is characterized universally by the capacity for community, man with man, with regard to something which transcends man as man.

The universal nature of man which consists in his capacity for purposive fellowship, partially satisfied within society, yet reaching longingly beyond it, especially through its most vital and creative individuals, roots in man's sense of right and in his sense of love. Man's reason is needed in order for this sense of right and

[3] Cf. Blanshard, *The Nature of Thought.*

for this sense of love to transcend the immediate, but reason is not original in the same depth-sense as the others are. Once upon a time man was called the child of God because of his capacity to reason. Reason was even called the image of God whereby man distinguishes himself from the animal world. But the sense of right and the sense of love are more elemental than reason. Reason refers to ideas which convey reality or, rather, which point to reality more than they convey it. Life relates itself to reality more through the sense of right and through the sense of love than through reason. Ideas tend to produce in us a sense of unreality, and when the mystic contemplates long enough, he may get this strongly into his very being. Then nothing seems compellingly real; everything evaporates into a sense of ideas. Students often experience how increasingly ideas remove them from the compelling nature of reality, not in the sense of more of freedom, which we feel at times, but in the sense of the unreality and unimportance of everything.

Man's sense of right is an elemental part of his nature. To be without all sense of right is to be less than human. Kant's investigation into the "categorical imperative" has an aspect of unshakable truth. Some thinkers, like Brunner, make this sense of right central to the image of God. He calls it responsibility, or accountability, or answerability. Man must answer to God's call. This answer, whatever be its content, is an inescapable part of being human. The content of conscience may vary, but the active capacity to react in terms of some sense of right is there, provided there is no moral disease present. The form is there regardless of the specific content. To have no sense of right whatsoever is to be below the highest animal level, where this sense exists, though here, of course, apart from free ideas and self-transcendence. Man's sense of right is in some way related to purposive fellowship. But when we have said that, we have also said that the sense of right is not merely formal in the sense of a complete relativism of morals.

The sense of right is, rather, organically connected with man's gregarious nature. To sin against the brethren is to sin against Christ, Paul writes. But this connecting of the social with the religious is integral to man's total nature. Each man is, at the same time, related to society and to the ultimate, and to both he is related organically. Society is not made *de novo* from discrete individuals either by contract or by circumstance. Society springs organically out of a relation to the environment where gregariousness characterizes lower levels of being and where the very perpetuation of itself depends upon mutuality. Aristotle is right that man is a political animal before he is an individual in the sense that he springs inevitably from a social vortex. Yet the same society is itself confronted inevitably with the ultimate, for to be human is to decide inescapably for oneself and for the group what is most important and most real.

If existentialism has any permanent truth, beyond the fadism of words and academic novelty, its truth is man's inescapable involvement with others and with the universe in which he lives. To disregard the total involvement and to speak of an ethical autonomy to decide one's world, in the sense of much modern humanistic existentialism, is to go no more than halfway with truth. The halfway is good, but when this is made into a defense against the fuller truth, the half-truth becomes really dangerous. For men are convinced by half-truths and often use their ideology to camouflage their escape from the fuller truth, not only camouflage it to others, but to their own selves. Existentialism as a total metaphysics, whether acknowledged to be so or not, is a pure pragmatism and relativism that destroys the foundations of civilization. Existentialism as a proper component of metaphysics allows for that dynamism which characterizes the universe and ethical choice alike and is indispensable to any adequate metaphysics, even as it must be a strong aspect of any adequate religious interpretation.

Man's sense of right is organically involved with both society and the universe. Morality and religion join hands not by choice but by nature, unless, of course, they are perverted by interpretation or practice. That is why the moralist answer to the Neo-orthodox by a man like H. D. Lewis is so unsatisfactory, for he tries to make the ethical field autonomous and self-sufficient.[4] One can see his rebellion against the extremes of some theologians who have discarded what Leo Baeck calls "Judaism in the Church."[5] The Jewish stress on righteousness, on conduct, is of utmost impor-

---

[4] Cf. *Morals and the New Theology.*
[5] *The Pharisees,* chap. 3.

tance, and Judaizing becomes bad only when morals become the way of salvation rather than fellowship itself.

How does our analysis of man *in loco naturale* fit into the discussion of whether man is naturally good or evil? In this dimension man is plainly both. The sense of right itself and its observance, however partially and imperfectly, are themselves good. Man's whole creative growth toward "the fullness of time" is that far good. There is a true preparation for fellowship on every level of life. If natural man were mostly evil, there would be no preparation for any fuller time. When most of the house is bad, it tends to deteriorate more and more; if, however, it is partially run down, but mostly good, it is subject to repair. A defensive and invidious Christian theology has tended to paint all human nature black in order to magnify the grace of God, but in so doing it has scoffed at His grace in creation and in creating. God has never left Himself without a witness anywhere; everywhere He is at work in history. The Spirit of God prepares for the Holy Spirit. The Old Testament prepares for the New. The old covenant prepares for the one founded on better promises. To say that the image of God has been totally destroyed by some "fall" is either to smuggle in a chronological fall by means of general experience or to vilify general experience.

This does not mean, however, on the other hand, that man is mostly good in the sense that he needs no salvation and can grow good by himself or be educated into the Kingdom of God by human means. That problem lies in quite another dimension of life. We affirm, rather, that though we be evil, we know how to give good gifts, that we can of ourselves judge what is right, that those without the law of Moses or of Christ have still the law written in their hearts and do by nature the things contained in the law because they are a law unto themselves. This is not a static law; it is no psychological compartment finished and sealed off until some fullness of time either for the old or for the new law. This is, rather, the work of the Spirit of God, dynamically operating with all creative urges and with all efforts for good. To reject synergism in proper proportions and in the right perspective is to deny fellowship altogether.

Obviously natural man is mostly egocentric; the problem

whether natural man is more concerned with self than with others and with God hardly exists, except for romantic speculation on the part of those who do not even know their own hearts. The problem is, rather, whether a Christian, and certainly whether most Christians, ever get away from this dominant egocentricity. The question is whether Luther, who maintained that God's grace in Christ comes mostly to people who are still in themselves basically sinners, is more or less right than Wesley, who said that God's grace in Christ comes after conversion, and particularly after sanctification, to men who are mostly new creatures in Christ, and therefore no longer live in themselves, even though sin may remain in their lives as a contrary force.

Yet, even so, we must remember the solid fact that natural men do astonishing deeds of self-sacrifice. Men have high enough faith, courage and love to lay down their lives for a friend. Higher love they may not have, though we wonder whether Socrates, for instance, did not show a higher love. Did he not voluntarily lay down his life for those Athenians who hated him and whom he wanted to help? How can anyone be acquainted with the classical writings of other religions, in any case, and not feel the nobility and goodness running through the best of them in every religion? Principal Murray of Chesthunt College, Cambridge, England, has pointed out how a certain tribe in Africa, even while untouched by Christian influence, had as their very meaning of man, denoting and connoting the picture of those who were judged righteous in Matthew 25, those who feed the hungry, visit the sick. It is even impossible to claim dogmatically that no individual, or exceptional individuals, outside of Christian history, have not risen to a personal fellowship of outgoing love, found in a source beyond themselves.

Certainly we must not darken the character of man for the sake of making the Incarnation, in one special sense, inclusively necessary. We must, rather, accept the fact that in Jesus, the Christ who is Agape became conclusively known and effective in human history. Even such a statement is only partially ascertainable and must rest, to a large extent, on a faith-judgment. What we can know is that the New Testament attributes such a life and teaching to him and that the power in the Early Church probably points to his life as the source for its fellowship power. After all, Jesus is the *mediator* of God through the Spirit unto the children of men, but a mediator whose real purpose and power are to lead to God Himself and to the saving fellowship. No theory about Jesus or about salvation ought to want us to misrepresent actual life. Natural man must be described as good or as bad in relation to his own knowledge of the good *within* the dimension of the natural man. When the light of Agape falls full on him, his depth of sinfulness is made clear, but then within a new relation, with regard to his potential salvation. Revelation is the disclosure of need by that which can fill that need, and not a strange light to be used for purposes of invidious comparison outside its own proper domain.

We must not forget, moreover, that the drive and desire for purposive fellowship which form the universal spring and structure of human nature, perhaps more drawing than driving, and also more of longing than attaining—a spring and structure organically connected with the environment—are due not only to the sense of right but also to the sense of love. What man loves is more important than what he considers to be right. No external rightness could possibly make man human; only when rightness is a matter, most deeply, of what a man potentially is can that rightness come to carry inner compulsion. Authority and motivation must be organically joined, if man is to find freedom in fellowship.

Man loves that which he most basically is. Love is the center of human nature, for love is of God, and God made man in His own image in love and for love. God made man for fellowship, a fellowship drawn into being through the creative processes by the lure of God's love from the depths of man's nature below and from the heights of God's revelation above. No life at any time, or in any stage of its being, is without this craving for love or without some capacity to give it.

In every person some Agape is found, some outgoing concern; and all such love is of God, for there is no other Source for it. Every man has within him God's image, however unearthed, however covered over, however twisted and contorted in relation to other leading drives. For this reason, mere rationalization never satisfies. Man longs for truth, for honor, for rectitude in his own eyes. Man longs to be whole. If he were totally bad, rationalization would be a seamless robe. There would be no rent in man's camouflage from others and from himself, through which to reach him. But man never can cover himself completely. All garments of evil, self-chosen or chosen by rationalizing groups, prove too short and too thin. That is why growth is possible. That is why conversion is possible. That is the cause of man's unrest in evil. We are made for God and are restless without Him, whether as natural man or as redeemed man. Our deepest nature is God's purpose for us. Our essential nature is God's creation in us. Our truest nature is not our actual, but our potential nature, what we are *to become.*

In this sense Vanzetti was right in saying, even in facing a probably unjust execution, that human nature is good, and that he would assert it even if he had to be burned a hundred times or chained for a hundred lives. When we see man torn as he is between what Allport calls "his own effective cravings and the harsh demands of his environment,"[6] we marvel at his capacity to endure and to make constructive choices. Man's nature is partially due to God's activity in him, partially due to the social situation in which he is reared, and partially due to his own choices. When we see the kind of environment which man faces, his insecurities and his true causes for fear, we certainly must own how much nobility there is in human nature in behaving as he does, though the largeness of the task, divided responsibility, distorted information, and, mixed with this, the evil of man's selfish drives, in groups and as individuals, bring about disasters which are never willed on the world directly by individuals of Satanic structure or stature.

Even Calvin, who held that "man is so enslaved by sin, as to be of his own nature incapable of an effort, or even an aspiration towards that which is good,"[7] had to admit that there is "no man . . . destitute of the light of reason," and that "the principle of it is innate in the human mind."[8] Reinhold Niebuhr has done us much good by stressing that social theory must recognize how much harm has been done because the liberal schools of thought have

---

[6] *Personality,* p. 118.
[7] *Institutes,* II, lv, 1; cf. also "such is the pravity of his nature that he cannot be excited and biased to anything but what is evil." *Ibid.,* II, iii, 5.
[8] *Ibid.,* II, ii, 14.

"agreed in rejecting the Christian doctrine of original sin";[9] but seen from the perspective of natural man we must acknowledge that the Spirit of God has been powerful in leading him from his animal background to his creative and constructive choices as a human being. We must never forget this animal background in appraising man's actual nature. Though man is, without a doubt, basically egocentric, in this perspective, he is yet also a man longing for his fuller destiny, capable of constructive and creative choices.

When we leave the dimension of the natural man and turn to man in the dimension of law, we are in a quite different territory. For before there is a law, "sin is not imputed where there is no law," even as there is also a subsequent stage characterized by the fact that "where there is no law there is no trespass." But in between these two stages or dimensions there is the necessary stage of law. We are here using the word "stage," rather than "dimension," to connote development and purpose. Stage as a term will suffice provided that we do not think in terms of mutually exclusive stages. A person in earthly history is practically always to some extent in all stages at once. At one moment a person can be in one dimension or stage, while, in the next, he is in another. But even while he shifts dimensions, he does not get, generally speaking, clearly out of any, but only shifts with regard to the dominant dimension. The use of both stage and dimension is meant to emphasize this relation between distinctness of status dominantly in active interaction with, at least possible, dynamic change, a change which actually is more frequent than we dare think, with our desire for external security and intellectual steadiness. Even so, in the larger picture, the dimension of the law is also a stage to be passed through. Naturally, we cannot make any abstract, formally fixed scheme out of these dimensions. The world has suffered too long at the hands of the scheme-makers. They come close to scheming in order to fence off their neat categories. Life is never like that. Life is a dynamic interaction of countless drives. There is, nevertheless, such a thing as a "master-motive" which organizes life, in spite of the swirling drives and desires which openly or subtly conflict with this "master-motive."

The coming of the dimension of law into history is not a sudden affair. There is no literal Eden, and never was. Man sprang historically, under the creative purpose of God, from an animal background. Then he came up through perhaps a million or two million years of prehistory, roughly speaking; then more suddenly, it seems, there broke forth a new, creative level where the sense of right and the sense of love used reason with relation to the environment to construct the beginnings of purposive fellowships. Long and slow was this prehistory. Swift in comparison is man's known history. The production of law must surely be traced far back into dim prehistory. Even animal life, for that matter, has a rudimentary sense of law, as anyone can attest who has watched animal group behavior with long and patient intimacy. Whitehead may have exaggerated when he used to say that dogs may be more moral than men, in their loyalty and understanding dependability; but to sever the emergence of moral law from animal history and from man's prehistory would be a capital mistake.

For this reason we cannot speak of any actual "fall," in any historic sense. We cannot even speak with Reinhold Niebuhr of "perfection before the fall" in an experiential sense, because we know of no such perfection. All we see is the possibility of a perfection which may be more in mind than in life, but which is, nevertheless, vitiated even in mind by the limitations and sinfulness of the chooser. Moral self-transcendence there is, but no perfection before the act. Many categories like "original justice" are due to a sentimental clinging to Biblical myths instead of facing the actual world of man's animal background and long prehistory. We know of no "fall" of man; we know only that man has always come short of the perfect law of God's Agape. It is the introduction of this law which actually makes man so deeply sinful. But we must never forget that this perfect law of the Spirit could not have been introduced before it was relevant, and it was not relevant until man had come far enough forward to be able to understand, and at least to face, its demands—at whatever distance and by whatever means. Before Agape could be declared as the only adequate law for human life, there had to be preparation. This preparation was mostly through man's prehistory; then through man's general experience in all lands before the coming of "the law of Moses" at a rather late period in Israel's history as a nation, a time very likely not far removed from the great prophets, whose writings were often classed together with it as "the law and the prophets," for more reasons, probably, than proximity in a Hebrew Bible.

"The law and the prophets were until John." Love fulfills the law and the prophets, but these had to come first. They are not of the new covenant. They are not the Gospel. Without them, however, the Gospel would have been irrelevant. The most important thing to notice here is that the purpose of the law is creatively to instruct man in right relationships. This is true whether the purpose of the law has to apply to man before he wants to walk in the ways of the law or afterwards, when, as converted, he wants to do so. The law is not to be thought of primarily as legislation. The law is not mostly juridical in any formal sense. The law is the understanding by the community, in relation to the Spirit of God, of the need for right relations and, to some extent, the content of right relations. Law, therefore, is originally a groping, half-conscious, half-fortuitous, half-deliberate combination of custom, creative public opinion, and gradual legislation, in whatever form and by whatever means of enactment and enforcement.

This is true of all law everywhere, in differing measures and combinations. The Hebrew Torah is to be considered mostly a dynamic way of walking together. Religious and political legislation have positive parts to play in man's preparation for the fuller fellowship. They become evil at the point where they falsely freeze history and demand that the law and the prophets be for man to serve rather than for the service of man. The useful Sabbath becomes a nuisance and a hardship when the pious priest and the pompous politician consider it as an institution to be guarded and served rather than as an instrument for rest and as the possible occasion for religious worship, and thus make narrow laws about it which hamper its usefulness and make it instead a burden to bear.

Christ is the end of the righteousness of the law, not so that he destroys the law as rightful relations, but in that the oppressive burden of the law is done away when God's love is seen and accepted as the basis of fellowship. Law, in the Christian dimension, has, in one sense, the creative function of finding and formulating right relations, in dynamic terms and by the whole community. But this aspect of the law is ever preparatory to the coming of the fuller fellowship. The further function of the law is to convict of sin. Man can never be saved by himself even though he kept the law perfectly. Salvation is not juridical in nature.

The fellowship dimension is the central dimension, as we have already stressed, and law is only a subsidiary dimension. The law is a servant to bring unto fellowship. The perfect law cannot be kept in one's own power according to God's wisdom in creation, in order that man might not be able to live perfectly for himself. Or we may put it, rather, this way: the perfect law of Agape involves a full fellowship love which is possible only by means of the full fellowship Spirit, even the Holy Spirit. The law, *as law,* is always beyond man for man's sake. God does not want, of course, to make man a sinner by giving him the perfect law, which includes the governing of his whole inner self, all his attitudes and desires. God means, rather, to make self-sufficient moralism impossible by putting the law as high as the demand for perfect fellowship love, which can come only when the self is surrendered to the fellowship itself, beyond law as law, within God's own love and power.

In the dimension of law, it is true that man is a sinner and that he can never be saved by his own goodness. We have seen the reason for this situation. This fact does not mean that he cannot do many good things. It does not mean that he is all bad. It does mean, rather, that we recognize his basic egocentricity which is given him for the purpose of making him free, and which becomes sinful when he persists in it against better knowledge, even when he knows why he should seek the fuller fellowship. But the purpose of this dimension is not, as some seem to say, to honor God by man's humiliation. The purpose of this situation is not to have men confess that they are sinners, unworthy, vile, and thus be saved by a grace that is unrelated to this situation. The purpose of this situation is that man might recognize how far short he falls of God's purpose for him, to repent, to change his mind, to let God reset his heart, *that he find the fellowship for which he is made.* The purpose of this unattainable law is thus through and through positive.

The purpose is organically preparatory. The level of creation is good in the way God uses it, and we must honor it.

We do not here, to be sure, want to commit what Luther said was man's final sin, namely, his refusal to admit that he is a sinner. But a groveling admission of sin, for sin's sake, is due to primitive fear and is on a far lower level than the Christian's thankful understanding that God has made him with such drives toward self that he might be real, but has all the while made possible a new and better relationship, for which every man is destined. When man truly sees this function of the law in this light, then even the convicting function of the law is through and through positive. The traditionalistic theology has been due to fear; what we need is a theology that shines straight out from God's gracious purpose for the world. Such a theology will not blink at the fact of sin; it will not underestimate its seriousness and its stubbornness; it will not shrink from seeing its depth; but it will triumphantly declare, and even shout aloud, that the faithlessness of man is in no wise to be compared to the faithfulness of God. This theology will take the love of God more seriously than the sin of men.

Some head-hunters in the Philippines used to treat their criminals wisely by declaring that the criminals were good, deep down, and, therefore, needed the help of punishment whereby the evil spirits which tempted them would be made uncomfortable and driven out. They knew enough to get the criminal on their side in their treatment of evil. Man, deepest down, is made in the image of God, in Agape. That is his essential self. If sin can be seen as not being essential to man, the essential self can be found and enjoyed through the full fellowship, when we do with understanding what we most deeply are and want.

Beyond the dimension of the natural man and the dimension of man under the law lies the dimension of perfection. This is the distinctive dimension of Christian social action. This is the dimension which is under the reign of the Holy Spirit. It is a relationship which is primarily constituted by the Holy Spirit. It is the dimension of the Kingdom of God on earth. It is the locus of the Church in the divine perspective. Perhaps the expression *in loco perfectionis* is not the best possible. Perhaps "perfecting" would be better than "perfection." Then the dynamic and the potential would receive the fullest stress rather than the actuality of attainment. Or perhaps we should use the term "sanctification," which has long Biblical and theological standing. Be that as it may, in contrast to *in loco naturale* and *in loco justificationis* we use *in loco perfectionis,* because this dimension will have to be distinguished from all the rest by the fact that here God is truly present in history as rightly understood and personally appropriated.

This is the dimension of Agape. To live here is not to live in oneself, but to have Christ live in the saint. Saints are such because they have recognized their own weakness and in utter humility and surrender have found the wisdom and power which are of God. Their gifts are of the Spirit. In their weakness is their strength, in that they make their weakness the occasion for God's grace to work. The works which they do, the Father worketh in them through the Son by the Holy Spirit. Need we emphasize that we do not speak of people as perfect in themselves or of a perfect Church as an institution? Is it necessary—we think not—to remind ourselves that self-righteousness is the very opposite of the righteousness in Christ which puts an end to the law? The dimension of perfection is the dimension of God's perfect presence and perfect work in so far as we are completely open to Him. Whatever part of us is open to Him He fills. As we open more and more parts of ourselves He becomes the stronger in us.

To open up to God is to surrender without qualification to the only One who is trustworthy beyond our fullest thought or imagination. We do not want to curb and to confine this relationship to any institutional connections, to any confession of historic creeds, to any kind of moralism of life or worship—we want only the reality itself to be the standard. Where God in Christ is, there is genuinely outgoing concern, rooted in trust in the Trustworthy; there is the dimension of perfection, there is the Kingdom, there is the Church, there is Christ, there is the Holy Spirit. We cannot start with the externals and from there determine whether or not Christ is present. His presence is what determines the rightness or wrongness of all else, as it is related directly or indirectly to His purpose. The tree is judged not by its greenness or its form, however verdant or correct, but only by its fruits. No other judgment can be adequate for the Christian Church and for the distinctive dimension of Christian social action. Daniel T. Jenkins has made out a strong case for the claim that Christian humility and service are the seals and signs of the true ministry; that true orders root in the Christian reality of God's kind of commission in Christ and not primarily in externals.[10] This is true not only of the ministry as a profession but also of all Christian life as a ministry to God and men.

The distinctive dimension of Christian social action is first of all, then, to be understood in terms of a new reality, the presence of the Holy Spirit, by whom it is constituted. It is not right to confine to this dimension the incoming of the supernatural into the natural, the superhistoric into history. Wherever there is a genuine emergence, nature is increased and changed. Wherever novelty beyond previous chains of causation appears, there is something from beyond history. But this is the only point where Eternity *as Eternity* breaks through, where what is determinative in eternity enters time. This is the only dimension where that which is eternally right and abiding enters history. This is the only place where the Eternal Purpose, not only as a means, but as an end, breaks upon the human scene. This is the only instance of "revealed history" within our process. The distinctiveness of this dimension underlies all other distinctions, the qualitatively final distinction between the Eternal Purpose and all the rest of historic process. This is the meaning of meanings. This is the form in which the category of categories can best be grasped. This is the decisive *kairos* which fulfills all other times.

The distinctive dimension of Christian social action is Agape, the greatest gift of the Spirit, because it is the gift of God's own self, the sharing of His own nature. What we sadly miss in the otherwise excellent books of men like John Bennett is the presence of this distinctive dimension of Christian social action. Wise men though they be, they have not opened up to us what constitutes the heart of Christian action. It is not man's wisdom, or experience, or effort, individually or socially. It is the active presence of the Holy Spirit. After an excellent chapter on "The Distance between Christian Ethics and Social Policy," and after having discussed four

[10] *The Gift of Ministry.*

social strategies, John Bennett goes on to discuss the fifth, or the Christian, approach. This is the way in which he summarizes this fifth strategy: it is "one that emphasizes the relevance together with the transcendence of the Christian ethic and which takes account of the universality and persistence of sin and the elements of technical autonomy in social policies."[11] His recognition of human sin in all actual endeavors to better society is indeed good, without which any social theory is obviously vitiated and made irrelevant. His stress on technical autonomy is one way by which he safeguards the doctrine of creation and precludes God's direct presence in all areas of life. Naturally, the combination of transcendence and relevance which he advocates is the very lifeblood of Christian social action. All this is good; but the one best thing is lacking, *the explicit recognition of the direct activity of the Holy Spirit as the incomparably primary dimension of Christian social action*—and of the Spirit of God, for that matter, on the level of general social action. To keep institutions under judgment because of their sins is one important aspect of Christian social action, but more important than any sin or any judgment is the positive, primary *agency* of God Himself *in history*. Without this we are shorn Samsons. When we have this truly, in grace and in faith, all the other approaches will fall into their proper places and proper proportions.

There are two matters further to remember about this dimension. Though it is constituted in its primary dimension by God, there is always the fallible human side to it. Thus is it always under judgment, and men in it stand in need of humility. As a matter of fact, since men in this dimension see their own sins in the blazing light of the truer reality, they particularly know their sin and feel the need for humility. Thus, in a sense, this dimension is peculiarly characterized by humility. The work done is by grace. The attainment is due to God's activity. How can man boast when he can give no increase regardless of how much he sows or waters? And how can man feel proud of the fruits of the Spirit when he knows that in himself he is thoroughly egocentric and under judgment?

The second thing to remark about this dimension of perfection

[11] *Christian Ethics and Social Policy,* p. 59.

is that unless it is characterized by real and dominant change, it is not Christian. Here is where John Wesley, in his emphasis on sanctification, was far closer than Luther to normative Christianity. We need, however, the stress of Luther and of Wesley in symphonic co-ordination. Apart from the recognition of the depth and stubbornness of sin, the perfecting is not of the actual man. Apart from the dealing with the body of death in strong terms and with its astonishing power for survival and resuscitation, we can have no real doctrine of sanctification. Many who come under the sway of perfectionist doctrines and claim the experience of total sanctification fail woefully to illustrate this power in life. Imagine what power history would see if we had a few saints dominantly open to God as were Jesus, Paul, or perhaps even Gandhi! Yet it is also true that some people who have taken the doctrine of total sanctification seriously have increased not in brittleness and priggishness but in quiet humility and sacrificial concern. We need very much indeed to read John Wesley afresh and to feel his fire with respect to this New Testament doctrine. Whatever be the exact combination of texts and their finer meanings in the New Testament, there can be no question about the fact that the New Testament means us to have radically changed lives by the powerful presence of the Holy Spirit.

Men like Sangster, Lindström and Flew[12] have put us in their debt by their discussions of this much neglected aspect of modern theology. Surely one aspect of the power of the Nazarene position in our day is its stress on walking in newness of life. A basic change of intention, of the set of the self toward God, of the total relation of the self to God, takes place in the conversion of man, however this occurs, when he decides to put God's will first in his life. This radical decision, with whatever conscious or unconscious accompaniments, and in whatever length of time, must involve change of authority and motivation and cannot be without change, if it is genuine, in actual life. Thereafter the constant walking with God, without which the Christian life cannot be maintained, must also, if it is authentic, be accompanied by actual change of life.

[12] Sangster, *The Path to Perfection.*
Lindström, *Wesley and Sanctification.*
Flew, *The Idea of Perfection in Christian Theology.*

The distinctive dimension of Christian social action is man *in loco perfectionis.* Though man is still imperfect through both finitude and sin, when he is open in intention and deed to the Holy Spirit, God performs through him the miracles of creative change and vital healing. But when he then faces history as a whole, he finds that other authorities and motivations hold sway. Man in the realm of the Holy Spirit must face the responsibilities of civil life where the majority neither understand nor accept the dimension of life which is basic to him. What difference does it make, then, whether or not a person is Christian *in loco civile?* Can he do better than to join the best relative force in history as far as practical action goes? Is the only difference between a Christian and one who is not, as Reinhold Niebuhr suggests in *An Introduction to Christian Ethics,* that the Christian participates in relative choices and political actions with humility and with the spirit of forgiveness and the willingness to be forgiven? No, the differences beyond these attitudes in actuality are at least two.

The Christian, regardless of what happens, remains in the distinctive dimension of social action. His "vision and authority," to use Oman's phrase, are of the Holy Spirit. His perspective and power are of Agape. His approach to all the problems of the world is through "the eyes of faith." His relation to all partial fellowships is through the full fellowship love. This relation is no external relation, but one that is through and through organic, by means of the deeper union of the Spirit of God and of the Holy Spirit.

Many sects have a believer's philosophy of social action and refuse to co-operate with the world at all. They feel no responsibility because the world is the Devil's and to participate is to besmear themselves. They mean well, but are unrealistic about the complicated nature of social evils. If they are always to use uncontaminated means, they must needs go out of the world. Against them John Bennett has rightly written his *Christian Realism.* Such people confine Christianity to the level of redemption; as though God were not Creator, and as though they were too good to do the "dirty work" that God has to do for our sake, by means of the austere and unsentimental operation of His wrath, which is a vital function, we must remember, of the Spirit of God.

Others give up belief in a distinctive Christian dimension, as far as social action goes. That is true of some of our so-called Neo-orthodox who seem to have no adequate theory in this realm. Some of them, of course, lean over toward individual salvation, complete other-worldliness, and the despising of the "liberal social Gospel," and thus really belong in the preceding paragraph. Others, however, draw a deep moat between the two realms, and yet operate on both sides through some splendid leap, while maintaining that the best we can do in the social realm is to prevent the worst possible evil. They do not speak of even the best possible choice, but the choice that is least bad among all possible choices. Of most of this group it can be said that they want to establish a purist Christian perspective, and yet at the same time have a hand in actual affairs. Between the two realms, however, they have no organic relation that makes this possible. Thus as far as Christian social action is concerned, there is, with them, generally no specific perspective or dimension.

When the fully surrendered Christian faces the actual world, he finds, to be sure, relative historic choices and imperfect means with which to work. But the use of these choices is not evil. The surrendered Christian must use the best available means to accomplish the best relevant ends. The use of the best available means in history is not to compromise, but to do God's actual will.

History knows little of perfect means. To live in history, *where God has put us,* is not automatically to sin. To live in an imperfect and sinful world by the grace of God through faith in Christ is, rather, to fulfill God's will in humble obedience. It is to "become sin" for the world. Sinning is not a matter of external circumstance or of historic involvement as such, but of man's personal response to God within his given circumstance with regard to that circumstance and actual involvement. Jesus did not sin simply by living in the Roman Empire or by paying tribute money that was corruptly used by a corrupt State. The total upshot of Jesus' life was to redeem the situation, even though perfect means for doing so were not available. With the world he had to live differently from the way in which he lived with his disciples, and to speak in indirect discourse or even in clever or evasive speech. But to accept the best possible means to the best possible ends, in the power and in the love of God, is not to compromise because those means were not altogether perfect and pure.

Nor are we responsible for all the consequences of our acts. We can act only in faith and love through the power of the Holy Spirit and leave the rest with God. If Jesus' refusal to become an earthly Messiah heavily conditioned Judas' suicide, Jesus is not to be condemned for following God's will. We are obliged to think straight on these issues and not to rationalize; nor must we remove the life of Jesus from history by calling it "on the edge of history" or "tangent to history." Our claim is that it is possible to maintain a distinctively Christian dimension of social action and yet operate without enfeebling compromise in the general social realm.

Others, again, give up the perspective of faith entirely and accept the general level of social action as adequate for Christians to use. Thus Rommen in his strong work writes: "Catholic political philosophy remains a philosophy of man, not simply a philosophy for the believer. The state belongs to human culture and to the secular order. Its root is the social nature of man. Its nearest end is the order of secular felicity, the *ordo rerum humanarum*."[13] The Roman Church believes frankly that there is a realm of natural law, common to all nature and accessible to all men, without faith. They have thus an order of creation which is quite distinct from the order of redemption, or of revelation. On the one extreme we have the religious with their councils of perfection; in between, the ordinary churchgoer with his need to live in both worlds; and on the other extreme, those who know nothing of a revealed order, or care nothing, but still can observe and participate in the demands of the order of creation.

We believe that this point of view has lost the relevance of the order of revelation and redemption dynamically for the whole world, and that its order of creation is itself conceived of too statically. It is refreshing to see many modern Roman Catholic thinkers operating with more existential categories. Yet how uncommon is this kind of thinking among numerous Protestant laymen, not to mention others! Business, they say, is one world and religion is another. The less they are mixed, the better it is for both!

[13] *The State in Catholic Thought*, p. 12.

The second respect in which our position differs from the idea that we can do nothing distinctive as Christians, except the introducing of humility and the spirit of forgiveness in social action, is that we believe that a Christian can and ought to refuse to participate when the choices which are available are not genuinely constructive. Instead of taking the least bad choice we ought not to take any dominantly bad choice. In that case the best means available is the refusing to participate. There is always a best possible choice open in history even though that choice be martyrdom and death. The best possible choice may not be at all in line with the demands of people in general or what is expected for us to maintain civilization, but may simply be the going to the Cross. That foolishness of God may be far wiser than the wisest wisdom of men, talking about our having to participate in the social processes all the time. There is a real place for social nonconformity that breaks the smooth reign of man's wisdom of complete social conformity and complete social relativism.

This talking about complete social relativism is dangerous and foolish and may be illustrated by an actual incident. A very distinguished world leader who did not believe in pacifism was one night defending his position at the home of a pacifist. As he happened to hold a most important position in the world organization of Christianity, it was acutely comical to have him confronted with the following question: "Dr. So-and-So, if you were out one beautiful night with a charming woman who was not your wife and she began to make improper advances to you, what would you do?" For a moment he was baffled, because if he admitted that he could refuse her, he would at one point have given up his complete social relativism, and if he gave the opposite answer, he would obviously reflect on world Christianity. But, true to his argument, he smiled and said, "I would ask God's forgiveness." But as far as real life goes, the situation cannot be turned aside by a joke. We are going to say that whether in participation or in nonparticipation, the Christian acts differently from the rest of the world.

Before we turn to the next chapter we ought to say a word about two topics of current interest that have such intimate bearing on this topic that omission here might prevent some from following along with our constructive argument. The topics are these: Is historic improvement on earth possible; and what are the distinctive standards of the Christian good?

Unless improvement in history is possible, why should we worry about world-transformation at all? Would it not be enough, in any case, to be sufficiently concerned with the world to restrain its evil and to permit the work of the Church to go on? Often Luther's position and subsequent Lutheran actions have been interpreted in this light, although, we think, with only partial right. Many people today, however, are very near to this kind of position. They feel that world-transformation is not a genuine part of New Testament faith, but is, instead, part of illusory and utopian liberalism.[14] Does history actually ever improve, and is improvement progressively possible? That question must, therefore, be answered genuinely. Without needless repetition we cannot here discuss the fact that a Christian cannot be unconcerned with God's world without denying both the fact of God's creation and of his own sonship. To be Christian is to share God's concern, through faith and grace, for the whole man and for the whole world. Thus world-transformation is part and parcel, irremovably, of the Christian Gospel, not as a secondary or separate part of it, but intrinsically and organically. The question we are now concerned with, however, is whether there can be any improvement in history as such and as a whole. Is improvement, we repeat, progressively possible?

This question can be decided only by the confrontation of the fact of creation with the Eternal Purpose. It could be argued, in the light of such a confrontation, that the reason for our participation in world-transformation is solely athletic. It could be said, with some reason, that we need to be concerned in order to learn God's concern in fact as well as in theory, but that our concern, nevertheless, does not change the actual world. Even such a position would go beyond those who hold that the world is simply a place to learn one's own despair in order to be saved by utter grace out of the world or beyond the world.

[14] Cf. Pierre Maury's statement that "the sin of modern man is that he 'believes in history,'" and the subsequent clarifying discussion in *The Church's Witness to God's Design*, p. 101, *Man's Disorder and God's Design*, Vol. II.

The positive function of creation, even in giving us being and understanding, cannot be avoided in any theory that will do justice even to the minimum facts. But we can say that we must be concerned for the world in order to develop our spiritual muscles, or, to put it in terms more congenial to others, to manifest the signs of the Spirit as the Christian witness to the world. The second way of putting it, however, confining our works to signs of witnessing, again misses any organic function *for creation* and consequently falls short of the full Christian perspective. It is less than fully purposive with regard to process as a whole, in the eternal dimension. We must show our faith by our works and also the why of our works, giving reason for our faith, that men may glorify God who is in heaven. What, then, is the purpose of works besides teaching us obedience and exercising our spirits?

We work, even as our Father works, up to the present, because God's creation is not yet finished. The statement that God rested on the seventh day is a concept that can make for a static view of creation and for a deistic understanding of God. This is, of course, a false view of God and of His constant activity in history. Creation was *completed* as far as the preparation for the purpose of God in history was concerned, but only *begun* as far as the outworking of that purpose goes. God did create, and now, beyond that creation, makes all things new, re-creates, transforms, develops. History can improve. This we must hold unless we are willing to fly in the face of all the evidence of the nature of process. We have found in *Faith and Reason* that process points, and can be understood only in terms of its truest pointing beyond itself. When we look back upon the last million years of human history and compare the last ten thousand years with the preceding part of the million, we are overwhelmed by the sudden shift, as it seems, of God's creative work in history. God means to do something with this creation. He has invested much work and thought in it. He is its Maker and Lord. To neglect the perspective of process is to slight God's patient work in creation. To scorn the perspective of process is to ridicule God's sense of time and proportion. The perspective of the Eternal Purpose must be related to the perspective of the historic process.

We must recognize, however, that there are limits, both above and beyond, where human history cannot go. A false optimism means not an ultimately inevitable victory of God, which is a necessary aspect of His sovereignty, but belief in an automatic and steady progress.[15] Such a conception eliminates man's freedom and makes for a divine determinism which would preclude the realization of the ultimate freedom and faithfulness in fellowship. Any dependence upon life-force, or evolution as such, or human nature as such, is not only fickle because of freedom, but also because the onward drive of history goes against the grain of human nature. We must not forget that man is bent in on himself, or weighted chiefly toward himself, so that automatic progress would be retrogression. D. R. Davis significantly maintains that the unity of mankind is the unity of original sin. In *actuality* this is dominantly true. Our own way of putting it is that mankind is mostly characterized, on the level of actuality, by the tendency of its members to draw apart and live for themselves, though the contrary driving and drawing are there, too. All possible progress depends upon the activity of the Spirit of God in history in relation to man's freedom, or, on a different level, upon the activity of the Holy Spirit in relation to man's freedom. The current underneath all currents moving them is God's eternal purpose; but this includes man's freedom and works within the conditions which God has Himself created for the effecting of the fellowship.

Nor is progress possible without suffering. We should always remember that truth is centrally seen in the Cross. Every life must be frustrated and led to self-despair. Toynbee is certainly right in saying that there has to be challenge in order for there to be response. When this challenge is seen in terms of the Cross, the necessity of shared suffering, of suffering for and with others, if there is to be fellowship; and when it is seen conclusively and empoweringly in the sufferings of Jesus as the Christ, then it becomes clear that without suffering there can be no progress in terms that have permanent meaning. Progress can mean only the effecting of Christian fellowship; that is the distinctive standard of the Christian good. Irwin Edman speaks of "religion without tears," but such a religion has little to do with the personal appropriation of

15 Niebuhr, *Faith and History.*

truth and goodness through grace and faith, finding its full satisfaction only in the full fellowship of God's love. Such progress often is conceived of in external terms. But external progress is no true progress *of history*. History is a matter of man's choice of community. External "progress" is merely the development of the means and media of community, but not of community itself. We must not underestimate how God has used the push of this kind of "progress," to demand the true, inner progress which alone finally counts. There is, nevertheless, no real progress in technological development, for external "progress" can lead to bigger and worse wars because we know bigger nations and have the more demonic powers for destruction. All true progress is of God and within His purpose for history.

We must also remember, in order to avoid a false optimism, that the spiritual life consists of immediate choices as well as the continuum in which these choices are made. Both are important. Since one side of life is the immediacy of choice as a constant recurrence, there can be no moral and spiritual progress in any final sense, for every moment has some freedom and is open to wrong or sinful choices. Life is no steady stream upward; it is almost like walking upward on an escalator that goes downward. Just to keep up where one is takes work; to rest is to go backward! The strength that comes from above for walking does not take the place of walking. Faith never takes the place of work.

Thus Kierkegaard is right that in one sense every person begins again at the beginning; and Tillich has also said rightly from this angle that there can be no moral and spiritual progress, since these are a matter of repeated choosing. But this is not the whole truth. Kierkegaard himself sees that in another sense every individual begins where the race has taken him up to that point. There are not only immediate choices to be considered, but the relevant continuum in which those choices are made. All creative newness and inventive "progress" are interrelated with the historic stage on which they appear. For them all there is a "fullness of time." Fullness of time is conditional upon both personal response and social preparation. It depends upon the continuum as well as upon the choice.

It is good, therefore, to have a high-grade civilization and constructive communities in which to live. We do not help our children to become great merely by bringing them up in unstable homes, conflicting church life, and confused community life. Only when the instability, which Whitehead and others claim make for creativeness, is the result of a restless adventure toward the better beyond the present attainment of good, can the most important choices arise out of a continuum. When stability is due to stagnation, nothing important happens. When stability is due to complacency, nothing constructive happens that is worth recording, because of the nature of the continuum. When instability is due to deterioration, nothing positive happens because of the nature of the continuum as such. When, however, instability is due to a divine unrest with previous attainment so that what is about to be born is more important than what is about to die, then creativeness characterizes the continuum, and this in turn becomes conducive to adventurous choices.

It seems likely that in spite of the fact that most people are talking about the disintegrative instability of our age, what really is happening, deep down, is the birth of an age of such power and creative drive that we cannot even picture it. God is ever far greater than all historic times of trouble, and for Him our age most certainly has a fullness of preparation, as the Christian ideals have been spread by modern means of communication and have partially penetrated the general human consciousness. These Christian ideals have received an exceptionally wide theoretic relevance and suggestiveness for actual applicability mostly within recent times. This, generally speaking, is a fact. A false optimism would rely upon the preparation and upon God's activity in an external way, whereas Christian realism believes that, if we repent, believe, and bear the fruits of faith, a new and better day is crowding to be born.

Just as there is a false optimism about history, there is also a false pessimism. This false pessimism founds itself, for one thing, on the idea that world-transformation is not according to the will of God. It forgets that we are bid to pray that God's kingdom come on earth. It forgets that God is not only Redeemer, but also Creator. It forgets that Christianity is concerned with the whole man and not only with discarnate spirits. Reinhold Niebuhr surely has a strong point when he says that in our day we cannot speak about sin without speaking about politics. That we see our sins in our day peculiarly in the socio-political struggle ought to be obvious. Christianity is concerned with spirit, mind and body, individually; and with religion, education and the social political order, collectively. False pessimism very likely arrives at the conclusion that God is not concerned with world-transformation mostly as a rationalization. This rationalization is perhaps due to its own downward perspective, to its looking more at the past of history than at the power of God. For much of the argument to the effect that history will not change is based on what is called a realistic understanding of history. The fact is noted that civilizations come and go and that no perfect civilization has arrived. From that fact the *non sequitur* conclusion is drawn that no improvement of history is possible.

But God, and not man, is the primary factor in the determination of whether or not there is to be progress in history. God wills it. For real progress is the effecting of the Christian fellowship.[16] The distinctive nature of the Christian good is ever Christian community. Whether or not that can be effected cannot be determined primarily from past experience. The history of man as a whole is not the final criterion of that progress, except to tell us that enough progress has been made for that fellowship to be a relevant option in history. The conditions for the fullness of time were prepared particularly through the Hebrew people. From Abraham to Jesus, however that history as such is considered, there real progress was enacted in life and teaching by the prophets. The coming of Jesus marked a discontinuous and climactic stage of progress. The birth and establishing of the Church was real progress in history. The spread of the Church and the gradual penetration of its message in people's consciousness was real progress. The application of Christian truth to society as a whole is a very recent thing, generally speaking, and indicates real progress. Progress there has been. Even if this civilization should perish, Toynbee surely is right that the

---

[16] Cf. "Yet ultimately, whether in history or beyond history, God's perfect will is to be accomplished." Latourette, *The Emergence of a World Christian Community*, p. 58.

Kingdom is a goal that transcends any civilization. The Kingdom is the perfect fellowship and its fulfillment. That fellowship alone is the nature of the true Christian good which measures progress. The measure of progress is the measure of the coming of the Church whether as revealed history or as latent history. In each case progress is measured by the kind of community which obtains in relation both to the ultimate and to human community. If our earthly history will end, moreover, man's history will still go on in God's way and in God's time, and there, too, will be God's will for progress. Only through history will history ever be perfected. Progress is coming in God's time and way, which is conditioned by the response of our historic freedom to His Eternal Purpose, which is finally certain but at no particular time of history.

That time and way, we repeat, is *conditioned* by man's freedom. Man's sinfulness is accordingly made a cause for dismissing the possibility of progress. Human nature is made the reason for history's remaining basically as it is. But man was made by God for fellowship. Though his actual nature is weighted toward self, his essential self is satisfied by nothing less than God's will for him. We may not see the total vision, and may give ourselves over, instead, to partial loyalties that destroy the age to be born. We may even destroy civilization. But this is not a real defeat of God. This is a defeat of His "intentional will" but not of His ultimate will. Heaven and earth may perish, but not the eternal Word of God. That stands as sure as God, and nothing can be surer.

Progress in history should thus be viewed, first of all, from the point of view of God's purpose; then, from the standpoint of man's nature; then, from the fact of his actuality. That actuality has enough freedom to cause real retrogression, stagnation and destruction. But man's freedom is never large enough to thwart God eternally. God alone is infinite and He will prevail. Progress in history must be measured by the effecting of the Christian fellowship and the kind of community that is akin to it. The more freedom and fellowship are actualized, particularly with regard to God's purpose, the more creation hallows God's name and makes progress actual. If through education, example, religious contagion or legislation, any societal situation can be made open for the Gospel to be proclaimed, there progress is possible in history.

Progress, obviously, does not mean human happiness or convenience. History can mean nothing except human experience before God. Earthly history is a small segment of this, important but not ultimate. *Progress, then, is possible in history even as the Christian fellowship is possible in history.* External conditions modify this situation the way in which the body affects the spirit. Communism, for instance, with all its atheism and materialism, may be a way in which the wrath of God is made to praise Him by preparing a better order of property relations. Within it, free from certain contradictions of capitalism, Christianity, when it has destroyed the hard shell by means of which Communism breaks through into history, may find a new era of creative fellowship and adventurous co-operation.

We must also remember that progress in history can never be treated merely collectively. Where there is freedom there is difference, and Jesus and Judas lived at the same time in history. Who can say that there was no progress in one life who grew in wisdom and stature while there was a spurning of new light and self-destruction in the other? Though Nero and the early Church lived at the same time, we cannot say that they progressed or went backward equally. Though we cannot judge as God judges, it seems legitimate to say that many in the Roman Empire lost ground and made rebellious choices even with regard to the light they did have (and the best that they had was rather bright); while some who lost their lives to the lions made great progress in history. The saints have made the world. Through them have always come creative power and light. Naturally, we cannot reduce history to the shadow of great men or to hero worship, but we can say that men like Saint Francis and Wesley profoundly affected their age and still live in historic power.

While freedom is individual, we cannot, therefore, say that progress is general, at any time, in any conclusive fashion; but we can say that there can be both individual progress and real growth, on the collective side, of the Christian fellowship in depth and range. Besides, we can say that there can be let into history enough light and spiritual power generally to change the external conditions under which men live so that the general patterns of thought, the way in which we work and play, and the way in which we treat one another and groups, can be more close to the Christian point of view and way generally than it was before. That is what God wants, for the fellowship to be effected and for creation to be used to hallow His name and to help humanity. In this deeper sense, possible progress is organic to the nature of history itself.

Perhaps we can summarize the general discussion of the possibility of progress, conceived of in terms of the distinctive nature of the Christian good, in the following way. Progress is as possible in history as God's eternal purpose for it. Human history on earth is, of course, only a small segment of history; for history, as a whole, is man's total preparation for paradise. Progress *toward* paradise means the effecting of the fellowship which God has eternally purposed and for the sake of which He has made the world. Progress *in* paradise means creative choices by means of which we grow in the good beyond the elimination of actual evil, where evil is defined as the frustration by sin or by culpable ignorance of the effecting of the Christian fellowship.

In this chapter, then, we have considered the distinctive dimension of Christian social action. We saw how the personal dimension is the most basic of all of man's relationships whether to God or to man. Within this total personal dimension there are two kinds of agents, those explicitly within grace, and those who do not recognize and accept this dimension of Christian fellowship. In other words, there is the dimension of those in the realm of the Holy Spirit and those in the realm of the Spirit of God.

When the next dimension, that of law, grips man's life he becomes more restless, whether in evasion or in earnest obedience. Yet either way he fails. When, however, man is released from this tyranny of the law from without, and finds full freedom toward God in faith and grace, he does not evade the problems of civil life but enters what Luther calls "a free prison."

Willingly he then takes on, for God's sake, which is also his neighbor's, the common problems of life, in all its relevant realms. There is a distinctive dimension of Christian social action which makes the only true progress possible in history, the progress of actual man toward the finding of the full fellowship which God has prepared for him. It includes both individual and social salvation, and beyond that the salvation of the means through which individual and social salvation was made possible in God's patient manner in history.

With this general summary in mind, we turn now to the fuller elucidation of the two realms of life and action which come together *in loco civile,* the realm of the Spirit of God and the realm of the Holy Spirit.

CHAPTER VI

The Translating and
Transpowering Role of the Spirit

We have now come to the nub of our argument. The distinctive dimension of the social action which can legitimately be named Christian is the activity of the Holy Spirit in relation to the Spirit of God. Too much of our thinking of late years along the lines of social action has been naturalistic. Somehow God has not been actually the prime mover, director and controller of human history as far as our practical considerations are concerned. We might have acknowledged this in theory, but even in this realm we have had a weak conception of the concrete and constant activity of God in history. God is great, beyond our every understanding, and His actual presence in history is its determining factor.

What Bevan says of God in relation to Christ is equally true of Him in relation to the Holy Spirit and to the Spirit of God.

> The Christian doctrine of the Incarnation is not another way of saying what the Indian means when he asserts the essential identity of man and God. The doctrine of the Incarnation has its point solely on the Hebraic presupposition of the otherness, the transcendence of God. It is because God is infinitely above the world that His coming down into the world is wonderful.[1]

The point is to unite a completely dominant transcendence, or a full supernaturalism, with an immanence which is organically united to it, yet also real. We must find the organic relation between an altogether independent transcendence with a creation

[1] *Op. cit.*, p. 76.

and history which are real and free within their scale of scope and meaning. Just as in Christology a great danger is to raise the Christ into a unique irrelevance or to lower him into our common impotence by respectively denying his humanity in all true senses, or denying his divinity in its full nature and meaning; so a great danger to the understanding of the Holy Spirit is that He is either raised into some pure spirituality on the level of redemption, which makes Him irrelevant for social action, or lowered into some historic or experiential reality, which shears Him of His full authority and power as God in history. We tend either to deify the flesh, denying the realities of its weaknesses in conjunction with the Word, or to humanize the Word, denying the uniqueness of Agape in relation to all flesh.

Yinger has ably put the same problem in the language of secular social action:

> If the religious group demands too much allegiance to the religious ideal, particularly in spheres which require sacrifices of things held dear in a particular society, it comes into conflict with secular powers and is either persecuted or neglected. On the other hand, of course, if it does not make demands on behavior, in terms of its norms, it is also without influence. The dilemma is to keep in a position of power without sacrificing the goals for which the power was originally desired.[2]

What we are after, in short, is the full power beyond history to change the world. We are concerned with relevant power, beyond the world, with capacity concretely and organically to change it. The answer which we have suggested is in terms of the relation between the Holy Spirit and the Spirit of God.

Actual history, in so far as the Church is truly present in the sense of the dominance of the Holy Spirit, is divided into two dominant parts that are yet united in the deeper Reality upon which both depend. Nor is this uniting merely substantial in the sense of forming the underlying Reality of both to which either responds according to the presence of this Reality in its appropriate form. This uniting Reality is also functionally present, though less directly than indirectly, since natural man is never totally bereft of Agape nor the spiritual man entirely free from the Spirit of God.

---

[2] *Religion and the Struggle for Power*, p. 18.

The Holy Spirit, however, appears in one area of social thought and action as Himself, open to the eyes of faith. In another area He appears as the Spirit of God. There He is often thought of as an "it," a system of values, some truth, or some common interest based upon limited loyalties, common needs, or common convenience. He may be thought of as God, even personally, but then He is used more than accepted for Himself; a God, at best, to be feared and worshiped rather than a Father to be loved and obeyed. Between these two realms, however, there is a permeable membrane, if we may use that figure. The Holy Spirit is on both sides, in one capacity or another, and therefore content can flow from one realm to the other and back again, but in so doing the context of the content and usually the content itself are changed. At least the appearance, or the functional understanding and acceptance, of the content is itself altered. Thus the main burden of activity goes on, in so far, at least, as it is truly effective, *in the Spirit,* not for the most part directly, but, rather, largely indirectly.

This permeable membrane between the two realms can be thought of in four distinct ways. The first is the translating function of the Spirit. When a thought or a word from the realm of the Holy Spirit reaches the realm of the Spirit of God, the specific import of its message is, if left to itself, distorted by the rationalizing power on the part of those within the realm of the Spirit of God. The new and distinctive context is usually rejected outright before it can reach in to hurt and to help the defensive self. The natural man receives not the things of the Spirit *naturally.* From the world the things of life are hidden by the self and his fellow rebels, and, therefore, there is no effective entrance into his life, via experience, via reason, or via expedience. All these ways are effectively closed. The self has retreated behind the moat of its own selfish despair. Fear has dug deep ditches between itself and the saving Word. The defensive self and the fearful world cannot and will not, or will not and cannot, hear the truth that alone can set them free.

But somehow the Spirit enters, via its different reality and context, into the sinner and makes him restless with himself when he hears a word and meaning which is spoken, not in man's wisdom, but in God's. Even the demons within know when the

Lord is near, and quake. All argument in terms of experience, reason and expedience which the Christian offers the unsaved in any realm, even the social realms, are torn to shreds by the unwilling and chained spirit because overt context clashes against overt context and the natural man both prefers and is bound by his own defensive context of meaning. Therefore truth that is not spoken in the Spirit lacks the power of becoming translated, of moving with living meaning into the man who does not share it.

But when the wisdom and power are of God, in the Holy Spirit, then that wisdom enters via its own private wire beyond man's conscious defenses and speaks with power by means of its own subtly translating power in the depth conscious. The voice of the Holy Spirit comes in by one voice up to the membrane between the spiritual and the secular realms, then speaks in another voice that is understandable to the natural man, perhaps more in terms of power and conviction than in terms of explicit meaning.

But not only is this permeable membrane of the Spirit able to translate the message from the realm of the Holy Spirit to the Spirit of God, or from the Spirit of God to the Holy Spirit, but it is also able to transform it. Truth is a relationship of each man to the Ultimate and to the proximate world. Religious truth is the unique relationship of each individual to God. It is a living, dynamic relation, constantly changing according to his concrete choices. The particular perspective from which one man views God cannot be taken by another. The particular dimension of being in which one stands cannot be exactly duplicated. Therefore the content of truth varies with each viewer and with each decider.

Truth is a matter of "how" in particular as well as of "what" in general. The general realm forms a bridge of communication, but, as far as religion goes, the general "what" is never enough. There is also a particular "how." There must be the click of personal conviction with regard to a personal seeing and to a personal content to which one can be converted. There is an inescapable, existential element in all religious truth which cannot be bridged in terms of mere ideas. Nor, on the other hand, can it be bridged merely in terms of human decisions, considered as arbitrary leaps of faith. There is a continuity presupposed for such leaps of faith.

That continuity, however, is from above, providing ground for the discrete discontinuities of the human spirit in its decisive leaps of particular faith decisions. That continuity is the work of the Holy Spirit. The Holy Spirit and the Spirit of God, in their respective spheres and in their joint activity, fit the content of communication to the concrete needs of each hearer. Therefore, beyond human knowledge and wisdom, it makes all the difference in the world, and beyond the world, whether the speech is made in the Spirit or whether the action is taken in the Spirit. A cup of water in Christ's name, actually and seriously in the Spirit, is different from any cup of water given out of sheer well-meaning or human friendship.

The third function of the Spirit, presupposed by these acts of translating and transforming, is the transmitting function of the Spirit. How can one human being speak to another and make himself understood? We take this for granted! He cannot do so, however, except for the active presence of the Spirit of God as the mediating agent, or of the Holy Spirit on His distinctive level. But transmitting from one distinct realm to another is even more mysterious and involved. It requires that the message go through in spite of all the interference that is purposely put out by the unwilling self. The transmitting from one realm to another, and back again, is due to the fact that not only is there a translating function at the point of the joining membrane, but also a transmitting wire, if we look at the situation in terms of some endowment, or a transmitting wave length and power stronger than any other transmitting power, if we look at it in more functional terms. This wire is the essential nature of man on both sides of the membrane in terms of God's creation and present activity in him. The transmitting reality of the Spirit is more powerful than anything else in human nature and history and goes from the depths of one person or group to the depths of another, though man's freedom can, of course, still reject and distort the message. In order for there to be something spoken, some specific content, on the horizontal level, where most social action and thought are carried out, God needs voices in history to take up the mouthpiece and use it—voices that come from sons who have listened carefully and well to the Spirit. Those who have heard the Word from above, and then speak and act in the reality of that Word on the social level, are those who speak to man's essential condition without either irrelevance or impotence.

The fourth main function of the Spirit with relation to these two realms, in their constant interaction, is the transpowering of the Word, whether in speech or in action. To translate is not enough. The Word must reach all the way into the essential heart of the hearer. To transform into the context of each hearer so that he hears in the tongue of his own specific needs is not enough. To transmit the Word is not enough even when translated and transformed, because the hearer must somehow find *the power* of salvation, and then *the power* of acting within this new context of the Spirit. Truth is not only meaning but also power. The new meaning, which is not yet within the context or content of the Holy Spirit, needs the power to rise to thought and action in spite of the natural resistance of the whole-context and whole-content of the natural man. This empowering function of the Spirit comes particularly from the realm of the Holy Spirit to the realm of the Spirit of God, when suggestions for improvement in the realm of the Spirit of God, or with relation to common needs and problems in the common realm of life, *in loco civile,* are made in faith, love and prayer by the spiritual man. God empowers those who pray to Him in sincerity and truth.

For this reason, a few individuals can change a whole vote. A clergyman, for instance, with some surprise commented that he had observed how a whole town vote was changed by the witness of one man. The group of deciding citizens were voting on some discriminatory act such as the limiting of all property in the town to the socially elect. They had already gone around the circle save for one man, and every one had expressed himself in favor of the discrimination. Then a quiet layman, sincerely Christian, ended the round by saying that he could not vote for the measure and face his God honestly. He spoke in the Spirit. Thereupon, one by one, the members of the group began to change their minds. This is what they, too, had most deeply felt, they said, but they could see the practical call of the discriminatory statute. Thus one man reversed the entire situation. This happens often when there is a creative minority, speaking not in human self-assertion and in self-sure wisdom, but in humble confession and faith. When the social action is approached in this manner there is a new power present.

While we are discussing this movement from the realm of the Holy Spirit to the realm of natural normalcy, or the realm of the Spirit of God, we must remember that this secular realm has its sacred aspect too. We must under no circumstance confuse the realm of the Spirit of God with the irreligious in the agnostic or in the "worldly" sense. Our previous discussion has attempted to stress the fact that most of the worship in this realm is in terms of limited loyalties and of partial perspectives. Often it is high worship, and when no higher is available, God "winks at" it as part and parcel of the age of innocence. But when a higher conception comes in, the old gods exist either as open idols or as disguised idols. Certainly idols are seldom worshiped knowingly as idols, but rather as divinities! Yet depth-knowledge has made much worship dishonesty within, and a matter of subconscious rebellion, wherever the total self has used his reason to rationalize the lower faith, which he wants to keep, into his highest possible faith. Thus the Old Testament God has become an idol in fact. The realm of law is good until the law of grace supersedes and abolishes it for the believer, who now gratefully obeys, and thus transcends, the realm of law by the spontaneity of the heart which keeps the law unconsciously.

Much of the realm of the Spirit of God is dominant within parts of the Church as a sociological institution and also within numberless individual believers. In this case the latter state is worse than the former. For now the state of natural normalcy, under the dominance of the Spirit of God, is still preferred to the state of genuine Christianity in the realm of the Holy Spirit. This state is nearly normal in so-called Christianity. Here is where self-righteousness and self-deception become man's worst enemies. Here is where harlots and publicans go into heaven before "Christians." For now the very fact that the self has hid himself behind the very words which can free him, but has changed their content so as to make the speaking of them of no effect, becomes the greatest possible obstacle to his salvation.

This self-deception is precisely the reason that countless people heartily enjoy orthodox talk, and any criticism of inferior or heretical teachings, because these words come to them through the screen of their own remaking and help further to secure them in their own subconscious deceit. "Orthodox" preaching very commonly adds to the strength of their camouflage. They crave it, resenting words spoken in the Spirit. When the Spirit of power comes in, with its soft, penetrating certainty, the self-righteous gather together in consternation "to crucify" the offender. Thus the Holy Spirit speaks not only in terms of newness and power out into the world, but speaks to those who are scarcely alive spiritually within the Church because of their self-righteousness. To them he urges either hotness or coldness, but not the state of being lukewarm because of self-comfort and of self-righteousness. Often those who defend the offense of the Cross are the most offended at its piercing reality, the childlike acceptance of God's love and power revealed by it.

We have seen, then, that the realm of the Spirit of God can have high worship, as of the Old Testament God or even of the Gospel in a perverted or in a theoretical acceptance of it, along with a practical isolation from its gifts and demands. Thus the state of natural normalcy can be very high indeed. But in another sense, there may be a higher and clearer conception of the social standards and tasks outside than inside the realm of the Holy Spirit. The reason for this fact is that the social aspect of religion has there become the center of sacredness, and has thus become developed to a heightened degree through the feeling of substitution, through compensation, or through a deep feeling of guilt which finds no expression and forgiveness in relation to a personal God of love, but finds for itself instead an intensified endeavor for self-justification in terms of social betterment. Thus those who find fullness of life and peace within the full fellowship love may not be equally developed in some social matters, because to them these are, after all, not central and eternal but secondary and temporal; while to those who make these their object of sacred devotion, they are central and primary, and cause them, therefore, in these realms to overdevelop, compensate, and perhaps even become prophetically martyred. But this is also one way in which God works. Tillich rightly affirms that the secular world with its understanding of practical issues can often be the conscience of the Church in these realms, even as the Church in its distinctive realms is called on to be the conscience of the world. Often actual needs have also pressed on people to champion progressive causes which have not been clearly seen as such by religious people, even by those in the realm of the Holy Spirit. Yinger points out that the

> church did not create the labor movement; churchmen did not make the original discovery that the demands of labor were Christian justice; that followed as a necessary consequence of the fact that those demands were crucial in the lives of a great many people.[3]

We tend to forget that God uses the "push of progress" to challenge the "pull of purpose," as well as the "pull of purpose" to challenge and direct the "push of progress."[4]

The Spirit moves from the realm of natural normalcy to the realm of the Church, uniting them both by His inner selfsame reality, yet also differentiating them both by His difference of operational appearance. Somehow, we have lost sight of both this distinctive perspective and this distinctive dimension. Perhaps the real reason for this loss is the fact that we believe too little in the actual presence of the Holy Spirit and too much in our own adequacy. Perhaps we, too, have to learn that in our weakness lies our strength. Perhaps we have to come to understand that even with regard to the practical realm of social action the foolishness of God, in preaching and acting the Word, is stronger and wiser than the strength and wisdom of man. For a new attack on our social problems, with fuller vision and power, we need a new acceptance in understanding and, above all, in personal appropriation of the distinctiveness of the Holy Spirit in His role as the translator, transformer, transmitter and transpowerer of the Gospel to all realms of life and to all conditions of men.

How, now, does this analysis relate itself to social action? The answer is that our concern is with illumination and motivation that issue in concrete action. We have shown how word or deed

[3] *Op. cit.*, p. 48.
[4] Cf. *The Christian Faith*, chap. 3.

in the Spirit gives new means of communication and new powers for motivation. Most effective social action according to our analysis is, consequently, indirect. Before we undertake that question, however, it is well to say that there is direct action in which Christians as members of the Body of Christ, concerned for the world, or the Church as a Church, can participate. This analysis is not meant to destroy the validity of direct social action. Nor must we think of action solely in terms of legislative decrees and juridical enforcement.

Much talk of fellowship is vain for its simply puts faith in knowing God's will in the human community rather than in the Holy Spirit. Much talk of fellowship is allegiance to a human group or heritage and not to the present, demanding will of God. Christian social action, in the imperious sense of that word, does not wait for slow-moving, cautious institutional channels to open up. They are plugged up by the common concerns of this world and share too much of the foolish wisdom of the world which shall perish. Direct action on social issues in witness and proposal, in so far as this refers to radical change, will be limited to the strategy of the remnant, the creative minority, except as the Spirit raises up the hosts to battle for the good in exceptional seasons of social rejuvenation and refreshment. Our jaded, cynical, disintegrating age cannot understand this. Only an age of the Spirit, fresh with divine vitality and creative urge, can sense this approach.

The full impact of the revelational norms on the traditional norms, of God's present Will on the actual societal situation, will most likely be incarnated in voice and action by only the chosen few who have dared self-surrender in the full context of the whole gamut of human life. Yet the Church in its wider and more ordinary sense, and sober in its worldly wisdom, can help by acting directly on the maintaining of certain areas of constructive living. The whole Church can address itself to the task of moral integrity, family solidarity, general social righteousness, temperance, community relief and rehabilitation, and international co-operation and good will. We must not, however, underestimate the necessity for constructive maintenance of the best in any tradition. No prophet could ever exist to the profit of the community unless his discontinuous position could be organically related to the continuity of previous attainment. This attainment has itself been bought at countless cost and is not to be scorned. Our freedom in the United States, in the best sense of it, is an example. Without it the prophet would not have the same chance. In present-day Russia he could hardly get started, much less get a hearing. Thus when the Church in endorsing the *status quo* is simply blamed as reactionary, it is falsely accused, for the maintaining of the *status quo* against the many-sided onslaughts of worse leadings is itself no easy task. The solid body of churchmen who, either individually or together as men of the church, keep endorsing and working in direct fashion for our present system of government and line of life cannot be sweepingly condemned for their reactionary refusal to become prophetic. They must be seen as the field where the main force is still the Spirit of God, but which is yet most relevantly related, in numberless instances, to the force of the Holy Spirit.

Since our whole third section will try, as best we can, to deal with concrete social issues, our interest here is chiefly in pointing out some indirect ways which are used by the Holy Spirit with regard to social action. Indirect action consists, first of all, in illumination. The question is not here one of direct confrontation in areas where there is a very sore conscience under the disguise of a fanatical ideology, but rather one of simple light for people to walk in. There can be no question that one of our greatest social enemies is still ignorance. Here is where we need the help particularly of our social scientists and educators. How can we expect complex, difficult social engineering to succeed in the face of the thick fog bank of popular prejudice and misunderstanding of the real issues?

Somehow, our churches can assume the responsibility of adult education, at least in small groups. Intelligent education is sorely needed. Even our ministry, in large numbers, are dependent mostly upon the propaganda of our great newspapers, the radio and the more widely circulated periodicals. A prominent clergyman, for instance, and an otherwise well-educated man, recently remarked that his Bible of foreign affairs was *Time* magazine! There is a difference, we hope, between the full prophetic Gospel of the Christian Agape and *Time!* Perhaps we can gain not only ministers but small groups of laymen for some venture of adult education along these lines.

Daring concern, lifted by God's strength, often goes beyond its own fancied courage, to accomplish important things in history. Thus, when Christianity gives men the reality of concern in their lives, when the Spirit implants care in their hearts, when God creates compassion in their thoughts, necessity and need become the mothers of creative suggestions. The Spirit still breathes over the chaos and incarnates order amidst prevailing confusion. If the Christian Church can become the fellowship of concern, enough and long enough, to raise up sons in its midst, who will apply, in the concrete world, the creative suggestions which can come from the Spirit, when they tackle social and political evil in daring faith, there will become evident one more indirect way in which the Spirit affects society.

There is also an indirect function of the Spirit in causing judgment and in causing tensions. Complacency and self-righteousness are ever the enemies of progress in every realm of life. When creative concern becomes itself the norm of transcendence, man cannot escape being judged in the precise place where he is. Thus the Church by proclaiming and the Christian by professing his relevant faith in that which is at the heart both of the Eternal Purpose and of every man, deepest down, both judge our social and political programs as inadequate, and thus prevent, at every point, self-satisfaction and complacency. They judge neither unto despair, for they have to show the practicality of the standard which they proclaim, namely, the active Will of God in human history; nor do they judge below the point where the highest creativity can come forth. And, besides, they judge not from without, but from within, as themselves under the same condemnation. There can thus be no brittle and self-righteous judgment that is truly in the Spirit who is Agape. The judgment springs out of creative and redemptive identification with the particular situation, and is thus a judgment based on pedagogical wisdom and patience. The truth is spoken in love, and both truth and love are necessary to the speaking in the Spirit.

Very likely the most important work done by the Spirit indirectly is through individuals who become personal examples and stimulants to better social aspirations and actions. Pribilla quotes in German from one of Augustine's sermons the meaty sentence: *"Wenn der hl. Stephanus nicht so gebetet hätte, würde die Kirche heute keinen Paulus haben."*[5] The world-shaking work of Paul was due, to a large extent, to the example of Stephen! Sometimes it seems that we miss seeing, as most important, one of the truest means for changing society, namely, the rearing and developing of creative individuals. The first Adam was a living soul, but through the second Adam we become *kindling* spirits. In the helping to develop genuine and strong individuals the indirect and the direct method come together. To change society we must change men. Toynbee, citing E. Meyer, points out that "the ideal of Philosophy is the sage who relies on himself; the ideal of Christianity is the believer who sinks himself into God."[6] To be with God is to be for others. To love God is to love the neighbor also. Thus the key to a Christian society is the Christian individual. We need, as Isaiah writes, men who "take root downward and bear fruit upward," whose roots are in God and whose fruits are for society.

We tend to forget that "personality is the absolute existential centre."[7] Werfel fears that "the future belongs to the drill sergeant in every sphere."[8] This can be true only of a disintegrating civilization, not of the Age of the Spirit. Socialization may mean collective planning in certain areas of life for the sake of producing plenty and giving men creative leisure. But unless the end of socialization is fuller freedom in truer and more important areas of life, including the economic in the most constructive sense, socialization is an evil to be fought. We have too much of a capitalistic preconception of freedom. Society cannot ever afford to minimize the individual, in any dimension. As Walter Muelder stresses, the larger unit cannot without loss to the community absorb the functions of the smaller. Kierkegaard made himself into "that individual" and felt that our real problem was that we escaped into the herd. The crowd, he maintained, is untruth. Estall has pointed out that both

[5] *Um Kirchliche Einheit*, p. 310.
[6] *The Study of History*, Vol. II, p. 563.
[7] Berdyaev, *Slavery and Freedom*, p. 26.
[8] *Between Heaven and Earth*, p. 60.

Kierkegaard and Marx used the existential approach as opposed to systematic thinking, one in the realm of the individual and the other in the realm of society. Kierkegaard had by far the deeper understanding of the individual, and Marx of social problems. Estall feels that we need a synthesis of these two existential approaches, if theoretically and historically such a synthesis is possible.[9]

Christian existentialism, however, does just this. Berdyaev, for one, has labored well along these lines. When freedom and faithfulness in fellowship based on the concrete love of God for each one in his particular situation is taken seriously, no individual is ever put into a secondary place, but every one is made absolutely important. As a matter of fact, the only vital place where the problem of community can be tackled is within concrete individuals as sustainers of social relations. Though religion may be "world loyalty," as Whitehead writes, nevertheless, basically it is ever "what the individual does with his own solitariness."[10] Social relations can, after all, be approached only through social agents, each one of whom is finally an individual.

Toynbee has profoundly analyzed the disintegration of the body social into the disintegration of the soul. Above all in importance is the individual, as such, and in relation to society. Upon the "Creative Minority" depends the health of civilization. Sociological statistics, over and over again, have confirmed how social opinion is set in communities by its few creative and thinking individuals. A Socrates, following his genie, helps project into history a whole stream of understanding. Augustine, taking from him and the fuller Master, shapes thought and life throughout the centuries. A wandering "madman," the saint from Assisi, had a profound influence on the centuries. John Wesley changed the course of the whole English stream of history. Moody packed more power into creative American civilization than most people are aware.

Institutions are more than the shadow of great men, but they are that, too. This much can be said and must be said: the individual can open himself uniquely to the Holy Spirit who alone can

---

[9] 1948 Report of the Week of Work, of the National Council on Religion in Higher Education.
[10] *Religion in the Making*, p. 58.

truly redeem and create the fuller Christian community and over-flow into a creative and healthy civilization. The individual is ever the door to a new world. Lyman has defined religion as "the fullest development of every human personality through the co-operative creation of a world-wide community of persons," and even more fully as "the maximum of harmonious interaction between the per-sonalities of men and the Deepest Reality of the universe.[11] This stress is, indeed, good, but how earnestly we need to guard the truth that as a *channel the individual is ever primary, the dis-junctive reality of the universe* the point at which fellowship be-comes conscious and understands itself, even though this can take place only in the fellowship context and from within the Spirit, the deepest Source of all life and of all reality.[12]

Perhaps a word should also be said about the cell as an instru-ment of the Spirit in His translating and transforming role. First of all, the cell cannot take the place of the individual. They cannot pray rightly together who cannot, and do not, pray rightly alone. There is no substitute for praying in the closed closet to a Father who sees in secret and who rewards openly in terms of the social answers to prayer. Only those have the keys together who have learned to use them alone. The keys are not arbitrary *ipse dixits* of privileged groups or ecclesiastical structures. The keys are the con-trol of historic power, when we are controlled by God in such a way that history can be shaped by us. The cell is no substitute for hard work on the part of the crucial participants, the individuals.

Nor are the cells Christian and socially effective unless they are without walls toward the world. Often they become groups that insulate themselves from the world, where real satisfaction is sought in fellowship and where much social examination is carried on within the group, but where there is mostly talk as far as help-ing the world is concerned. No cell can be Christian unless it is a fellowship held together by its constant attention to God's love for the world. Another danger of isolation and insulation is that the consensus principle of the group becomes mistaken for God's

[11] *The Meaning and Truth of Religion*, p. 86.
[12] For an excellent discussion of the prevenience of God and the secondary primacy of the individual in social transformation, cf. Whiston, *Teach Us to Pray*.

revelation. The vertical, and not the horizontal line, must ever be primary, though both with regard to historic continuity and with regard to contemporary community we need the reality and the strength of the subordinate role of the horizontal dimension. When consensus becomes the final principle of truth, however, God is often debarred from the group and the prophet is silenced.

Often, too, the cell can become a separate strand within a church, putting itself, perhaps unwittingly, on a different level from the rest of the people. The cell, of all things, becomes the occasion for spiritual pride. The very nature of the cell as concentration in Christian nurture and work soon makes people join it who are spiritual misfits in ordinary groups, who develop a false intensity in their cell interest, and who severely criticize the church from a superior point of view, even though they could not themselves stand, in the first place, the wear and tear of ordinary routine and togetherness. The cell, if it is to remain Christian, must never become a second kind of church nor be preferred to the church. Cells can concentrate, with loving abandon and with quiet wisdom, on the steady transformation of the actual church toward the Christian pattern, but must not live as though they took the place of church life at the depths of a person's allegiance. Summer camps and college cells, especially, must watch themselves lest they take primary interest in themselves and in their own work, rather than in the full and normal work of the church of Christ.

The basic rule for the formation of the cell ought to be its naturalness. There is a prayer group of lonesome Christians in a university. There is a group of frustrated ministers who come together once a week to pray, or yet another time to study and to discuss. There is a group of church-school teachers who have common problems and precious burdens to carry and who begin to pray purposefully together. There is a group of congressmen or senators who know that in their own wisdom they shall fail, and who kneel in common seeking and finding before God. There is a group of railroad porters who need the power to do their work as Christians and who want to carry the load of the world with Christ.[13] There is a group of labor leaders who feel that the destiny of labor depends upon Christian and creative leadership and who

13 Cf. Samuel Shoemaker's writings for many illustrations of this kind.

therefore need to share their common problems regularly before God. There is a group of businessmen who feel that a new day must come in their line of work through those who offer up their problems, for strength of spirit to prevent their being defensive, and for strength to become creative. The most natural cells consist of natural arrangements. Artificial cells can be formed, but they seldom last unless they are active communities led by a great man of the Spirit. Natural cells, like students in one seminary dormitory, are far more likely units for the Spirit to use. Where common interests, relations or vocations bring people together anyway, there is the best seedbed for Christian cells.

The first rule for all these cells is that they should be from God for men. When the divine Agape becomes a cell's center in Christ through the Holy Spirit, the cell needs constant self-examination and self-nurturing, but the self never can think now in terms of itself, or be bound by itself, but becomes a creative and redemptive force for the world. By the fruits of the cell it must ever be judged, whether they be peace and joy and longsuffering, and whether they be the increasing and deepening concerns of redemptive compassion. A cell cannot consistently exist as Christian without becoming the center creatively of world-transformation.

But this means also that if the cell becomes merely activistic and does not put its fellowship with the Father and with the Son first, it is also not Christian. The root must bear fruit, but there must be a root. The cell must find depth by the primacy of worship, by the rendering itself up to God; by the walking together in the genuine fellowship of the Spirit; by the deeper disciplines of life and heart which come from working together unsparingly on common projects—disciplines, however, which to be Christian in nature must be carried with joy and thanksgiving; and by the kind of study which causes the soul to wrestle long and hard with the spiritual powers of untruth and evil which rule our present world-mind.

Such study ought to be of the spiritual life, of the Bible, of Christian history, of Christian theology, and of its constant and concrete application to contemporary life. The many road blocks to full faith and free fellowship in our own minds ought to be removed by the arduous co-working of consecrated thinkers. Then the nourishing food of faith for a new and better fellowship ought to be produced. Beyond that, but in conjunction with it, there ought to be action projects whether of direct social action or of immediate social helpfulness. In all these ways, faith, mind and the open hand co-operate to make the cell a well-rounded and God-grounded center of world transformation under the translating and transpowering direction of the Spirit.

But as we have said, the cell cannot take the place of the local church or of the Church Universal. The cell, in the proper use of the term, is not a church, but only a special mobilization point in the church. The church, local or universal, must represent the total community in the sense of man's total interests. A labor cell, for instance, can be especially concerned with the question how labor can become Christian and forget all about the problem of education as such. The church, however, must maintain the centrality of the Christian faith with regard to all human interests. Even where the community is mostly specialized, like a college church, the church cannot be the church if it becomes a cell; that is, if it looks at everything from the peculiar slant of the college situation. A labor temple is not really a church unless it transcends the labor situation and looks at life from the viewpoint of the centrality of the Christian faith with its equidistant radii to all human interests. As a matter of fact, to maintain a labor temple or a college church is well-nigh impossible. It means, at least, almost inhuman transcendence of interests and concentration on all of life from the Christian point of view. A minister paid by manufacturers is not a Christian minister unless his function is to transcend the manufacturers' point of view to correct their angle of vision in terms of the relevance of Christ for all of life. A church is a Christian church in direct proportion to the active presence in it of the leveling power of the Gospel, where at the foot of the Cross all ground is level and all interests are of equal impotence, because God is completely concerned with all legitimate concerns of men. To say that the church must take the side of labor because labor is oppressed is to distort the Gospel with its equal concern for the oppressor and the oppressed. The church is never a partisan to a class struggle. The church is God's whole Word to all men and to all conditions of men.

The local church, and not the cell, therefore, is the crucial area for Christian social action. The local church should be the center of all the cells. Into this fellowship of all concerned each cell should pour its own lifeblood and specialized vision and skill. The local church exists for the central light of the Gospel to shine illuminatingly, judgingly, and healingly on all areas of life. The fellowship itself, with God and men, is the Eternal Purpose which is the ground and goal of the historic process. The Church is the heart of the fellowship. All communities in other realms of life are the latent church and have their reason for being in their serving the fellowship or in the preparing the people who have that kind of fellowship for the fuller fellowship in the Spirit. All social action is for the sake of the Church with a capital "C," for the effecting of God's own end for history.

Social action is a matter of stewardship, from one point of view; a matter of pedagogy, from another; and a matter of the outworking of Christian concern, from a third point of view. But social action is not the reason for the Church's being, either in local living or in universal existence. The Church must face out and not in on itself, in a world of need, in order to be itself; but this concern is real in itself and the fellowshhip has its own end and reason for being, even eternally, and must not be reduced, in reality, to an instrument for social betterment. The Church, therefore, cannot maintain its Christian reality or function unless it makes fellowship with God and with the saints central to its life, a fellowship which then by means of its own nature performs responsible acts of concern for the world as a whole.

The central figure in this task of local transcendence and inclusive interpretation should be the regularly appointed minister. How this can be done is another matter. First of all, he ought to have competent training in the central meaning of the Gospel, and a Gospel which has relevant meaning for the community, being not a mythically historical or a merely personal Gospel. When an event in history loses generalizable, contemporary meaning, with full respect both to the need for inclusiveness and to the need for particular practicality, that event is that far myth as far as religious availability is concerned. When salvation, on the other hand, becomes personal apart from the organic solidarity of each man with

God and men, in responsibility and concern, based on gratitude and faith, that salvation is escape into self-security and is in no way Christian. Unless the Gospel, then, which the minister has received as a trust, is completely relevant, he has not the Christian Gospel.

But the training of the minister's mind is not enough. He must be trained in universal compassion and courage. This can come only when the Gospel becomes the power that *lives him*. Our seminaries should be not merely academic, "worldly" professional schools, but schools of the prophets, or even better, of the saints. How this is possible along with rigid and critical scholarship is a question that we must face. Perhaps the seminary chaplain will be the most important man on the campus, and must be selected because of his central function. Perhaps every professor must dedicate his life, and all professors together in a new and personally humbling way, in order for the Christian fellowship on the seminary campus to be deep enough and strong enough to give to the students the vision and the power of the kind of local ministry which is needed.

After that, each minister should read widely and carefully the central contents and applications to life of the Christian faith. He should be a first-class student at least in effort. This involves time and energy. Time must be had for the Church's rethinking its own central task through the ministry in the light of the Christian faith and of the needs of the world. Christian energy and courage come largely when the minister lives with his Bible and with great devotional literature, especially with the lives of the saints, and as he thus learns whole new sources and methods of motivation. The intellectual and spiritual stature of the minister, in relation to the concrete problems of the total scale of life, as far as possible, will greatly determine the social efficacy of the local church.

Sometimes it has seemed that if each minister could be paid from a central source rather than by the local congregation, he could be financially freer in relation to his congregation, and perhaps feel freer to prepare himself properly rather than cater to lesser needs of the community. But this would perhaps alienate him from his people and cause mischief with his message and leadership. The local man cannot, anyway, force the people to transcend their prejudices and part-seeings from some vantage point above them. He must win them by the power of his insight, the realism of his analysis, the consistency of his Christian perspective, and above all, by means of his living, acting and speaking in the Spirit.

The whole conception of the Church has to be rethought. When the world is perishing for lack of light and power, we cannot afford to be preaching stations with occasional meetings. The Church, to command for God and for the people, must wake up to its opportunity to give wholeness and meaning to all of life by itself becoming whole-time for God and for the world. When the minister and the people together, in humble patience, study the ends, the means, the motives and the methods for lovingly and wisely changing this distraught world, we shall see a new all-round power and a naturalness of believing.

Obviously this involves that the minister and people alike find their walls of partition, as far as in them lies, broken down in relation to other religious groups in the community. Ecumenicity, if genuine, always begins at the grass roots. It begins with the individual Christian, in whatever station, transcending his own situation by the power of Christian concern and by his living from God for the world. Ecumenicity is not mostly a matter of officials joining organizations, even though they be world-wide. Ecumenicity is the limitless love of Christ overcoming differences and creating the unities of common concerns. Only in so far as organization expresses this reality is it finally significant. In the local community this is crucially important. Unless Christian churches co-operate, they deny, in the central core of their life and message, the nature of the Gospel, and prevent it from being preached. What else is preached is rather unimportant, if, in life and thought, creative co-operation under God is not vitally and overflowingly proclaimed.

The degree of real Christianity present in a church can be measured almost directly by the fruits of actual co-operation. The most important single thing that can be done to change the community is for the local churches to exhibit the grace of creative co-operation within and among their fellowships, a fact which will naturally, in time, lead to the more effective uniting of both spirits and bodies in the full fellowship love of Christ for the world. Unless, then, the middle-class church on the common, the small, ivied, socially exclusive church on the side street, and the factory workers' church on the other side of town can truly come together in spirit and in deed, beyond differences of cultural background and financial and social standing, there is no hope for either a vital Christianity or for a creative civilization. Christ is kept out. The Holy Spirit is quenched. The reality of the Christian message stands and falls, for the world, with its power to transform, in actuality and with regard to one another, those who call and profess themselves to be Christians.

The fellowship must also learn to work wisely and well with other community groups. The members of the church are also members of the community. There they often hold positions of responsibility. If from their church life they get the facts and the responsibility, a great and natural opportunity for world-transformation is already open to us, particularly in any culture where Christians are not rejected outright because of their faith. Nominal membership is obviously of little or no importance to social action. Only men of faith and prayer, who act in the Spirit, will do.

I trust external manipulation less and less. Unless we can get at the heart of people, at the core of their very being, we shall change neither them nor the world. Social action, too, to use Douglas Steere's phrase, must be a "beginning from within." In his book, *Doors into Life,* he has shown how creatively social activity comes from the acceptance of God for what He is, and not first of all for what He can do or cause us to do. The peculiar thing is that the more gratefully we accept our lot in God, the more strength of life and freedom from tension we have to change that lot and truly to help others.

This is the power that must overcome the world, the faith in the Spirit that all of life belongs to God and must be used to His glory and to the highest possible human fellowship in, under and with Him. Even if such faith drives people away from the Church, nevertheless a creative and redemptive tension arises in the community. But we must be careful lest, on the other hand, people should be driven away from the church and from its members who participate in public life because these representatives are falsely pious and impractical.

Local ministers and laymen, however, need the wider vision and contact of the association and of the total Church. The association, the synod, or what corresponds to it sectionally, should be more than an occasional meeting or an over-all organization. The association, both for the ministry and for laymen, ought to constitute living cells for worship, study and action. When the association acts for the local church because it is from it, as far as possible, and because it is giving its best back to it, then there never arise needless functionaries who speak mostly for themselves. Here, too, there must be the same natural drive toward ecumenicity, as there are constant cross-reference and interaction among the associations on the part of the different households of faith, until we make the home large enough, according to God's original blueprint, to house us all within the same walls, which are built by the world from without against us, never from within against the world.

National and international work should follow the same pattern. The Spirit must be primary. That would surely mean a new way of working at our religious headquarters. Often God's work becomes as secular as selling sewing machines. Church officials are rushed with numberless rounds of activities. Some of them are men of real spiritual stature who manage to find time, anyway, for consistent and exacting devotional life. But what would happen if we actually believed that to find time for the Spirit as individuals and as groups has to come *first* on the agenda? What if periods of personal and cell devotion should be the *primary* task of the day? What if Gandhi, Jesus and Paul are better examples of getting things done *that matter* than are most of our machinelike business executives? This suggestion may seem preposterous and unrealistic to an age that does not really believe in the primacy of the Spirit, and in the actual presence and guidance of God. Often, men of large responsibilities in Christian work are God's biggest problems!

The Church would have an entirely new power if the leaders were prayed for fervently and believingly by all local and sectional groups and if all believed that no money was ever better spent than for the time in which the leaders find perspective and power through the Holy Spirit. If this Spirit becomes real, the time to raise money, which now is not a little time, will be free for worship. For when people believe, they give and give generously. If all Christians gave a tenth of their income and if some gave more, how much time would not be saved that is now used to raise funds, and how free would not our officials be from the pressure of money-minded men!

We may ask why so much resistance to progress often comes from those responsible, whether from board officials or from big-church ministers on decisive committees. Because of selfishness, inertia, fear for causes in which even they have not succeeded with all their work? To some extent, yes, all of these. But mostly the answer is that these men have not the time nor often the inclination to be saints of God open to the Spirit, partly, perhaps mostly, because of the setup in which they are caught. What we have done is to make the "realistic," businesslike men head of our national church activities. When these men are also men of the Spirit, creatively daring under the guidance of God, all is well. As surely as Christianity is not a myth but an operational reality, we must have the central organizations of our church bodies oiled by the Holy Spirit. A praying leadership and a praying church will produce both vision and competence. Competence in vocation is a definite fruit of the Spirit.

It seems also that if the church is really alive, through and through, it would send up, on a national and international scale, some kind of legislative and advisory body where all the local and sectional groups would come together. This should not be appointed from above in a haphazard fashion, but should comprise the representatives of the groups themselves democratically, in order that these groups would then receive back, as from their best selves, both advice and leadership. When "the churches" become the Church, through federation or organically, they can easily carry this kind of overhead structure rather than the present multiplication of the same functions through scores and hundreds of denominations. Such an overhead organization would be the voice of the people themselves under God for the world, though it must be open to the creative criticism of its own creative minority. It should be backed from the very local church through each sectional division all the way into the national and international areas by means of cells of worship and of devotion and by means of cells for study and for action.

The guider and perfecter, however, must be the Spirit. He alone can help us work out these arrangements or find better arrangements within which to work. The Church itself, through its own representatives, under the Spirit, will then have to decide to what extent direct action or indirect action will be its method. At present a split church tries to lobby into action certain measures whereas other churches or religious groups put up counterpressures. If the Church becomes one in body as well as in Spirit, which God grant for the Age of the Spirit, it will find more orderly and organic means with which to work within political and social channels. Our first task inescapably is the grass-roots reality of church union. But if no interest is taken in the rest of life, as in the secular fields, the attention to the inner life of the soul and of the church on themselves may itself become a flight from the real change of the heart which includes and, therefore, dares to tackle what is without. The two tasks will have to go hand in hand, but by all means the major proportion of time, prayer, thought, and energy will have to go into the renewing of the life of the Spirit, without whom nothing can be according to the power of the Eternal Purpose. Church union is mostly a mockery unless there be the genuine union in thought and life of the Holy Spirit.

Amsterdam, for instance, may go down into history partly as an attempt to salvage traditionalistic Christendom from the fuller truth of a better faith and partly as the yielding of important churchmen to popular pressure for the unity of Protestantism in a showy but largely innocuous manner in order to salvage the structure and reality of denominational sovereignty. It may be basically of the nature of the same false-front effect given by the League of Nations and the United Nations. Such half-hearted measures, however, pressed defensively into being, can become actual channels for abundant grace if the Spirit is allowed at the broad base of the church to become potently active, and then either deposes or touches creatively the leaders of partial loyalties. But the unity that counts is unity in the reality of the Spirit.

We end these two sections of analysis with the strongest stress we can possibly put on the primacy of the Holy Spirit for Christian social action. Unless prayer becomes more widely real in Christendom there is no authentic Christianity, and if there is no authentic Christianity there is no use in talking about the relation of Christianty to society at all. Far better to have this truth known and constantly held before us than to use light words which have no power in them to save. If the church is to influence the world to a new level of life, its transforming power must come from its own having become, in large measure, its God-intended self through a new rebirth of its own life and faith. Our analysis is true and effective only to the extent that the Christian faith is real and effective in history.

SECTION III

CONCRETE CONSIDERATIONS

Introduction

Since this work is not a social ethics in any comprehensive sense, but merely the foundation for such a work, we are limiting to three topics the more concrete application of our method. Such limitation will bring out the purpose of this volume, namely, to illustrate the applicability of the Christian faith to our present problems. In order to do so we must show two things: first, that the Christian faith contains within itself clear, general directives for the solution of these problems; but, secondly, that these directives can never be completely explicit without denying the existential nature of our situation. The need for faith and for growth through responsible decision would be done away, if man could know directly, and in detail, what the right thought or the right choice would be. Whether such knowledge could be obtained through reason or through prayer, from within the created self or from the Holy Spirit, matters not. In either case the concrete directives for thought and action would deny the whole reason for the level of created existence, as we have found it throughout our investigations.

The three topics which we have chosen are war, property and education. That these are all at the forefront of present concern can hardly be denied. If the Christian faith has concrete considerations to offer to indicate the lines along which these problems can be solved, while still leaving it up to us personally to appropriate these lines of approach through both daring faith and careful investigation, it will have satisfied the evidence for its relevance and reality, for which we have been seeking. Yet such is its nature that the fulfillment of our search becomes what Hendrick Kraemer is reported to have called "a subversive fulfilment," for, at the end, we find ourselves not the judges of the Christian faith, but, instead, judged by it. God is gracious ever to allow us to stand over it and judge it, in order that we may find Him faithful, and accept His judgment, not as an arbitrary decree based on power, but as the austere, yet tender, judgment of the omnipotent God who is, nevertheless, all the while, our loving Father.

CHAPTER VII

The Christian Perspective on War

Nothing is more precious than peace, by which all war, both in heaven and earth, is brought to an end.[1]

To deny *that* is to deny the intrinsic and self-sufficient reality of Christian fellowship. Striving is, ultimately, not for the sake of striving, but for the sake of finding. What we find fully satisfying at the end of our striving is fellowship with God and men according to His power and purpose. Both Augustine and Aquinas knew that even in war men seek their true peace. They knew that "to confound the nature of the good life with the striving for it not only suffuses the moral life with a priggish insincerity, it destroys the springs of all fruitful moral effort."[2] Most of us know so much strife and striving that not only is the reality of peace questioned, in the depths of our emotions, but also even the desirability of it. Only the experience of occasional moments, or longer periods, of real peace can make our hearts quest for it, over and beyond the questionings of our minds and the uncertainties of our emotions.

Especially true does this become when we think of war and peace in a political sense. For we have hardly known anything except a truce based on weariness, the need to stabilize internal situations, and the vain hope of some victor's peace. The hope has been vain, because the idealism which has intermingled in the shaping of it has been all too heavily mixed with the camouflaged pretensions of power politics. To the Christian faith, therefore, the problem of peace looms as large as, if not larger than, the problem of war. To

[1] Ignatius, *Epistle to the Ephesians*, in *The Ante-Nicene Fathers*, Vol. I, p. 55.
[2] Demant, *op. cit.*, p. 16.

a large extent, because we want to escape what we call "peace," we have war. In other words, our periods of political peace are not peace. Demant is quite right in saying that "the causes of war lie much deeper than the will to war or absence of the will to peace."[3] Many may find more peace in war than peace in peace. Often open conflict is easier to bear than unfocused tensions all entwined with specific points of aggravation. We rightly shudder at the shallowness of much political pacifism at this point.

> War in modern times is the most blatant expression of the tragic nature of man. It appears as the final result of a number of forces in society which operate in peace-time without any consciously aggressive intention. . . . It is regarded increasingly as a calamitous necessity rather than a deliberate enterprise.[4]

At bottom, the approach to war is bound to be theological, at any rate for the Christian. We cannot, moreover, get the picture of the Christian faith and war, except in terms of the Christian faith, for the Christian faith is our ultimate, all-inclusive perspective. This means, of course, that the problem of war must be related more to God's eternal purpose than to immediate human choices. All superficial preachings of moralism and all thin, rational explanations will have to be surrendered to those who prefer to find their securities in terms of partial perspectives. Those who seek the full truth, however, must remember that God has made this kind of world and that we have no right, therefore, to deny that wars, however indirectly, have somehow a place in it. We must also ponder such facts as that wars, as Sorokin's careful studies in *Social and Cultural Dynamics,* Volume III, point out, occur mostly during man's creative periods, and decrease in number as disintegration of civilization and culture sets in. We can also observe that "the twentieth century is a century of disasters: disasters exploding in the midst of an exhibition of vitality such as has not been witnessed before in human history."[5] On the other hand, since God is, above all, the perfect Creator and Redeemer of this process, we have, even more, no right to think of war as a permanent or necessary part of process. The Christian faith, in any case, can neither explain

[3] *Ibid.,* p. 98.
[4] *Ibid.,* p. 92.
[5] G. V. Jones, *op cit.,* p. 14.

war, nor help us to get rid of it, if it merely condemns it from some
lofty level of a perfection of history which has never existed. The
Epistle of James may explain wars as coming from the lusts that
war in our members,[6] but the prior question is always whence come
these lusts, and what purpose do they play in a world made by an
all-loving, all-wise and all-powerful God.

The perspective which we must rather take is the confronting of
man's actual history, through God's long work in evolution, with
the perfect end promised by the Eternal Purpose. There is a long
distance, in human terms, from man's animal history to his Agape
history. All idealisms that neglect or minimize the actual, play us
false; and all actualisms that deny or minimize the ultimate power
of the Ideal Reality also play us false. To change the actual we
must first understand it. "In the long run, it is probably easier to
direct social change by working into the faiths and loyalties of the
group rather than counter to them."[7] This is true in that men need
to know why they have their allegiances, if they are to find, freely
and for themselves, the delivering allegiances beyond their present
faiths and loyalties. With this approach we shall try to understand
the nature of war and how to get rid of it.

One of the real reasons that modern theology does not strike
fire with the man of today is that theology usually fails to come to
terms realistically with modern knowledge. We know now that
there was no earthly Paradise six thousand years ago. We know
that man, instead, has come up from nature through a long, long
process of evolution—a long process, that is, in comparison to historic time in the sense of recorded history. And yet modern theologians still all too often keep talking about original perfection or
perfection before the fall. They speak of the image of God as an
endowment that man has forfeited through sin. Very often the
actual historicity of the earthly Paradise or of the fall of Adam are
denied, and the language is called symbolic.

To be sure, there are aspects of experience which can bear this
out in part, but only in part. Every human individual is born into
a social heritage of sin. Were he naturally good, he would, never-

[6] Chap. 4.
[7] Atteberry, Auble and Hunt, *Introduction to Social Science*, Vol. I, p. 5.

theless, soon be taught the ways of sin by society. The prehistory of man shows that history was not originated in perfection, for man came from a snarling, brawling animal background. The choice can be viewed ideally in the abstract much more rightly than it can usually be carried out into action. Nowhere, however, is there perfection, in history or in experience, from which man has actually fallen, and which can account for this kind of world in such a way as to exculpate God for having made it. Somehow we back away from connecting God organically with this kind of world. Much of social idealism stems from some primitivistic utopianism, which prejudices to begin with the realism of its Gospel of Hope. We have, rather, to start with the history, the prehistory, and the experience that we actually know. In this case prehistory is the long, muddy flat of animal evolution (not to go back farther) ; history is man's arduous climb up the steep cliffs of historic difficulty at the tremendous sacrifice of the many, and of the creative, sacrificial few; and experience brings to man's vision even before the choices are made, the imperfections of his finitude and the sinfulness of his actual nature. Only God, or possibly also the sinless saints—if any—can make choices which are pure or perfect before the act.

In other words, our actual conflicts now, whether internal disturbances or wars, are simply a continuation of the general struggle in nature, as they are modified by man's humanity. To say, therefore, for instance, that "history is the action, while nature is the stage,"[8] is to oversimplify the problem of man in nature. We have no simple person-to-person relations, but a person-to-person relation within nature and with nature heavily in the persons, and all within God, and God within the totality of relations. If we are to discuss war intelligently, we shall have to begin with the facts as best we know them. This involves the acceptance of a process of evolution, an ascent from the low forms of life to the higher. This does not mean that we accept any specific theory of evolution, be-

[8] Kean, *The Meaning of Existence,* p. 36. Dr. Kean actually is not guilty of such an abstraction, for he defines history as "man's experience in his encounter with the physical world and with other human beings" (p. 33). His relation between history and nature, however, has never seemed sufficiently organic in origin or in full interaction. He lacks in the development of the purpose of nature and in an adequate understanding of freedom in fact.

cause very likely we are still to find out far more than we can now imagine, and truth cannot be fettered to any of its mileposts in man's history, without losing its power to guide on along man's further search into the meaningful mystery and mysterious meaningfulness of his quest for reality.

For, from one point of view, it is true that there has been evolution, that man has ascended from the animal world; though much of the animal is still in him, to plague him continually in all his social relations. But God is the Creator of this order. God is not the Creator to our knowledge of any mythical or imaginary earthly Paradise, but of this actual world as seen in evolution and in history. But this evolution and this history are not, on the other hand, the primary perspectives of explanation. God is.

"In the beginning God created the heavens and the earth." Man came then, through conscious disobedience, to know good and evil, and, in this respect, to enter a new stage of possible spirituality. The fact is that "in the actual world things are not true to their essential nature."⁹ Man's actual nature, as we have seen, is not his essential nature. The future tells the truth about man far better than his past, for it is through the future that his real, eternal nature comes to fruition and is revealed. As far as war is concerned, for instance, there can be no question that man is naturally warlike in the sense of his actual nature. We do not have to go much beyond that fact to explain how wars can happen. But in his essential nature, as seen in the highest truth of history, in the life and teaching of Agape, man is not warlike.

We do not conceive of nature as mainly warlike even on the animal level. Conflict, as such, is never the mainspring of life. Even in the animal world nature operates in uncountable creatures seeking their kind of satisfaction, in their kind of day and in their kind of way. In so doing, they get in one another's way, which frequently results in a fight. The proportion of fighting to peace we do not know. Some have made the claim, after years of investigation, that it is the peaceable and co-operative animals which for the most part survive, that theirs is the greatest adaptability, the supreme capacity for the kind of fitness which is needed in order to survive in the struggle of evolution. But we do not want to pitch our in-

⁹ Demant, *op. cit.,* p. 11.

vestigation on this level, which seems definitely inconclusive as far as the question of war and peace is concerned. Instead, the more important fact is, perhaps, that on this level the creatures seek peace and plenty; and the seeking for plenty, according to their natures, often breaks the peace. A further fact, moreover, is that even when the creatures have plenty, they kill for the sake of killing, as a weasel in a chicken coop, or fight for power and prestige, as bucks for the leadership of the herd.

From the point of view of Agape, the only full norm for inclusive interpretation, there is, on this level at least, very little self-giving for the sake of the common good, although even that is not absent on the level of natural drive, as seen in the mother bird risking her life for her young and the bee stinging away its life for the sake of the hive. But most of it seems to be the fight of pigs for the trough or of the jackals for the carcass. Between certain animals there seems to be almost continuous open conflict, if the occasion occurs, but the occasion, somehow, is usually avoided because animals learn to know and to respect each other's relative strength in fighting. Birds at a feeding tray will yield, even when extremely hungry in snowy weather, to birds beyond their strength. But if two birds of the weaker species come together, they will often challenge and distract the stronger bird, and thus obtain food. Then fighting occurs of a sniping variety. Often the birds, however, will wait at a distance until the stronger has eaten his fill, thus preventing the arising of the occasion for fighting.

Anyone who has watched cows, day after day, until he knows them intimately, and all their little habits, knows how hierarchically a herd is organized. Cows come home in certain order a good deal of the time; each cow has found out, through experience, her relative strength or courage in relation to the rest, and usually keeps her place. If she happens to stray for some grass and gets out of line, she acts considerably upset and is often badly butted. At times there will be brief fighting. Usually, however, she recognizes her position and avoids a scrap. This order is also based on custom, it seems, because as the cows lose strength through age, they are not replaced in line by the mere fact of youthful strength. Studies have been made on hens, showing how each hen knows its place in relation to the rest. Anyone who has watched young roosters fight it out for position among themselves, and then with the older roosters, has observed how hierarchical again the structure is. *Order depends upon recognized structures of behavior.* Fighting develops when those structures are either changing through growth or through new arrivals, or when the old order is being challenged, or when by mistake some members of the cow or chicken society, for instance, get themselves into a false situation.

Perhaps we should lay special stress on the fact that conflict is both between groups and within groups. The small birds fight the large birds as a flock, the sparrows, for example, co-operating to fight the hawk, although they quickly return to fighting among themselves as soon as the danger from without is over. How they will co-operate to fight a snake, or distract it, as it climbs the tree for the eggs in the nest! Yet how they will pick on each other when the snake has gone! Gray mice will fight the brown mice for the grain bins, and then fight each other for a coveted corner. So humanity fights, group with group, and members within the group. Often the fightings between groups help to overcome or to suppress, at least temporarily, conflicts within the group. Family quarrels can be patched up quickly when neighbors try to intervene, by the whole family's turning on the neighbors! Obviously, much of this fighting comes from insecurity within and from lust for place without. Animals and men fight for food to eat, shelter, for their own needs, and then for place and prestige among themselves, for what they consider to be their social needs.

But part of this need, curiously and significantly enough, seems to be the need to fight. They need to become themselves through fighting. Fighting seems to be a creative need, beyond mere self-preservation. From the lowest levels of animal life, where life leaves off being mostly automatic reactions, to our own most advanced social struggles, there seem to be both inter- and intragroup struggles. What is the meaning of this, and how does it relate itself to the nature and function of the individual and the group? That is the question which we are asking.

When we see that God has created this world, and that we are a continuation of the animal world, we can understand that, in one stage of our life at least, God made us to fight. The Gothic ideal of manhood, the manly man who dares to fight, has a real root in reality. Animals do not sin in fighting, but act the way God made them. The tiger simply does not take by nature to the eating of grass. By nature and circumstance we, too, in one stage of our development, are made to fight. What, then, is the place and function of strife, of war, in the divine economy of creation? Strife exists in order to differentiate individuals and groups for the sake of preparing them for fuller and better community. Group conflict and war are, thus, part and parcel of growing men and growing history.

There is value in the process of strife and war, and in the goal which follows when strife is over, and when swords are beaten into ploughshares. God has made a process full of strife; the challenge is to make it creative and to get beyond the process to its end. Hegel is right, in one respect at least, that God is a man of war. God seeks to create no placid peace, apart from creative strife. That way He never made the world. See what fun young animals find in fighting as they match their strength. Though there be hurt in the wild woods, there is zest in the kind of life that tears and is torn. In human life even sadism and masochism have their rightful parts in the drives of life. Aggressive and regressive characteristics join their notes in the full symphony of life, and become bad only when they become matters of mental illness. What crowds rush to see the boxing match, the wrestling exhibition; what throngs clamor for "fight" in the football game! The fact that so few in comparison go to art exhibitions is not only a matter of lack of culture. The fighting game, team against team, brings out the whole man in an active challenge. Many have "found themselves" in war; many have there awakened a sleeping heroism, a sense of importance, a sense of responsibility and concern, who are bored insufferably in peacetime, dabbling away at impersonal tasks that lack challenge. Daring and creative risk bring out both creative and sacrificial characteristics.

Even the Christian faith must be the Christian conflict, if it is to be real and vital in this stage of history. Instead of conceiving of Christianity as the fight to the death with evil, with principles and powers, within and without, as the heroic life, we have often allowed ourselves to think of it as some kind of comfort to hide from us the real world, or some sort of means with which to overcome its evil by a kind of magic incantation. Young people are rarely challenged by "applesauce" faith. Unless Christianity has within its very bosom the drive to conflict and to war, it has not the full solution to our concrete problems.

Sorokin points out that if we want to disturb the old order we must be "ready to see violence and to be a witness or victim or perpetrator of it. This is true for all nations and groups."[10] Christianity is bound to seek to disturb rather than merely to defend this old order, and must, accordingly, be ready to send a sword into the world rather than peace, where there is no true peace. Hartshorne insists that the noble pacifists can be "easily matched by the nobler [sic] warriors."[11] Our age is electing warriors to leading civilian positions. Instead of merely cursing militarism for this fact, we ought to see that the age calls for courageous planning and wisdom, which is not always found among men who worship peace for its own sake.

Gandhi rightly preferred courage to the general avoidance of fighting evil, and approved of participation in World War I, for instance, rather than of the kind of pacifism that simply bemoaned human evil and did nothing about the situation. This preference he is also reported to have kept to the end of his life. Unless strife can be positively and constructively transcended, in spirit and means, from physical to other levels, it is better to participate in the physical strife on the side of the greater truth and justice than weakly to bow out of the arena entirely. If we are to treat the problem of war realistically, this place for strife to precede peace and to create the conditions for it, must be clearly seen and acknowledged.

But though there is a place and function for strife, even for war, in the divine economy, there is a more basic place and function for peace, since that is the goal of reality for process. This goal is present from the beginning. Within the process of strife is a process of peace, even as within the process of peace there is strife; but the beginning and the end of process is the reality of peace. Here we must be careful, again, not to identify peace with the absence of all strife. Peace is creative and harmonious life, individually and

10 *Cultural and Social Dynamics,* Vol. III, p. 478.
11 *Man's Vision of God,* p. 169.

in fellowship. The origin and basis of life is structurally peace, not as the absence of strife, but as the presence of positive living and satisfaction. Strife is a necessary incapacity through immaturity to grasp the reality which is essential to man, and thus natural to his deeper, though not to his actual, self.

There is much transcendence of conflict which finds the deeper reality of peace even within the conflict. The *Bhagavadgita* is deep testimony to this truer reality of peace within struggle and transcending struggle. No wonder it was Gandhi's favorite book, even more precious to him than the New Testament. Hinduism has a sensitive insight which has not always been seen or developed at this point in our Western all-outness for struggle or for peace. Nirvana, too, pictures a peace which is more than the harmony of our kind of struggle, a peace so deep, yet positive in being, that our ordinary earthly imagination is kept out from it by an eternal: "not so, not so." The Buddhists have much to teach our crude worshipers of heavenly harps, though even these harps, of course, can be symbols of the deeper harmony, beyond the reach of explicit human experience. The reality, however, lies in the "whirlwind heart of peace" during the struggle and in the reaches of creative and harmonious peace after the struggle.

How to describe this peace, however, in terms of fellowship rather than of nothingness, in terms of creativity rather than of stagnancy, in terms of life rather than of death, without using the categories of our small scale of earthly experience as the norm for the heavenly, is hard to know. Our best description is the Agape fellowship in God—from, through and for Him—with our fellow men, in countless stages of creative growth. Creative strife works within creative peace, providing life and goal for the process, until in God's time and way the destructive aspects of strife, which are the ignorant and the rebellious use of our freedom, are done away. The meaning and end of creative strife is creative peace.

In order to present the background of the problem of war and peace in the light of the Christian faith, we must at least touch on the question of natural law, for war has been considered a necessity, a sacred duty to the nation as an embodiment of natural law. In this connection it is well to see that when creation is understood as a dynamic, continuous process, rather than as an arrangement made at the beginning of a specific, once-for-all creation, the perspective on natural law changes radically. Natural law now becomes the temporary validity of such structures of behavior, or such stabilities in the environment of behavior, as best minister to the function of that stage. Consider, as an example, the question of marriage. There is nothing wrong in promiscuous sexual behavior in rabbits; there is nothing wrong, on its level, in the patriarchs' having more than one wife; there is nothing wrong in the unusual sex customs of so-called primitive peoples, where, for instance, the chief will offer his wife as bedfellow to his most distinguished visitors as a sign of his willingness to share his most intimate possession. Because of the kind of fellowship, however, which Christianity teaches with regard to marriage, that is, an insoluble union of two moral equals, under God, for society, promiscuity and the sharing of wives are definitely sin. Behavior can be judged only with regard to accepted standards, socially and personally, *as far as development in history goes.* It can be judged absolutely only when the absolute purpose of freedom and faithfulness in fellowship is understood as the proclamation of the Eternal Purpose.

Even then, however, there can be within this framework real, actual developments. In heaven no one will marry or be given in marriage. Marriage is a closed community, in one respect, for the sake of developing intensive fellowship among its members, as well as for the sake of having children. That is why anthropologists find some kind of structure of marriage and sex regulation in every kind of vital community. It may happen, however, in the distant future of human history, that children will be bred by the community in only the strongest mothers by artificial insemination from the strongest males, according to undreamed-of methods, knowledge, and scientific control of genetics and eugenics. This may involve changed sexual behavior, allowing possibly for a new freedom and creative fellowship on this level, within, of course, a higher spirituality than we can now foresee; or else it may involve a radical recession of this "sensate culture," and the arrival at a new ease of community through new means and methods, where freedom and faithfulness of fellowship under God are practiced even more fully, and sex as sensuous gratification and invidious separation is successfully sublimated.

The point is not to close the door to development within the relative areas of life, on account of structures of behavior which are now based on "natural law." Our present sexual situation calls for a new study of it that will not be based merely on doctrinal prejudice or on social taboos. This may lead to a fuller understanding of "the new freedom," or to a new Puritanism that will be less repressive and more spiritually and artistically creative. The function of natural law is to provide what John Dickison has said of the American Constitution, "a framework of order within which change can proceed without endangering stability."[12]

The first part of this chapter on war and the Christian faith is intended to stress that we have to begin with our animal background if we are to be true to the facts of the past. This background, however, is not seen rightly except in relation to man's foreground, which is the determinative factor of his destiny, because this is where we see the Eternal Purpose which is *more* than society and which is yet through and through *for* society. The point is to fit both of them rightly together. God is to be seen for the world in the Agape that, to the best of our knowledge, characterized at least dominantly the life and teaching of Jesus. In any case, whatever the historic problems, there is where He is to be understood—in the responsible concern which creates and redeems in order to effect the perfect fellowship. God is to be seen and to be understood in His Christ. As such, through Christ, as the immanent God, the objectively incarnated part or person of God. He is organically connected with every level of life and with every stage of its development. To each level He is related differently according to its need and its circumstance; yet He it is still, even though He is operationally different. He is not different from Himself in Himself, but different *as the interacting Reality* at each level of life, in so far as He is differently understood and accepted.

In other words, natural law is a dynamic function with different operations and meanings within different stages of development and circumstance. Within each stage there is dependable stability, except as this stage is giving way incipiently to another. There is

[12] Cited in Atteberry, Auble and Hunt, *op cit.*, Vol. II, p. 568.

present at least a needed relative stability, which is God's work at this stage. This understanding differs from that of those who hold that there is a permanent natural law, permeating continuously all creation, and from that of those who hold that God keeps giving concrete commands, but never lets Himself be bound to any predictable structures of an organic character. This point of view fails to grasp the reality and purpose of a semi-independent realm of creation. Both Toynbee and Sorokin, for instance, have seen that there are erratic fluctuations in any society, because freedom makes no outcome causatively predictable; but they have also seen that the destruction of any civilization is not only a judgment of God for man's sins of omission and commission, which it is, but is also the exhibition of *a structural relatedness* to something beyond itself, seen in faith as the Kingdom of God.

No discussion of war and peace in the modern world seems adequate, it must be stressed, that does not focus on the fact of our animal background and of the animal passions that still dominate much of our living and thinking. Man has just begun, within the historic twinkle of a few thousand years, to face the problems of the conscious control of fighting, in terms of government and police power, and most of his concern about the control of war falls within the last fraction of that twinkle. That is our perspective from the past, but that perspective must now face more demanding perspectives from the present and the future. Before we make this confrontation, however, we need to get our eye on the problem of justice, because much Christian discussion about war eventually comes down to the idea that love is a luxury which we can afford in times of peace, but that when there is a question between peace and justice, we must by all means choose justice. Brunner, Niebuhr, perhaps Archbishop Söderblom and others seem to hold largely to this point of view. Justice, they seem to say, is the balance of power politics toward the best achievable by a wicked world, and, therefore, love has no relevance to the power struggle as such, but is mostly limited in direct efficacy to personal and small group life, and to such areas and times as it can possibly be profitably and meaningfully employed in the wicked world of wiry realism.

As soon as we take seriously the depth and power of original sin, moreover, they say, we realize that love operates in a different realm from, and with a different coin from justice, so that only the foolish "children of light" could be perfectionist and pharisaic enough not to realize the irrelevance of this method to the processes of power politics. We must, consequently, try to fix more fully the relation between love and justice before essaying to treat the problem, as such, of the spiritual status of war in our time.

According to our relative view of the content, though not of the form, of natural law, we must obviously see justice as relative to time and circumstance. *Justice, at any point in history, is the equal application of the content of community, custom and law in relation to the depth-dynamic influence of the intrinsic nature of Eternal Reality, partially within, but dominantly surrounding that content.*

The definition to the effect that justice, on its content side, is the equal application of the content of community, custom and law does not mean, of course, that the content prescribes equality of place or of opportunity, or equality of trial and of punishment. If, for instance, the rule of a primitive tribe is to expose all aged and sick who cannot move along with the tribe, justice, on this side of it, is practiced if all are exposed. If one or a few are allowed to spare their parents, justice is not practiced. There may be, for that matter, primitive needs for certain rules that we do not fully take in. Injustice, in terms of content, is done when the rules of the group are not applied fairly according to the customs of the group itself. This is what is meant by the equal application of community, custom and law. The difficulty with this point of view, however, is that justice is not here a revolutionary or even a reformatory word, but expresses, rather, the equal application of the rules within the behavioral structures of the given societal situation. Justice based merely on the content and meaning of the group, however, is always limited. In order to fix more fully and definitely the nature of universal law and justice, which transcends the boundaries of group justice, we shall now have to discuss the relation between eternal law, natural law and positive law.

Our view of eternal law is that it is the full order of God's eternal purpose for man. Law, ideally and generally speaking, means the functioning of right relations. This approach goes deeper, of course, than prescribed or positive law. Effective law for the prescription of conduct or of behavior, whether of individuals or of groups, depends consequently a good deal upon the power to control or to enforce such conduct or behavior, in order to maintain or to establish right relations. As Ellul rightly maintains, law without sanction is unthinkable. Enforcement is thus a vital aspect of law itself. Unless God had power He could not command as well as attract. Unless a government had some control or power for enforcement it could not enact laws, but only pass resolutions or give advice. Yet mere might fails, on the other hand; for law, to be effective, must be at least relevantly right in order to adjust group behavior in relation to its actual content of consciousness and structure of behavior. There must thus be a proportionate element of wisdom and rightness in all exercise of effective power.

In God, all love, right and power are perfectly combined. He, therefore, being the creator and maintainer of all and everything, is the source of all right relations. The eternal law is, therefore, Agape, the very structure of God's purpose. Agape is the foundation of all right relations, and thus of all law. Every concept of law must ultimately lead back to God's Agape for its justification and legitimate power; for human power is all delegated power for the sake of the free creation of this fellowship based on love.

But eternal law is perfect only in heaven; on earth the Agape fellowship is far from real and full. Eternal law is consequently irrelevant, as it is, to the process at its early stages and, therefore, eternal law has to become transmuted into natural law. This natural law is the *stability which is necessary for any community, for its purpose, and at its stage of development.* The eternal law shines through experience at any stage of process as the background of this attempted stability.

Niebuhr has caught something of this in his statement to the effect that "every human society does have something like a natural law concept; for it assumes that there are more immutable and pure principles of justice than those actually embodied in its obviously relative laws."[13] Tillich calls this eternal "the unconditional,"

13 *The Children of Light and the Children of Darkness*, p. 68.

which is the background of the striving of all kinds of communities. Yet natural law is more than the vague shimmering through of the eternal. Natural laws are actual structures present in history for its epoch, for its *kairos*. These structures express the Eternal Purpose for that time. *The very form which contains the content contains also a structural mold which slowly shapes all contents.* This plastic mold is shaped immediately by the actual content within history but permanently it is shaped by the Eternal Reality which surrounds it. The categories of men's consciousness are not nonexistent. They are plastic molds which allow for the slow pressures of God's purpose without destroying man's freedom. Only thus can there be real growth in history, with God as the main giver and leader of such growth. The form of human experience is not empty. Through all communities operate certain samenesses of human nature, of earthly environment, and of the total relation of both of these to God's present providence in history and nature.

The eternal law is thus structurally present with the epochally changing natural laws, giving them permanent purpose beyond their temporary meaning.

Powerful prophetism springs from such an understanding of God's law. Yet such direct, divine presence in history and in nature is only part of the story of law on the level of creation. In order that we might find for ourselves God's way, nature and history are semi-independent.

The nation may be taken as an example of natural law. The nation was not before yesteryear in history. The year after tomorrow it may have ceased to be. Does this mean that the nation is not from God? This does not at all follow. The nation is from God for its time and for its purpose. Before the need of this stage arose, the nation was not necessary in history, and was not from God. After the day of sovereign nations has passed, nations which cling to sovereignty will be sinning against God. But while there is need for nations, they express, through their function in the divine economy of history, God's purpose for mankind.

We have defined the eternal law as the flexible fullness of Agape. This is "pure possibility" unmixed with historic ambiguity. The natural law we defined as the highest relevant epochal stability, stemming from the eternal law and undergirding all legitimate positive law. Operative positive law is *the concrete enactment of statutes, based on adequate sanctions, representing the will or the good of the community or dominant powers in the community.* The natural law can never take the place of positive law, for that is man's concrete responsibility as co-worker with God.

> This "law of nature" is not, and cannot be, in itself a code. It is no substitute for statute law. The natural law requires that motorists should not drive to the danger of the public, but it cannot prescribe whether the rule of the road be left or right; that is a matter of custom or of legislation. . . . But the concept of "natural law" is vital to the political philosopher as providing both the ethical foundation for the State and an ideal and limit for human legislation.[14]

This background of natural law, under eternal law, for positive law, is very important. The natural law, however, always owes its absolute aspect, which is the more important, to the eternal law, to the Gospel, while the relative aspect relates itself appropriately to the particular historic epoch or stage of development. The major perspective on development is always the divine, not the historic. The positive law is then judged in terms of the natural law either as destructive, or as a fair approximation to it, as the relevant enactment of it or, again, as ahead of the societal situation, anticipating either wisely or prematurely, a new level of living. The forced declaring of Japan to be a pacifist nation under positive law is an example of this kind of legislation, which has more foundation in wish and in theory than in the development of most of the people themselves.

All this comes down to the plain fact that the *justice which springs from the eternal law is redemptive justice.* Redemptive justice is Agape-action aiming, completely and constantly, at the attainment of the fullest development and opportunity of each individual, group, and of the total community.[15] Thus civil oppor-

---

14 Micklem, *op. cit.,* p. 64.

15 "Even as I please all men in all things, not seeking mine own profit, but the profit of many, that they may be saved" (I Cor. 10:33). Cf. also "In the absence of peace and concord, man's mind must be disquieted by contentions and fighting, and hindered from aspiring to God. And therefore the divine law has made provision for the preservation of peace and concord amongst men by the practice of justice. It commands that to every man be rendered his due. . . . But it is not

tunities such as the right to an education, to responsible free speech, or rights such as the right to a fair trial, the right to participation in political decisions, the right to the minimum needs of health and housing, the right to no discrimination on account of religion, race, sex or color, can be promulgated within this total concern without limiting justice to a defensive attitude and action. Christian justice operates thus with certain objective areas and structures, for the sake of the common good.

Justice no longer demands the preservation of the better of two sovereign states for the sake of preserving the best kind of political order, but, rather, demands creatively and redemptively that nations surrender their sovereignty to world government, however constituted. Nations as final entities of power are now beginning to become as outmoded as the smaller political units which the United States once began subsuming. As we shall see, both positively and negatively wars are anachronistic in the light of the actual development in terms of which natural law and justice must be established. The argument that we have to forsake love to establish justice, by means of war, is no longer defensible.

On the other hand, absolute pacifism or complete nonviolence, though very much to be honored as exemplifying the eternal law, forsakes the constructive obligations of man as a creature, to whom God has entrusted or delegated power to be used together with others for the common good. We can and must renounce war, without renouncing the constructive force of civil government under judicial processes or without renouncing the constructive role of world police. Absolute pacifism is based on a faulty the-

---

enough for peace and concord to be preserved amongst men by precepts of justice, unless there be a further consolidation of mutual love. Justice provides for men to the extent that one shall not get in the way of another, but not to the extent of one helping another in his need. One may happen to need another's aid in cases in which none is bound to him by any debt of justice, or where the person so bound does not render any aid. Thus there came to be need of an additional precept of mutual love amongst men, so that one should aid another even beyond his obligations in justice. . . . It is evident that love suffices for the fulfilment of the works of justice. Hence it is said: *Love is the fulfilment of the law* (Romans xiii, 10): to commend which fulfilment there are given us precepts and counsels of God concerning works of mercy, love, succour of enemies, and the like deeds of kindness, which overflow and run over the measures of justice." Aquinas, in Rickaby's translation of the *Summa Contra Gentiles, Of God and His Creatures,* pp. 294-295.

ology which, explicitly or implicitly, refuses to accept the actuality and instrumentality of process. Usually such pacifism fails to notice the difference between the Eternal Purpose and the cosmic process. But is not the using of means which are imperfect in the light of the end, or when compared with the eternal goal, after all a compromise, and how can a Christian compromise his holy Agape? Agape is never a compromise because it uses imperfect means, for history exists to be perfected. Agape exists to create redemptively *out of the imperfect and the sinful the perfect Christian fellowship.* Let us be very careful here. The fact that force has to be used is no compromise. God uses force continually and is not thereby compromised. "To recognize that only God can perfectly combine power and goodness is to understand that power is not evil of itself."[16] "There is no power but of God."[17] God uses physical compulsion, and His children must do so, too, to accept the responsibilities on the level of creation. God takes life, and there is no reason that the taking of life must constitute an absolute difference between the function of God and the function of man. Naturally, there must be the fullest possible respect for personality and the most intense concern possible for each to come to his fullest development. But perhaps for the common good, individuals, and especially states, have to make choices which involve the taking of life, and which are still constructive choices. This life is not all there is for God or for us! Agape always chooses the most constructive choice possible, redemptively and creatively, including the choice of nonparticipation *for* the world. It does not, therefore, compromise in any of its legitimate actions. To declare that the use of imperfect means is *ipso facto* compromise is to deny process as the method of the Eternal Purpose, to claim, in fact, to be better than God!

Naturally, the Christian, combining attitude and action, works with a different motive from the non-Christian. When he cooperates with the world and works in it, as he should, he may work for common objective measures, but his attitude leavens the situation with a new Presence, even of the Holy Spirit. His motivation for justice is redemptive to the point where he may work, for

[16] Niebuhr, *The Nature and Destiny of Man*, Vol. II, p. 22.
[17] Rom. 13:1.

instance, to end the war, yes; to prevent another by preparing the conditions for peace, yes; but beyond all political measures and conditions commonly aimed at, the Christian goes on to work for the complete acceptance of the Agape fellowship. If this is denied for the sake of co-operation; if for the sake of fellow-feeling the person denies his Lord temporarily, so to speak; if common measures for justice are treated as enough; then indeed the Christian has lost his savor and has become no better than the world.

With this general background, we are free to state our position. Conflict as an aspect of life will exist as long as life is creative. Insecurity and ill-will belong to history, not to eternity, in so far as eternity here means the fullness and fulfillment of the Eternal Purpose. Wars between and among nations belonged to the historic epoch, when the nation as nation had a necessary place in God's historic purpose, and was, therefore, part of natural law. But this epoch is now past or passing, and with it the place of the state as a sovereign entity under God.

The pull of God's purpose, in terms of His highest revelation in Christ and in the Church as Agape, is now demanding not only political unification, for progress and development of community to reach a new high, but above all a new revolution in the spiritual life to be followed by consequent revolutions in all spheres of life. The bestiality of man, amply revealed of late, and the impotent goodness and dignity of man both tell us that for us to go into the new gear of civilization, made necessary by technological revolutions, we must go even more decisively into a new spiritual gear, or die by our own hands. The Church is in a peculiarly strategic position of privilege and responsibility to lead the advance for the coming of the new day, if we will have it. The individual Christian, as the cell in the body, is thus bound for the sake of society to let God perform a miracle of healing and creative life in him beyond his utmost dream, and to show society a new way by renouncing war as now, at least, no longer constructive, even as maintaining the state, and by showing the positively co-operative way to the new epoch which God is waiting to let be born. That is our thesis, which we shall elaborate briefly.

We have already shown that there was need for the state as a unit of power over a stretch of history while man developed up to this stage of consciousness and width of vision, under the tender but austere hand of God in history. But the present stage of the state is its passing. The state's positive function is now for it to become subordinated to world government, and exercise within it regional or representative jurisdiction. That this thesis is true I shall not try to document. The question is not that it needs to be done, but rather how to do it and how to get the general vision and power pressure to bring it about. The last question is peculiarly our own. The Roman Catholics stress "the Principle of Subsidiarity," namely, that "society is for man and not vice versa."[18] By this rule the state, to serve man best, must now be willing to lose its sovereignty in order to gain its own true end.

We say here, again, that war is now no longer constructive, even to the maintaining of necessary sovereign states, except as interim instruments to effect world government, and, therefore, refusal to participate in war is not based on the avoidance of responsibility of the citizen to the state for the exercise of constructive force. The state has a right to demand such obedience only as long as it has itself a real purpose under God and uses legitimately the power which has been allowed it by God. When it does not do so, as in an unjust war, or in a generally nonconstructive war, the citizen refuses to obey, serving God rather than men, or even serving his reason and conscience rather than the reason of men who are blinded by narrow vision and narrower loyalties. If a Christian, or any other person, is still convinced, of course, that more can be conserved or created by war than without it, naturally he must follow his conscience in this regard, and no one is to judge his decision, as far as his spirit goes, though we can disagree as far as the objective analysis goes.

What is actually happening is that we are in the final stage of a long process that began with our animal background, wherein small groups became organized and then became fulfilled in larger. This stage is the consummation of that whole process. Wars come from many predisposing causes and break out from varied precipi-

18 *The Philosophy of Being*, Proceedings of the American Catholic Association, 1946, p. 113, citing the Encyclical, *Divini Redemptoris*, of Pius XI.

tating causes, because they represent a generality and totality of conflict and change between groups, and are partly like a natural calamity in nature. We, therefore, find very little hope in the consummation of the final stage except through the surrender of force to an inclusive and unitive authority; for force without a common spirit and mind will never give us a peaceful world.

Our greatest hope, then, is that partial, physical force, backed by inclusive spiritual force, will be surrendered to plenary force for the good of all. Two reasons for this hope are these: *Positively*, the conditions for it are ready in terms of technological facilities of communication, for the conquering of time and space. The world is smaller now to control as a whole, than any one great empire in the past, in terms of time needed to reach its utmost parts with adequate physical force. The means of education and the dissemination of ideas are similarly ready. Religions of superstition and myth, the defensive resorts of closed societies, are also caving in under the universal spread of science, and man longs for the more dependable faith, equal to his horizon, and yet receding in mystery far beyond it. Such a reliable universal religion is now also being proclaimed, to fulfill all others. Particularly in terms of political experience we are becoming ready for one world. We have had the League of Nations, and as Richard Vaughan says, "Victories are always won first in the ideal." Now we have the shadow of the reality in the United Nations.

Positive negotiations and every conceivable constructive co-operation alone can win communist nations toward effective world government and prevent the kind of war which promises seriously to set back or destroy Western civilization. We need to be more honest and ready to surrender divisive force to unitive force. The more democratically this force is controlled, the better; and the more freedom it does and can allow, the better. But the need to hold one world together will require the right raising, control and use of force within a framework of freedom and rights.

These privileges, naturally, cannot be forced on the world from the outside, without educational and spiritual content and response from within. The social engineers, helped by the wise in faith and insight and the strong in common co-operative concern, will have to work out the arrangements and techniques of the use of force that will allow for all possible cultural and political pluralism, including social and religious freedom, that will yet be relevantly applicable to each part of the world in terms of its past history and present circumstance.

Negatively, wars between nations, or the imposition of external unity on the world by one nation, now fall into a new category of frustration and futility. Modern warfare is no longer a limited liability; it is very likely an uncontrollably totalitarian destruction. In the period 1901-1925 in nine European countries the casualties amounted to 22,035,150; or in four countries during the same period, 38.9 per cent of the participants.[19] But what of the new, indiscriminate warfare covering the whole earth as in World War II? Think what has happened since! Think what is now true of atomic bombs and gases, or unimaginable biological warfare, now known to both sides in any struggle.

> The twentieth century, so far, has been the bloodiest period and one of the most turbulent periods—and therefore one of the cruelest and least humanitarian—in the history of Western civilization and perhaps in the chronicles of mankind in general.[20]

Consider what our scientists are telling us with one strong voice about the modern inadmissibility of war. Think also of the new dimensions of depth-knowledge and the general forfeiting of the common intellectual, moral and spiritual barriers of humanity against barbarism which such a wanton, indiscriminate, wholesale destruction of civilized life would involve. Just as for the first time in history the positive conditions for world government are at least incipiently ready, so negatively, the conditions for any constructive or just war seem beyond moral justification. In any case, the conditions which made group struggle meaningful, at least in some attainable results, now seem to be permanently gone, calling for a new international approach to war. Natural law and justice, as well as Christian concern, positively and negatively now join in the rejection of war.

It may be, of course, that war will come, be short and thorough in nature, and give us, by means of it, an externally united world.

19 Cf. Sorokin, *op. cit.,* pp. 336-337.
20 *Ibid.,* p. 487.

History has moved this way; seldom has it moved in the way of the several Colonies voluntarily becoming the United States. The kind of weapons which we have may be the right ones for a final unification of the world and for its universal control by one nation with limited police force, or army investments. Or it may also be that one world will come through a succession of Communist revolutions and the spread of the Union of Soviet Socialist Republics, putting Christianity to the crucial challenge to transform communist faith and life *from within,* no matter what the cost to itself. The hope and possibility are that nations may find enough sense to surrender effective force to a world organization, including the right of economic arrangement. If this can be brought about mankind would be spared, at least, the sufferings of Armageddon, or the setback in all our basic potentials of civilization and culture.

History is hard and dangerous to judge, although we have to survey its possibilities. Merriam urges that

> the hope that the Christian ideals of freedom, equality, responsibility and universality can become the operating principles of a world order is based on the assumption that some group will understand the rational use of force or coercion in behalf of those ideals.[21]

We urge that the democratic nations take the lead in such pooling of force for the common good and in finding the spiritual perspective and power to make force less and less necessary.

Jones writes that

> without being superficially optimistic (on the contrary, it claims to describe man exactly as he is) Christianity encourages the hope that, because God is Sovereign, nations will enter into reasonable relations with each other and will be driven by force of circumstances to realize that it is through the de-moralization of politics that the greatest disasters overwhelm society.[22]

This appraisal of our situation contains much truth and wisdom; but the crux of our problem is that nations are not Christian, some not even in profession, and that history, as far as man goes, moves more on the level of force and need than on the level of reasoned

[21] *Op. cit.,* p. 179.
[22] *Op. cit.,* p. 145.

or concerned decisions. Yet if there is enough pressure from within and enough faith that the good choice is a live option, namely, the evolution into a united world, where force is actually surrendered to a higher representative power, this devoutly to-be-longed-for event may come about.

Our thesis here is that both before we get one world externally, and particularly after we get a new world, we need a whole new spiritual revolution and level of life to cope with our larger togetherness and our new technological dimensions. Modern man has to choose between meaningless existence and the heroic challenge of war, which he yet loathes. The lack of control of science and the insecurities of an economic system where man dreads his own abundance, lest it lose him his job and his meaning in life, have increased his tensions which, in all ages and by his very nature as a human being, are severe enough anyway. But modern man is close to being collectively psychotic. Man now needs a larger perspective and a more piercing and powerful faith in which he can honestly and devotedly believe with his whole normal self.

If we attain one world, we shall have cheap and plentiful atomic energy. This may lead to the need for a close and general supervision of life, lest the few destroy or come to control the many to exploit them. The only way freedom can then be achieved will be by such development of freedom within, through a new spiritual revolution, through the attainment of a new level of life, that shall make freedom and faithfulness in fellowship through common concern and the joys of creative co-operation a reality. More than ever the divisive tensions must be outmatched by the tensions of unitive concern. The need for the Christian faith will be greater the larger the unit of togetherness, for the Christian faith individualizes, particularizes, with a redemptive justice "unto this last," springing out of creative love.

When Christians in theory become so in fact, they have the solution. Athanasius, in fact, knew the solution!

Strange to relate, since they came over to the school of Christ, as men moved with real compunction, they have laid aside their murderous cruelty and are war-minded no more. On the contrary, all is peace among them and nothing remains save desire for friend-ship.[23]

No wonder that Christianity, when it was really believed in and practiced, even though imperfectly, of course, was a power to turn the world right side up! While accepting the positive function of the State, all authority rightly used being from God, the Early Church refused for generations to deem either war or totalitarian-ism to be constructive use of force. How much more today should we follow that example! Then the Early Church recognized that the fullness of time had come on the level of redemption, the renouncing of war by the community of the cross; now we must recognize that the fullness of time has come also on the level of creation. The special challenge of our age is to renounce war while creating the positive conditions for peace.

The Church as a total sociological institution, to be sure, is now slow and conservative. We must not pin too much hope on that body without, nevertheless, underestimating what can happen, even through it, if prophets are raised up and followed, first even by the faithful few, and then by the many. The Church is now, however, too feeble, as a whole, even to become one Church in the sense of overcoming its senseless denominational sovereignties. We must not be overoptimistic about the Church as a social and political example to a divided and dying civilization. We must, rather, find the power of fellowship, through concern for the world, borne high on faith in God.

This fellowship of constructive concern for the universal good must "seek peace and ensue it."[24] It will run the way of God's commandments when He shall enlarge its heart,[25] but not before. It will then dare to deny war by offering instead its own kind of un-breakable community in Christ. It will work like a mighty army, but positively, motivated by a common concern which grows organ-ically out of its new creaturehood in Christ, for the kind of uni-versal civil rights and general constructive behavior patterns which

[23] St. Athanasius, *The Incarnation of the Word of God*, p. 90.
[24] I Pet. 4.
[25] Ps. 119:32.

can constitute for our new epoch the patterns of stability and opportunity for man to grow and work.

We do not want, of course, to blueprint any future arrangements of law and order. That is the function of the social engineer. The theologian's business is to give the perspective of the ultimate. After that, we need appropriate social engineering and legislation in terms of laws, rights and responsibilities. But beyond these, the fellowship will offer all men a new faith for a new day, true to the best that we know and applicable to our everyday life. However external political unification may be brought about, the providing of a positive meaning for life, *the peace of creative satisfaction,* is the real task of the Church. The world in general cannot lift its life above narrow loyalties and visions because of fear, and lack of answering emotional associations in its life. This is true both before and after political unification, before and after catastrophe, before and after any external change. The Church, on the other hand, should be there to prove *the reality and practical power of the Christian faith.* If it cannot do this, or, at least, if this cannot be done, Christianity must wait for a new and better faith.

The Church, besides, bears the burden for becoming one world in itself, under God, and for giving the world creative power through the Holy Spirit and thus to raise the pressure and pull of mankind to the pitch where world government can become a fact. "The intervening stage between 'the government of the Spirit' in personal experience and in the State is the government of the Spirit in the polity of the fellowship within the Church."[26] The Church should be an example and should provide the power. If we are to have a new world community, we need a world ethos. A world ethos, however, can come only out of a world faith. Christianity stands compromised through its poor history, an insult to its Lord and to its saints. Can the inner fellowship of full believers, who take their Christ and their Church more seriously than anything else, achieve the surrender to the Eternal Purpose which shall bring a new level of life into the world?

Particularly we ask if the inner heart of the church, at least, is willing even now to renounce war unconditionally as a part of its own distinctive fellowship life for the world. When war has

26 Nuttall, *op. cit.,* p. 119.

broken out some Christians have had as their *primary vocation* the faithful witness to God's will and way with the world beyond either side of the struggle. They have enacted, in fear and trembling and in deep humility, God's eternal wisdom, and fought for this over against the partial goods and evils on either warring side. They should, however, have acknowledged that though "the sons are free," they thereby also might have neglected their duties on the level of creation to maintain constructive force, as far as the stage of process goes in which war was waged; but they were already so far beyond this stage that they could hardly think or feel their way back into it. The vertical dimension where war appeared mostly as a total evil and an anachronism, had for them become real enough to blot out the choices on the relative political level.

These pacifist Christians, or vocational pacifists, when genuine, have been the forerunners of a new and better day. When pacifism is not a false over-againstness, a blanket condemnation of force, but the humble witness to an unbreakable fellowship in God's love, it is God's continuation of the Incarnation, a perpetuation of the Cross, and an illustration of the Resurrection in the midst of common death.

What, then, is the relevance of the Christian faith to the problem of war and peace? It cannot and does not profess to solve technical problems. It cannot force faith and make men accept the Christian way of freedom and faithfulness in fellowship through trust in God's all-sufficient love and power. To do so would be to deny man's freedom, the good gift from God. But it can demonstrate in thought and life that there is no other way through which the world can be saved. The proportion of peace in the world is the proportion of man's acceptance of God's purpose.

A secular social scientist declares that "the international political organization is not in accord with the other fundamental aspects of modern international life."[27] True, there are many positive technical, economic and cultural relations beside man's international conflict. But these objective achievements are only fragmentarily analogous to our real problem, for this conflict among nations is

[27] Atteberry, Auble and Hunt, *op. cit.*, Vol. II, p. 742.

quite in line with man's basic conflicts within himself which will make any external solution of peace unsatisfactory by itself. There is no other way to real, deep and effective peace. Personal peace must precede world peace, though the externals of world peace can to some real extent precede much personal peace. Somehow this whole-response is the only one that can lead to true peace. Perhaps we have to gain, practically and generally, the sound wisdom of the Act of Horodlo, A.D. 1413:

> Nor can that endure which has not its foundations upon love. For love alone diminishes not, but shines with its own true light; makes an end of discord, softens the fires of hate, restores peace in the world, brings together the sundered, redresses wrongs, aids all and injures none; and who so invokes its aid will find peace and safety, and have no fear of future ills.

But remember we must that the only source of love is God's will, and as Dante said, "in His will is our peace."

The Christian faith, above all, needs to be spread from pole to pole, and to become the steady background of a universal ethos. An effective missionary outreach is a necessity for world well-being. For the Church must not only renounce war to work for world government, now and during its being effected, but will have its constant and unimaginable job to saturate the whole world with freedom and faithfulness in fellowship within, and radiating from the Agape life. World government alone will not solve our problems. It may even increase them in some ways. Only the finding and the living of the releasing and meaning-giving Christian community, in a new dimension, will ever solve our problems.

CHAPTER VIII

The Christian Perspective
on Property

In the economic realm Christianity today confronts actual problems with critical decisiveness. Will it side outright with either system in the global struggle, or can it give a different answer from either? Or is economics a realm outside the perspective and power of the Christian faith? It must give some kind of answer; although the way of putting the problem and, therefore, the answer to it may not conform to the usual questions which are being asked.

As a matter of fact, economics, man's organized control of things, well illustrates the relation between spirit and body in the Christian faith. They cannot be studied except in their total interrelationship. They must also be seen in the light of the larger purpose which holds them together and guides them on. Both man and economics must finally be studied in the light of God. For this reason we must refuse to accept Sorokin's accusation that to attempt to establish "causal-factorial relationship between religious beliefs (as a system of meanings) and economic conditions (as a system of vehicles and agents of an economic system)"[1] is to be guilty of the "misconception of the Componential Structure of Sociocultural Phenomena."[2] We agree, rather, with Parsons that

the inescapable conclusion . . . is that on an empiricist basis there is no place for a logically separate body of economics. Economics must be merely the application to a particular body of concrete phenomena

[1] *Sociocultural Causality, Space, Time,* p. 57.
[2] *Ibid.,* p. 52.

of the general principles necessary for understanding human conduct. . . . Economics then becomes applied sociology.[3]

We should naturally also go one step further and insist that economics is always *applied theology.* Obviously, as a partial perspective, there is a real and needful place for economics as an objective science. There is such a force as supply and demand which conditions economic behavior, even though it does not determine it. There is such an influence as the law of diminishing returns. Our whole behavioral pattern, under whatever economic system, presupposes certain predictable relations without which our total organization for the control of property, could not be carried on. There are definable categories of economics. Labor, everywhere, is the expenditure of physical, mental or spiritual sacrifice for the sake of producing certain goods; capital involves produced goods that are then engaged in the production of more goods. Those who today tend to stress merely the subjective side of life neglect or belittle the reality and truth of creation. Economics is more than a phase of the spiritual life. To minimize the purpose, function and scope of objective science is foolish and detrimental to human welfare. And it is, besides, to refuse to accept God's way with the world.

Those who stress economics almost totally as a science, on the other hand, are usually those who have become so involved in a partial perspective that they either have forgotten the larger perspective and functional relationship of economics or else have suppressed this unwelcome truth into the subconscious. The hope of all separate sciences, however, as Whitehead maintains, is to find the fuller perspective of Truth and to make progress by mounting up to the fuller vision on each specialized subject. The task of the Christian theologian is naturally not to decide technical questions of economic theory nor to chart social engineering along economic lines; his task, rather, is to ascertain the relevance of the Christian faith for economics, whereby the Christian can make more intelligent faith and life commitments in this sphere, and whereby the economist can have suggested to him the larger setting of economic theory in order to guide him both in the further interpre-

[3] *Structure of Social Action,* p. 173.

tation of his subject and in its more wide-visioned application to social life. Such a perspective is needed by the Christian citizen and statesman in days like these. Economics is basically, then, applied theology. Archbishop Temple's fervent insistence that economics can never be subordinated to the truly human unless we subordinate the human realm itself to the divine realm is both painfully and hopefully true; painfully, because we have thus far failed enormously; hopefully, because economics can be controlled for the general human good.[4] Our first job, accordingly, is to affirm that all property is from God and to fix the place of property in the divine economy. Only thus shall we operate consistently, from there on, in the light of the perspective of the Christian faith.

As far as human life goes, it is hard to know when and in what ways the sense of property developed. Certainly in the earliest hunting, agricultural and pastoral stages there must have been the presence of some tools, of herds, and of grazing grounds. If the general use of uncharted land, as for instance, for hunting, can be called communism, there was, of course, such a state; but this state was, then, mostly on the animal level, with the hand of each against the hand of each and all. As soon as there was differentiation of property and repeated use of the same tool, there was a defensive sense. Even "instinctive" tribal collectivisms were closed, not open, societies. The point is that, instead of pure spirits only incidentally or marginally connected with nature, we have men who are nearly shoulder deep in animal life, who gradually acquire self-consciousness and the consciousness of others, perhaps mostly through their relation to nature by means of their development of property. Civilizations have come and gone, just as evolutions have come and perished before them, but still the process has gone on and on.

Man has answered God's push to live in terms of need by means of the utilization of nature to meet those needs. Up to now, man's *main* history has been shaped by his endeavors to meet his physical needs; that includes his whole technological history, in one way or another. His cultural and spiritual developments have been dependent upon this material base. The more man is removed from

[4] Cf. the whole tone of Temple, *The Church Looks Forward*, on this subject.

his direct, personal relation to nature and caught up in the complexities of our modern technological world, the more he becomes dependent upon his fellow men. As he becomes more interrelated to and dependent upon others, the more spiritual power is needed to keep him living peacefully and creatively with them. Though man may think that he is the most important power in gaining freedom from fear and want through the creation of property, actually the most important power, indescribably, is God, who has controlled and directed the whole process to His purposed end. Man's total economic history has been the basic external means by which God has guided man's social and spiritual history; for God made both man and his environment, and has dynamically concurred controllingly in the history of their interrelations and interactions.

Man's natural and cultural history are dynamically interdependent. This is the total historic perspective. Man's response to this total drive and direction comes both individually and collectively. In the long and large perspective, all human responses are vertical in nature. They are responses to the Creator, whether directly or indirectly. Individually, man needs property both to internalize and to externalize himself. The truest inwardness, therefore, is in relation to God. By means of dependence on outward circumstance, man fails to find complete self-sufficiency and therefore self-satisfaction. To learn the secret of man's dependence upon God is one of life's deepest and most profound lessons. Schleiermacher was not far wrong when he made this into the religious category itself. To learn that man cannot live without progressively controlling nature, by making it into property, something "proper" to man and for man, which is part of his very earthly life, is to learn a second deep truth. Ritschl saw much of this truth, and though he is accused of making God into merely a means to man's control of his environment, Ritschl is greatly right in his basic insight, for God is humble enough to allow Himself to be used for man's ends, while always controlling and correcting those ends for His final end with history.

Not only should property engender the sense of dependence, but it should also lead in the experience of the individual to gratitude and service. Thank offerings go far back into primitive religions. The harvest festivals have been the immemorial expression of man's sense of gratitude for the filling of his needs. As what is proper for his bodily sustenance and health is obtained, man should learn to know its source and purpose. Ultimately all property is from God, all possessions of external goods and services, and the meaning of property is not known or accepted, *existentially*, until the individual becomes truly grateful from the heart. As he externalizes himself in terms of responsibility and creative activity, he also internalizes himself in terms of gratitude.

Property exists in order to teach us all to know and to love God and others better through service. Others need. We have wherewithal to help them. We cannot truly help them without understanding them. We come to know them as needers. Or we need, and are helped, and come to know others as helpers. Or we all have needs together and work to fill those needs, and in so doing we learn co-operation. We may be using others' property in so working, but no work is ever legitimately performed which does not involve the investing of the product with value. To say that the only value is the value of the work directly put into the product is, of course, a shortcut that fails to arrive at the destination of the full truth. Even Marx, in his discussion of the labor theory of value, realized that capital is cumulative, that reserves must be taken out for repairs, replacement of capital, or the building of new capital, etc.[5] Capital extension is sacrifice by the consumers for the future good.

The understanding of this co-operation, both by the past and the present, is part of the Christian consciousness of vocation. To work is to *col*laborate with God and with men within the total matrix of property relations. To work in the Christian spirit is to serve. Through serving, we externalize ourselves and internalize others. The way in which this is done is the criterion of Christian vocation. Luther had this New Testament conception of vocation as a divine calling. By the spirit in which we work and by the way in which we work, we witness to God in Christ for the world. Vocation is a way by which God forces us out of self-sufficiency

[5] The new reader of *Das Kapital* is usually surprised by Marx' realism at these points.

for the sake of facing others.[6] We learn to know others as needers, helpers or co-operators. How we then react to those whom we come to know, and with whom we have to work, is another thing. The truly Christian answer to this divine push, of course, is in terms of the pull of God's purpose for the full fellowship to be effected. Thus through property man learns to know and to live with others in needing, helping and co-operating. Service to God and to man through the legitimate use of property is one of its intrinsic purposes for being.

Property is never properly used unless it is from God for the full fellowship in the spirit of a free faithfulness. Yinger points out that the Puritans stressed individual responsibility rather than social obligation.[7] Troeltsch writes that the outstanding characteristic of the Gospel Ethic is "an unlimited, unqualified individualism," that the real question was man's "unconditional obedience to the Holy Will of God."[8] But Christianity knows no such distinction between personal responsibility and social obligation, between the holy will of God and social service. The content of the Christian consciousness is always a community consciousness. When a man is away from home and walks in a distant city, he is still a member of his family, and the content of his consciousness is ever colored by this fact. There is privacy and individuality in Christian fellowship, but only as partial experiences and perspectives. The plenary experience and perspective are ever social, a divine sociality. Man is a socius more basically than an individual. The sociality, too, is ever within a cultural-natural whole-environment from which we must not abstract falsely. Even Cicero could write that "there are by nature no private rights."[9] By nature, in the full light of Christian truth, rights are redemptively social; they are opportunities for world-transformation. A lesser use of them never rises to the Christian level of motivation and value. Even the understanding of the past is actually transmitted to a large extent through property. We have books, libraries, school buildings, museums, art treasures, and many other ways by which, through transformed

6 Cf. Wingren's excellent study, Luthers *lära om kallelsen.*
7 *Op. cit.,* p. 96.
8 *Social Teaching of the Christian Churches,* Vol. I, p. 55.
9 Cited in Fletcher, ed., *Christianity and Property,* p. 56.

nature, history is recorded and inherited. Thus social history is experienced by means of property, while property, in the terms of capital, forms the steady background and foundation for social history itself.

Perhaps we ought to see that one function of property in the divine economy is to help us to discipline power. Obviously this can, and to some real extent must, be done by the external belongings of police departments and armed forces, in whatever sense and on whatever scale these may be needed. Police clubs and international airplanes may be social property, used to discipline power for the common good. But this is not an adequate answer to the problem of power. Power must be controlled mostly from within. For us to control power rightly we must first be controlled by God, whether externally through His pedagogical patience, or internally, by being constrained by His love and by the sharing of His vision.

Property, moreover, is the external elongation of ourselves. It is, to some extent, our objectified selves. We should be a true society, and property consequently should be social in nature. Only as we as individuals and as a society rise to the real meaning and reality of the common good, can we use social property for social ends. This means that the desire for private power, competitively in an invidious sense, made objectively possible for a good part through the presence of private property, must be disciplined and erased through new motivations of the Christian community consciousness, and through the increasing organization of society to accord with such social incentives and rewards rather than with individual success and with invidious satisfactions. Veblen knew all too well how much of economics is a matter of "invidious comparison" and of "conspicuous display."[10] *Power welding fellowship rather than dividing it* is the place of property for society in the divine economy.

Merely to describe the actuality of the power struggle is, therefore, not Christian realism; that is the realism of the world. To describe the actuality of the power struggle with a firm conviction that power belongs to God, and that power can, therefore, be controlled by the Creator in the creatures He has made is the only Christian realism. Christian realism has for its correct criterion

[10] *Theory of the Leisure Class.*

not the description of actual history, but of actual history in the light of God's purpose and power. History cannot be measured by the past; *that* is faithlessness to God, and *that* is a failure to see that history is turning a corner. The high and holy faith that power can be socialized because it is given by God for society is the only Christian answer to the problem of power. When we are controlled by God through a new level of life in the Spirit, we shall be able to make through new sources of property power, a new world beyond our imagination.

Property is not only *from* God, but *for* man. The basic formula that must govern Christian thinking regarding property is this: property is the means of freedom and faithfulness in fellowship between God and men. Complete stress must be laid both on the liberty and on the responsibility, both to God and to men.

Property, in the first place, is freedom from God, freedom over against God. For our own good, God has made man considerably independent of Himself. If we were directly and constantly dependent upon God, we should have very little opportunity for free choices. We should hardly be free agents, finding for ourselves that God's way is best with us and for us. We should either be forced to obey God arbitrarily in order to get what we need, for a price, or we should be completely determined, with little or no moral option, except possibly in attitude, for we might adopt the position which William James in "The Dilemma of Determinism" called "soft determinism."[11] There would, however, be little real freedom in fact. But as it is, we are free to store things in barns and build ourselves bigger barns. We are free to store the manna for other times than for the Sabbath. Property is properly ours, even over against God, in the sense that the husbandman has gone away for a journey. He is not with us directly to give constant and detailed commands. He has given us pounds which we must invest or hide in a napkin.

God has given us an amazing length of rope. We are quite free in this life to hang ourselves with it. Adam starts by hiding behind external things, the bushes, and he and his wife from each other, behind fig leaves. Man is not completely without a place on

11 In *The Will to Believe and Other Essays in Popular Philosophy.*

earth which is properly his own over against God. Property bestows on man at least a pedagogical freedom, and may eternally be an aspect whereby the spirit individuates and expresses himself. Roger Hazelton says that we must be keenly sensitive as Christians that bread is more than physical, that it has spiritual meaning and implications.

But not only does property make man to a large extent temporarily free over against God, a freedom which is genuinely felt and lived by man in the now, but property also makes the individual free over against society. There is private enterprise over against God, and there is also social enterprise over against Him. There is, besides, private enterprise over against society. Property is the means for freedom and faithfulness in fellowship. In an effective and satisfactory society there should be enough private property for the individual to be able to initiate creative activity for contribution to the common good. The individual should not be trammeled, as far as his needed material is concerned, or as far as a real degree of responsible choice concerning it goes. He should have freedom of travel and of change in his investment of value in productive property. He certainly should be free to have the permanent and secure use of personal effects and the belongings of home. He should have enough property to be allowed to contribute significantly to religious and other worth-while purposes, placing his own life, his own stake, in such enterprises. Individual initiative and personal enterprise are essential parts of meaningful life, and any system that denies the individual such freedom goes contrary to the grain of God's eternal purpose with property.

Perhaps one of the most important spheres for individual and group freedom in the future will be the possession of sufficient private property to enjoy creative leisure. More and more free time, particularly in the atomic age, will make the fullest and freest use of property for play, art, travel, and other forms of recreation more and more necessary. We may have to learn increasing public playing and mass entertainment, collective creativity in the realm of common leisure, but nothing can quite take the place of personal associations with intimate bits of property, like the underlined and thumbed volumes in one's personal library. Perhaps housing will become a critical test for our appreciation of private life, of personal freedom. Every individual should have a room or rooms where he can be by himself. If in the dim future the family should change its basic pattern into a more communal institution, the children will, nevertheless, need privacy, probably through property possession; for children brought up by the litter without a chance for solitariness can never become truly and fully human. The crowd kills depth of inwardness. The collective kills personality. Man needs not only faithfulness but also freedom in fellowship. He needs very much, by nature, to be by himself free from both God and men, and sometimes with God free from men. Any use of property that precludes large areas of private living and of private power by means of personal property is unchristian and unsatisfactory.

Perhaps we ought to notice here that the reason there seems to be enormous effect of income upon incentive power is not only a matter of greed or of mere having. Man is more than an economic man. He is a man who wants to be himself, to be his best self, to amount to something. In any culture, perhaps, this involves earning according to the patterns of behavior characteristic of its economic setup. To accept oneself, therefore, is to have care concerning property. To press on creatively is often connected with the incentives of income which to a great extent are our outward tokens of achievement. Veblen is certainly right in his psychological interpretation of much economic motivation. But our present culture is peculiarly an economic culture, as George Kelsey has ably developed.[12] Because of this fact, there is this enormous effect of income upon incentive to work.

Incentive of personal achievement ought to be in any culture. But take away the present setup of competitive incomes as a large factor of the social consciousness, and give us instead a society which values social service, and there will no longer be the same incentive power on the part of private income.

As a matter of fact, some department stores have found that mere raising of personal income did not raise the standard of efficiency, as hoped, while the making a game of the work in such a way that there was group competition for far less personal in-

12 "The Challenge of our Economic Culture to the Churches," an unpublished address.

come, in terms of prizes, changed the efficiency of the same workers radically for the better. In other words, the workers were not after money merely; they wanted meaning and challenge in their work. This would indicate that man is not a mere economic man, but a social creature subject mostly to social incentives. Private incentive there must be; economic life, within its vast complex of impersonal empires, will have to become genuinely personal at its grass-roots. Property and the production of property must not lose private meaning and personal incentive; but such personal stake in property can be combined with social motivation and meaning, and even largely fulfilled in them. This meaning must always include personal freedom, freedom to understand one's own place in the total property relation and one's own function in the production, including one's own sharing in the social rewards of labor. Such reward should include the rewards to property for privacy, and for personal creativity. Without such rewards, there cannot be maximum incentive, for one of man's main drives is frustrated, the drive to become and to be oneself.

Man also, if he is to be creative, needs security, to a certain extent, both individually and socially. To be denied personal freedom is to be frustrated.[13] When freedom is threatened, man is insecure. Proletarian socialism in its early history was largely a humanitarian movement, *a personalistic movement,* a revolt against the machine, against the impersonal life which came to dominate society. The machine seemed to become the master and man to serve the machine, instead of the machine serving man. As labor conditions have become far better and as the opportunity for creative leisure has increased, much of this revolt is dying down. Man still fears, to be sure, that machines will displace him and cause unemployment and lack of reason for living as a social contributor. The answer to that, however, is that we must learn to use the machine more fully and better, allowing all men, through wiser social planning, more and more material for creative living and leisure. The real problem is not of overproduction but of underconsumption. Man needs to be delivered from the thralldom of our present economic system into a fuller economic freedom.

Man needs freedom from the machine, from the impersonal.

[13] Cf. Dorothy Fosdick, *What Is Liberty?*

This will come as Christian vocation gives meaning to life itself and as there is more opportunity for creative leisure. He also needs freedom from things by the having enough of them. "Reasonable material security is a basic essential of life."[14] Now, it is true that a Christian has no right to things or even to life itself, if his life can be better used through the losing of things or through the giving of his life. To surrender this perspective is to surrender Christianity. Nor can a Christian ever have security in this life. His is a pilgrim life. Yet for creativity he needs the general predictability of a secondary security, which is always open, nevertheless, to God's inscrutable providence. Christianity is synonymous not with poverty or absence of life, but with richness and fullness of life, both in spirit and in body. This should be the normal and natural state.

When things have to be sacrificed for a cause, a Christian must do so with freedom from self-complaint and with joy in helping, in aiding God's cause for man. Augustine rightly writes:

> But as to those feebler spirits who, though they cannot be said to prefer earthly possessions to Christ, do yet cleave to them with a somewhat immoderate attachment, they have discovered by the pain of losing these things how much they were sinning in loving them.[15]

And:

> As for the good things of this life, and its ills, God has willed that these should be common to both; that we might not too eagerly covet the things which wicked men are seen equally to enjoy, nor shrink with an unseemly fear from the ills which even good men often suffer.[16]

This is certainly an undeniable Christian insight; but the further truth seems to be now that history is turning a corner from chronic scarcity to constant abundance. Certainly there is potential abundance, if men stop producing negative goods, stop wasting God's gifts, and use the undreamed-of resources of modern science to release creative energy and to produce ample sustenance with which to use this creative opportunity on a world-wide scale. That

---

14 Atteberry, Auble and Hunt, op. cit., Vol. I, p. 620.
15 The City of God, in The Nicene and Post-Nicene Fathers, Vol. II, p. 7.
16 Ibid., p. 5.

means that God seems to be offering us a new freedom from the burdens of want and giving us a new freedom from things through the abundance of things.

But society also needs freedom from oppressive individuals and groups who use property for their own power and satisfaction. Micklem rightly complains that some defenders of our kind of capitalism "will tolerate no restrictions upon individual initiative or personal enterprise. They are liberal only to the extent that they wish to be liberated from all social responsibility."[17] Society needs economic freedom by having restored into its own hands the power over economic processes. Property is from God for man in freedom and faithfulness in fellowship. Some forget all about the faithfulness and interpret freedom as their right to do what they can. Might becomes right and political freedom is abused, "behind stage," by economic power in such a way that political freedom becomes empty. Economic security must be obtained through political control by the people of all the property which concerns the common good.

Obviously, to be successful the operation to save mankind will have to be much more than economic in nature, but the economic aspect must not be underestimated or undermined, for it is possible to operate upon the physical body and thus help a person, even though mere bodily health will not give that person meaning and zest in life, or determine the kind of conduct which he is to choose. We shall have to operate on our economic body, even though the method is far from a cure-all.

> The gain of the monopolist [for instance] is usually the loss of the community, because the average standard of living can be raised, not by restricting, but only by increasing the production of the goods and services that the people want.[18]

From such abuse of economic freedom on the part of the people by the economically powerful few we need to be delivered. We need to regain the perspective of the Early Church which accepted regulated possession and use as the best system, in which the means of production are held and used for the common good, and

[17] *Op. cit.,* p. 96.
[18] Atteberry, Auble and Hunt, *op. cit.,* Vol. I, p. 455.

the necessities of consumption adequately provided for all. The idea is summed up in Saint Augustine's combination of the relevant texts from The Acts, "They had all things common . . . and distribution was made unto each, according as anyone has need."[19] Gregory's principle that "the social use of property is a matter of justice and not of generosity,"[20] is important for it shows that property belongs by right from God for freedom and faithfulness in fellowship. To put it in Micklem's words, "No man has the natural right to the possession or use of private property to the detriment of the common good."[21]

The first section of this chapter discussed the fact that property is primarily *from* God. The second section dealt with the fact that property is *for* man. In this last section we want to consider the redemptive and creative functions of property. In the main body of the book we have treated, in the plenary Christian perspective, the relation among world-transcendence, world-affirmation, world-renunciation and world-transformation. These must be applied to property in the right perspective and proportion.

Property must be affirmed as good, within this perspective. Christianity never makes poverty an end, but fullness of life in its every realm. If poverty must be endured or chosen, it must be for a redemptive or a creative cause. Poverty as such is absence of life. If God wanted us to profit by poverty, His task in creating that, or the conditions for it, would be easy indeed. Instead, He has so made the world that when we first seek the Kingdom, *which we must do together,* we can have increasing abundance. Then "these things [are] added unto" us.

In some circles there seems to be a certain hallowing of not having. There seems to be a real prejudice against those who have. To be sure, it is as hard for the rich man in his own power of property to enter into the Kingdom of Heaven as for a camel to go through a literal needle's eye. Both are impossible with men, for no one can ever be saved by his own effort; but with God it is possible. If it is not possible, then Christianity is the rationalization and self-

---

19 Fletcher, *op. cit.,* p. 71.
20 *Ibid.,* p. 70.
21 *Op. cit.,* p. 102.

comfort of the poor and the unfortunate. Trust in riches is certainly the root of all kinds of evil, but unless Christians can have the power to have God's riches and use them, there is little positive power to Christianity. Christianity is not first of all consolation for the lack of life, but the having of life, and also the victory over the means and media of life, where the fellowship is understood as indescribably more important and satisfying than all the means to it. There is a stress on *abounding* in Christianity, as it is found in the New Testament, which should become increasingly true with the progressive spread of the influence of the Christian faith. The fact that we are now entering into an economy of abundance is a token of this fact. To be able to be victoriously Christian in an economy of abundance is a test of the power of the Christian spirit over things.

Thus all things from God are good and to be received with prayer and thanksgiving, but world-affirmation, unless thoroughly within the Christian perspective and power of world-transcendence, can become the occasion for pride and the hardened heart. It might lead to the forgetting of our offering up of what we have "that there be equality." Pride and the hardened heart are twin temptations of the well-to-do life. That is why world-renunciation must always be one aspect of world-transcendence, as long, at least, as we live in a world of need. For poverty has its temptations, too, like envy and bitterness. When those who have, allow those who have not to suffer, while they thank God for what they have, they lead the poor into temptation as well as deny in their own lives the essence of the Christian faith, redemptive concern for each and all in every area of life. As a matter of fact, we ought to recall Gregory's maxim that "when we administer necessaries of any kind to the indigent we do not bestow our own, but render them what is theirs; we rather pay a debt of justice than accomplish works of mercy."[22]

All property is God's for the common good. It belongs, therefore, first of all to God and then equally to society and the individual. When the individual has what the society needs and can profitably use, it is not his, but belongs to society, by divine right. In this way we can have neither private property as an uncon-

[22] As cited in Fletcher, *op. cit.*, p. 70.

ditional right, nor can we have a totalitarian society where the individual is a means to a collective end. If society has not reached the point where it legislates in a free and understanding spirit to this effect, it is up to each individual and group to live up to this to his own maximum capacity, beginning not with the dry trees, but with the live trees.

World-renunciation, in this sense, is thus a matter of redemptive living, whether it be called justice or love.[23] It is something which the Christian owes others, whether by the compulsions of duty or by the constraints of love. Blessed be he who feels no compulsion, but has found the liberty, in this respect, of the sons of God.

This simply means, as we found before to be our main conclusion, that, if we are genuinely Christian, *for this history* world-transformation is our chief perspective and motivation. We live for the sake of effecting the fellowship. Property, whether used by us or by others, must be used and given to this end. Property, under God, in the Holy Spirit, perhaps *into* the realm of the Spirit of God, must ever be used redemptively and creatively. For the individual Christian, or Christian family, this means the using and the giving of his income, under our present economic system, with a view to where it can do the most good in effecting the Christian fellowship. Naturally, we must not be self-conscious and institutionally bound as far as our understanding of this goes.

In the modern world we must give more and more impersonally. As a matter of fact, effective aid must come less and less from giving, and more and more from doing, from the creating the effective economic system where giving becomes less and less a matter of supporting subsistence needs and more and more a matter of co-operating in creative enterprises. Yet as it now is, we must be rational and careful in our giving. Without losing the personal touch of intimate giving, we have to give our main contributions through large agencies that reach effectively and well into the areas of need. The careful giver makes it a Christian responsibility to figure out where he feels his own money can be most helpfully given. The Christian family consults long and well over the available choices. Giving often reveals to us our actual faith.

[23] For an excellent discussion of such justice cf. *King, The Holy Imperative*, pp. 63-64.

If we say that we want to give all to "actual needs" and then give all to physical relief, it means very likely that we believe very little in the intellectual, moral and spiritual needs of mankind. If we say that we want to give all we have to missions, that may mean that we actually have little concern about bodily needs, and consequently slight one part of God's full equation. If we give nothing to educational institutions, that may mean that we have "practical" minds and actually do not believe in the cultivation of the mind. If we want to give only personally, that may mean that we do not trust others, even Christian organizations. If we want to give only impersonally and indirectly, we may be humble and want to keep out of the way, but it may also be that we have an exaggerated sense of self and do not trust God to give with the direct gift the grace of a humble personality, in whose compassion there is no condescension or superiority. By observing our own inclinations about giving we can often discover and test our own faith, for we tend to give in line with what we actually believe in and are concerned with.

Personal giving, or family giving, should, above all, be preventively redemptive. Many will give for relief, but they cannot be touched by the need to prevent further relief. Many will give to the victims of war, but they will give nothing to help prevent war. Many will give to those oppressed by our economic system, but they will give nothing to organizations concerned with improving this economic system and doing away with such oppression. The Christian approach to giving is the actual taking hold of present need, but even more the preventing such need by the redemptive use of property.

The redemptive and creative use of property is not only a personal or family affair. It is, particularly in our age, mostly a social concern. Often we have thought of stewardship in the private sense of the personal generosity of the individual. Social stewardship involves the use of property by society under God for the common good. Our formula for this is freedom and faithfulness in fellowship. We have seen how this formula precludes either private capitalism or totalitarian communism, since property by divine right is social in nature, while including every individual as God's end and a consequent sharer to his maximum needs, as far as possible, in the use of property.

We take for granted that equality in the sense of an invidious measuring of oneself in terms of others is definitely sub-Christian. There is, to be sure, a sense in which the New Testament rightly insists "that there be equality." But this stress on equality is simply the stating of the social nature and responsibility of property. When people have all things in common, according to the New Testament formula, nothing worse can happen to the community than that all are filled with the evil eye, measuring their own portion precisely over against the other man's portion. There is a Christian communism. (Communism is a right good word. We have falsely surrendered this ideal to the Marxists. They gain much support from using it, for it is revolutionary in intent. Yet the revolution which can make this formula work is none other than the Christian.)

The Christian stewardship of property starts with the assertion that under God we have all things in common. No one lives unto himself alone and no one has property unto himself alone. Each one lives as a fellowship member and each one has property as a fellowship member. This is Christian communism. Only when life is conclusively motivated by the Holy Spirit can there be the spirit of community, which can get beyond private profit, or the kind of mass state where the individual or group is fully integrated.

The concern of this community spirit, however, is not equality in any invidious sense, but rather the maximum contribution of the individual to society and the concern by society for the maximum opportunity of the individual. For the common good the distribution of the rewards of society ought to be "from each according to his ability to each according to his need." But "need" here must not be interpreted mostly as consumer's need, as the opportunity for private enjoyment. Rather, the first need in a creative society is to contribute meaningfully to the maintaining and transforming of society.

Obviously there must be no reward except for labor, no reward for speculative activity or "finagling" of finances, no living on the work of others without personal contribution to it, except, of course, for those unable to work, who have all the rights and privileges of those who can.

The actual problem of social stewardship, in one of its largest aspects, is the complex and enormously vast economic system in which we live. The indirection of control and the impersonal nature of large-scale corporate activity are hard to imagine throughout their wide reaches, and impossible to hold back by personal intentions, however good. Mass production is part of modern life and is here to stay. It is not only a burden on our backs, however, but primarily the opportunity for fuller freedom and creative leisure for common man. Some keep pounding home the limitations imposed on personal living by modern mass production. It is high time that we began to realize and to make effective the opportunity for a new kind of life which this combination of mass production and specialization has made possible. The division of labor can become the occasion for the solidarity of the more direct forms of communal life. The concentration of technics and the concentration of economic power are the opportunity for the subordination of the material side of life and the lessening of the economic hold on life. By providing more abundantly and generally for the basic needs of life, including adequate personal freedom for creative leisure, we can help to usher in a new age.

Every temptation is the chance for fuller social and spiritual victory. Every relevant limitation, as Paul Minear keeps saying, is God's opportunity, if we trust Him, to make it redemptive or creative in some way. We are, for instance, up against the problem of concentrated economic power and of the ever-growing power of technology, threatening democracy and personal living and values. Here is the challenge of opportunity, however, for "the economic answer to economic chaos is planning."[24] The fear of planning is to a great extent due to poisonous anxieties injected into the social stream by special interest groups, especially through their now complex and concentrated power in the whole fabric of the social life. The newspapers both whisper and scream this fear. The radio takes up the doleful tune. Numberless circulars in the daily mail insinuate themselves into our consciousness. Politicians

[24] Jones, *op. cit.*, p. 168.

in numerous cases harp on it. Social planning has become a hob-goblin with which to frighten the children of men. Yet it is true, in a large measure, that the inefficiency of our system of life "de-rives fundamentally from the dominance of individualism. It is indeed ironical that the very economic liberalism which played such an important role in the rise and early spread of the democratic way of life should in the twentieth century be the basic cause of its decline."[25]

Yet, naturally, this fear is not without foundation, for does not the planning together of the total economic life easily lead to totalitarianism? Is not economic freedom the precondition of po-litical and personal freedom? Is not the danger real, however, that "in our complex society it may well be that planning nothing will eventually be overcompensated by planning everything?"[26] Mann-heim has battled with the problem of how we can have planning on a level of freedom within a planned society. To this question the only adequate answer is the obvious one. Unless we are able to achieve a spiritual and social level of political life, a way of living co-operatively together, precisely in relation to this new concentra-tion of technological and economic power, we shall all fail of constructive civilization. The kind of temptation offered by our present type of opportunity for privileged economic power and backstage government by special interests is certainly not the an-swer to our problem. Our kind of economic behavior is not appro-priate to our kind of economic situation. Neither is any sort of social planning that is based primarily on fear and force. Bureauc-racy and bungling are the results in that case. Only social planning backed by the creative dynamic of a religiously-rooted community can answer the problem. What is needed is a new kind of man and a new kind of society. To get *that* we need a new dimension of religion.

If Christianity is to be the world religion, it must be tested in the hottest flames of world need. Religion must become central and not peripheral, if we are to use our economic system satis-factorily. Economics is applied theology, and theology in essence is ever existential. By the fruits of economic planning for a free

25 Atteberry, Auble, and Hunt, *op. cit.*, Vol. II, p. 602.
26 *Idem.*

society, where the physical has been made less central by the meeting of its primary needs more easily and adequately, the power of the concrete Christ in this area must become known. Naturally, this will need careful social engineering. We shall obviously need critical and creative legislation. Most certainly we shall need world government and the relief from the oppressive burdens of armaments. Unquestionably we shall need to work out and to support wisely and vigorously bills of rights within the fuller stress on opportunity, obligation, and concern.

Already the American public has gone a long way to approve of this course. The Social Security Act of 1935 is the open rejection of the older kind of extreme individualism. That act in turn will be changed and improved for the fuller common good. The states are separately undertaking similar actions, often in conjunction with the central government.

Economic power and technological might must be controlled by spiritual and social power expressed in a freedom obtained through social planning. Yet such planning depends upon ease of economic regulation. While most of the means of production are owned by private members of society or by special interest groups within it, such ease is nearly impossible to obtain. If all were saints, perhaps! But they would even then be severely tempted saints! Private power tends to tempt to corruption. We do not believe, of course, that absolute power corrupts absolutely, for God is not absolutely corrupt! All power is from God for a good purpose and does not corrupt, for corruption is in the human soul. But granted an imperfect and sinful soul, power constitutes a temptation to inward pride, self-importance, hardness of heart, desire to control others, or to a means for evasive self-enjoyment. Hand in hand with the spiritual rebirth and power should come the socialization of property in the sense of the public ownership of the means of production.

Communism scares us. Having surrendered this great word to he Marxists, we are now on the verge of losing the word "democracy" as well, in many areas of the globe. Yet whether we call it socialism or communism, whether we call it Christian economics, the classless society, or "economic democracy," technological development throughout the whole world is ushering in a new era.

The right course for the Christian Church is not to fight the flood of the future, but to have ready for it the larger stream of God's eternal purpose within which to cleanse and to redirect it. This brings up such issues as capitalism, communism, or other choices, whether intermediary or more lasting.

Let us first take a look at capitalism. Our task is to suggest implications of the Christian faith. In the first place, then, "all forms of productive capacity are ultimately capital and are to be traced back to the same complex of factors—inheritance, the activity of the individual owner and other persons, . . . social processes and accident."[27] There can be theoretic capitalism of the free market, as in Adam Smith; there can be monopolistic capitalism; there can be a mixture of the two; there can be state capitalism; this, in turn, can be controlled by a dictator, a power group, or by a democratic, representative government. There can be and is, furthermore, a mixture among these forms, and perhaps still other combinations of actual "capitalist" systems. Nelson Rockefeller has described a concerned capitalism where ownership would feel Christianity responsible for the workers and for the needy. The state can perform this function of care under our present system or, for instance, force manufacturers not to cut down work irresponsibly. In discussing our own system we must not discuss a caricature of it.

Furthermore, capitalism as we know it has changed indescribably for the better during a hundred years, shall we say, doing away with undepictable child labor, female labor, sweatshop conditions, below subsistence pay, etc. We have no right to discuss modern capitalism in terms of the industrial revolution or the Wesleyan revivals; that simply is not fair. Actual capitalism is a complex affair and a dynamically changing system. For our purposes, however, we want to confine the term to monopolistic capitalism, or at least to corporation capitalism, where restricted competition is now mostly a dead issue. There is no use in discussing the capitalism of the nineteenth century as the capitalism of today.

We must ever remember, furthermore, that no economic system is the expression of its theoretical justification or ideal description. Every economic system is a composite of conflicting tendencies and

27 Knight, *op. cit.*, p. 114.

the actual compromises of forces. Certainly the spiritual, the social, and the ethical ingredients have their power as concrete forces. We must understand the total human dynamics of a social situation if we are to describe it at all adequately. Human nature vitiates any economic system; and human nature vitiates any system at all, that actually operates in history, including most decidedly the Christian Church as an institution. Human nature also partially redeems any system, so that actual practices and life, within it, are very near the general level of social attitudes and practices. With this in mind, we must grant that present capitalism is a mixed economic system and modified most basically by the people who run it, as they are more made by the external situation than they are spiritual masters over it in freedom of soul. We cannot, therefore, discuss any ideal capitalism nor any ideal people. We know both factors too well. Nor can we discuss capitalism as "a quest for purely individual profits,"[28] without having committed what Whitehead calls the fallacy of misplaced concreteness. What we have to discuss is an actual system of economic organization, evolved out of concrete history in response to actual needs and human situations including human nature, and still open to continuous and radical evolution.

When that is done, there can be no abstract criticism of capitalistic economy as though it could have been avoided, without positing an ideal humanity and a historic wisdom, *after the fact,* which is utopian in nature. Capitalism meant the development of man's productive capacities and the concrete tools for ever-increased production. In this process human life was abused in the same way that wars or internal conflicts have caused human misery. Such development of productive capacity was necessary to the coming of a new and better age, at least as its material condition. During the development, new fortunes made a new culture possible, through philanthropic endowments. There was a new opportunity for foundations for research, for institutions of learning, along with the enormous development of the technological means of communication of mind and body, which conditioned the becoming of a whole new kind of consciousness. Along with this

[28] Fanfani, "Catholicism, Protestantism, and Capitalism," pp. 178-179, in Yinger, *op. cit.,* p. 73.

came not only fortunes for the few and a chance for the fuller conditions of cultural life, but a broadening base of those who could afford it, plus, most importantly, the general education of the masses of people which made possible "the century of the common man." Then continuing developments made for shorter and shorter hours, giving a new chance for life to the multitudes.

At the same time the total standard of living has been continuously rising *in spite of wars and catastrophic destruction.* The productive capacity of the capitalist system and the general lift it has given to the conditions for further cultural and spiritual development are amazing. Not to be thankful for the capitalist era, as a whole, is to fail to see the push of history and the power of the fuller Purpose within cosmic process. The latest developments in medicine and in technological skill and resources are now beyond our imagination in their implications. God's push has been powerfully preparing the conditions for a new day.

We must be thankful to yesterday for its sacrifices of goods and services for today. Not only did capitalism achieve a totally higher balance of goods for all classes, but it achieved the savings which today are the capitalist's goods, knowledge, and skills which can prepare for the better tomorrow. But actually what has happened by the main thrust of events, at least, is that capitalism has saved up for us the means for a better day.

We must also recognize the solid fact that during the era of capitalism we have developed the truest political democracy known to man. It has effected, or there has been effected during its tenure, the widest genuine political participation known to the history of man. Feibleman in *Positive Democracy* claims that political democracy was a corollary of economic urges to freedom. The capitalist, in order to justify to himself freedom in the economic realm, had to espouse its cause generally. Though there is some truth in Gandhi's return to the weaver's loom, and in contemporary American urges for decentralization, like Bordosi's, nevertheless, the clock of history should not be set back. The way to meaning and freedom is not back before the present producer's power, but right through it by means of its more social direction and understanding.

Then again, in no civilization so far has labor had so much actual power and freedom. The workers of the world are becoming educated; they are becoming organized in a new depth, they are becoming politically adept, adroit and powerful; they are becoming employers of legal talents and of means of communication to present their point of view. As a matter of fact, given political democracy, we wonder whether labor would not actually be the gainer for giving up its stress on violent means of conflict, if instead it concentrated its gigantic sleeping power on education toward a new world. Early strikes accomplished little objectively because government was far too much on the side of capital, except to make the masses conscious of their own plight and potential power. Now the giant has awakened and can control more and more the processes of government, as labor learns to offset the power of the interest-controlled press and other means for the presentation of political issues. Labor is often blamed for supporting capitalism and for being far too conservative. But labor can see the total gains of mankind in most brackets, and the opportunity for even a much better world under a free system. Capitalism has been in an increasing sense an open society, and will remain so unless it is frightened into a muddled mood of repressive defense by the fastest growing movement on a world scale in the history of the world: Marxist communism.

This communism is a prophetic movement giving hope to the masses. As an economic system it, too, is a mixture of religion and sociology. It is strongest as a protest movement against the unconcern and contradictions within the capitalist system. Marx was without question a prophetic personality who expressed in history the revolt of the masses against the unconcern and iniquities of modern industrial society. Our own criticisms of capitalism will for this reason come mostly as part of our discussion of the rise of Marxism. After that we shall discuss the failure of Marxism to solve today's problems.

Capitalism played its part in history's rough but effective way, in its era, but now we need something better. Kagawa criticizes capitalism for exploitation, accumulation of capital and power in the hands of a few, and an ever-increasing proletariat. Others criticize it for the materialistic, individualistic stress it puts on profit and on property. Others see its trouble in its indirect and divided responsibility. Others again emphasize the waste and insecurity of the cyclical "booms" and "busts." Anyone who has read Bellamy's *Equality* will never forget the parable of the water pump, where water is bought for profit and price by its fetchers in an ever-recurring cycle of overflow and emptiness; whereas the whole situation could be prevented by the common sharing of labor and reward, by the acceptance of social equality as a desired state of life.

For our purposes the two real reasons for passing beyond capitalism are (1) the concentration of economic power in the hands of a few that makes political democracy difficult in actual practice, and (2) the artificial restriction of the market for the sake of private profit.

We are also convinced that the capitalist system as a system is not now most fully conducive to a democracy of the whole man, including economic democracy, nor is it now the best system to effect maximum output for the highest material basis of civilization. On this score the Christian view of work and Karl Marx's labor theory of value, in their general intent, agree solidly, and on this main point Marx's basic criticism as to the contradictory nature of capitalism is amply valid. The new and better world, on its material side, cannot be based on the artificially limited market, on profit as the mainspring of social incentive, and on a competitive economic behavior that is continually making nation fear nation and group fear group, which finally has to seek expanding markets, wanting both to sell machines and to keep others from using them, and which puts on people's backs the burden of armaments for the sake of keeping the system going. A new world needs *now* a better handling of our problem. Why do we not, then, choose Marxism?

Marxism was and is good as a criticism of the contradictions in the capitalist system, as an indignant protest against the subordination of the masses to economic interest, and as the bringer to man's awareness of the large place of economic conditioning which actually exists in man's total history. But Marxism is bad theology and bad anthropology, and consequently cannot escape being bad sociology and economics. Alexander Miller's idea that while Christianity is the right ultimate faith, Marxism may be the right scientific sociology is hardly warranted, except in spots.[29] The Marxist view of the ultimate, while disclaiming metaphysics vehemently, is the eschatological drive inherent in history whereby man passes from a primitive communism through a capitalist economy of class conflict into the force-free days of the classless society. History is thus ultimately good in nature and sovereignly certain. This dialectic materialism is far from materialistic cynicism. It is the expression of the highest hope of the Hebrew religion, as the general hope for all mankind, couched in economic terms. Not the content of this hope is at fault, but its source and ground. Without the Eternal Purpose, the better history will not come.

Anthropologically, too, Marxism is bad because it believes in the inherently good man, when he is cleansed from the selfish drives generated by a vitiating economic system. Man, however, is sinful by nature and cannot be saved from the outside in terms of environmental transformations alone. Sociologically, again, the real change will not come through economic means, certainly not by themselves. Add to this the method of class conflict as the means of a new day, and we can see no real hope for the effecting of fellowship according to the Eternal Purpose.

But at least, when Christianity lost nerve and despaired about historic hope, Marxism maintained the faith. When Christianity lost faith in man, Marxism held that man could know a new classless day and a force-free society. When Christianity wondered whether man was not caught in an economic system and in external circumstance, Marxism believed that man could revolt against such bondage and overthrow it. Marxism took over and expressed with confidence much of what in Christianity gave man hope. Perhaps actual Christianity has grown weak and weary and needed a new form in which to express its permanent truth. For actually there was more hope and faith in Marxism than in much actual Christianity.

Nor was Marxism a world-weary sentimentality about people and events. It knew that the means are sanctified by the ends, if the ends are truly proper, and if the means are truly appropriate and effective to those ends. Marxism thus embodied much of the lost Christian depth faith, giving men courage and hope. This it

[29] Cf. *The Christian Significance of Karl Marx.*

coupled with its actual appeal to the interest of the rising masses, who were being educated and beginning to sniff the air of a new day. Besides this, Marxism also appealed to the oppressed colonial peoples and the downtrodden races. For Christianity merely to bait and to blame Marxism, and not to see its deeper truth and reason for success, is to miss the real point of modern history.

Atheism, utopian anthropology, and violent class struggle are not the right theology, anthropology and sociology, but underneath these lie the understanding that the original purpose for creation was good and that man's essential and final nature is good, and that real struggle with evil in corporate form must precede the coming of the better day. When this depth faith and realistic understanding are superarched by the fuller faith, corrected by a more searching realism, and operated within the Agape spirit of true concern for all, Marxism can already begin to be seen for its degree of true worth as well as for its proportion of real error. If Marxism should conquer the whole world, this might be merely the prelude in economic arrangement to the blossoming forth within it of the deeply-sowed seeds of Christian faith and expectations. Marxism may be God's means to Christian fulfillment in history. Much blood may have to flow and much witnessing may have to be done through martyrdom, but in the long run we can do everything for and nothing against the truth. That Biblical insight is sound.

Yet we hope that a partial perspective like Marxist communism will not win the historic day. We hope, rather, that Christian communism will win the day. That such a new economic system is coming seems altogether likely. The question is only how to make it serve as freely and as fully as possible the Christian ends. Perhaps we had better speak of a democratic socialism as what we have in mind, or better, of a Christian democratic socialism, in so far as any of these words can be properly and meaningfully used to indicate a real social content. Without democratic processes public ownership becomes totalitarian, a small group deciding for all the rest, and whether it be tyranny or paternalism, a nondemocratic government robs man of fullness of life. Without Christianity, moreover, or without religiously motivated responsible concern, democracy will not work.

We shall merely indicate needs of today which must be met by any economic order that will serve the new and better day. History has turned a corner in this field, too, and we cannot look back. To look back is to be unfit for the Kingdom. Herbert Gezork has preached a memorable sermon on the text: "Ye cannot return whence ye came." Though the present situation may seem a wilderness making the fleshpots of Egypt attractive in comparison, the only way that can be successfully taken is ahead, though the people and powers who oppose us may seem like giants. Marx rightly maintained that capitalism has solved the problem of production— and for that we cannot be thankful enough to it—but that it fails to solve the problem of distribution. Economic organization ought to have one end in view: increasing efficiency of production for the sake of consumption by all in order to prepare the conditions for a new and better life.

Economic reward, moreover, must be subordinated to fuller personal values, within freedom and fellowship under God. Saint Paul kept hammering home this theistic perspective: "in the Lord."[30] We must bring economics into an organismic atmosphere, under God for all men. Economically this means the bringing of our economic power under democratic control, delivering individuals and groups from temptations of power and pride, at least in this realm. Control, for the social good, should be in government hands, we think, by more than supervision, and really by effective ownership, in order to prevent certain "kitchen cabinet" rulers from causing conflict and exerting constant political pressures. What is actually happening is that business, through monopoly or political privileges, taxes the general public for its own private benefits. And that is wrong both in principle and in practice.

There are, to be sure, economic advantages to large-scale business, benefiting the public, and certain economic laws which restrain monopoly practice from extremes; but the point is that when this large-scale planning and advantage of production are centered in the government, the agent for all the people, we have combined the need to keep large business, and to increase it, without the direct popular control of it, and with the general public's reaping the benefits. There can be, of course, and constantly is, control

[30] Cf. Acts 16.

without ownership for the public good, and this can be justified by the social nature of property. But perhaps Marx's maxim is clearer, namely, that collective labor necessitates collective capital, involving ownership.

Sweden has gradually worked out a "middle way," combining private property, co-operatives and state socialism, under socialist direction. Certainly that process is still going on, for the middle way surely will not remain that way with time. England is plowing its deep furrow, with earnest intent and sacrificial discipline. Other countries, outside Marxism, are also moving in the right direction. Socialism is a long-range trend called for by the nature of technology and by the ongoing historic processes themselves. Many, if not most, of the stresses of socialist thought have already been accepted and incorporated into current legislation. Our present American government, by the standards and thought of a generation ago, would now be labeled definitely socialist. A Chinese financier, in private conversation, maintained that when you get an effective income tax really distributing property for the sake of the common good you are already socialistic!

Some, like Kagawa and Carpenter, favor a more social use of property through co-operatives. Some first-rank businessmen, who dread communism and are far more satisfied with things as they are, have, in conversation, urged this approach. Though social engineers may see how co-operatives can be used in a transitional capacity, the problems of co-operatives within our present society are great and the dangers which threaten them grave. If there is ownership of the producers' goods, production, in any case, is the fullest kind of co-operative endeavor, provided there be real and efficient democracy. On the side of consumption, however, it may be that consumers' co-operatives become the best way of handling our problem. If the way we look at things be changed for a more co-operative way, and if social incentives and practices are generally strengthened, this may be precisely the best way to deal with this side of the economic process. Certainly the co-operative way would strengthen local responsibility, would enforce, or at least be conducive to, the co-operative attitude, and would prevent the undue competitive and financial motivation on the part of the more privately successful. If this cannot be managed, or some similar or substitute way that abets social incentive and prevents temptations to financial invidiousness, perhaps a thoroughgoing Christian communism, except for private articles and tools for creative and adventuresome leisure, may be the only way out of our problem.

The second need of an economic system for the new and better day is authentic democracy. This presupposes moral power and purposive education. Though democracy cannot be equated outright, on the human level, with Christianity, it comes close to it. By the nature of reality God is, of course, the author of all things and makes the good possible. He is in a different dimension from creaturely decisions. What kind of world we are finally to have cannot have been decided from the beginning by democracy. God has decreed it for our own good. Yet, even so, God is not willing to rule puppets, or to command arbitrarily. He wants understanding, loving, and willing children who co-operate with Him, in a co-operative enterprise where all will see why they do what they do, and, seeing God's way is best, will want to do it.

This state of affairs comes close to the spirit of democracy. Democracy is not a shibboleth; it is the normative nature of right government. Its form may change. We perhaps should have more functional rather than geographic representation. The initiative, referendum and recall responsibilities might be more widely and efficiently used. There can be more local participation in politics and more co-operation between alert churches and the political government, as well as numerous other changes and improvements which are open to a dynamic, creative and morally purposive society.

But without genuine democracy we cannot adequately meet the needs of a day of world-wide problems, and of general education. Particularly dangerous is economic ownership by governments unless their base is broad and steady. State control or ownership can lead to bureaucracy, political oppression, thwarting of creative drive, indifference, officiousness, pride of place and power, irresponsibility, "passing the buck," and what not. Such evils as these are nonetheless also present in any and all systems, for they are part of our actual human nature. As a matter of fact, we may meet more officiousness in privately owned places like railroad stations than we do in post offices, where many employees are conscious of the responsibilities of being public servants. Though no generalization can be made, it seems, systems may have their temptations in a peculiar degree, but a socially conscious democracy, in all spheres of life, is certainly the goal of freedom and faithfulness in fellowship at which to aim. If this is attained, an effective beginning is made toward the solving of our social problems, though imperfect and sinful man we have always with us, until God's full day and light set in for our history, here or beyond, in God's own time and way.

Economically speaking we are on the borderline of a new era. To get it we need the abundance of economic democracy to serve as the material basis, delivering us from the continual burden of material concern. Subsistence existence or below is not conducive to high living in any realm of life, except possibly for the socially irresponsible because of vocational preferment, for the sons who are "free" and cultivate the better part of life, for the good of common humanity. Jesus' and Saint Francis' lives we cannot judge, only thank God for. We now can have what Kirtley Mather calls "enough and to spare"; if we stop wasting, if we stop producing negative goods like war armaments, and release instead our productive capital from the strangling clutch of artificially limited markets. What we need is creative daring and freedom for general fullness of life. Christ came that we "might have life and that abundantly." The New Testament, particularly Paul, likes the word "abound." Our creative capital ought to *abound,* to overflow, to the glory of God and to the help of man. This creative use of capital for the common good presupposes a genuine democracy of high educational, political and economic efficiency.

But, above all, we need the spiritual motivation. Never was an age more generally wistful and truly seeking. Marxism sees this and has set out to meet the need of the common man, clamoring for a new day. And it is being believed. Its inadequate myth, in the plenary perspective, is operationally dynamic. Yet we know that Marxism sweeps the world on borrowed faith. The dynamism which Sidney Hook and others point out as the strength of Marxism, the refusal to live behind the walls of a static metaphysics, and its operationalism, are part and parcel of the Christian faith.

Nowhere has genuine widespread democracy lived, apart from

Christian roots and nourishment. It takes thousands of years, says Whitehead, for an idea like freedom or democracy to take widespread root under ground and then to shoot forth plans with power. Needed is genuine economic democracy, which presupposes responsible freedom and creative concern. What is needed for a new world internationally and economically is thus a new level of life, the Christian life, with all its actual involvements. Christ has gone out "conquering and to conquer"; his white horse may have to go to the bridle in blood, but his steed is a steed of peace.

Some fear to apply the word "Christian" to civilization. Yet "the earth is the Lord's and the fullness thereof." Creation belongs to God. From the Eternal Purpose to the most practical aspect of cosmic process the relevance of personal purpose and social motivation obtains. "Behold I make all things new" is a promise at the heart of the Christian Gospel, and economic processes and behavior partake of it.

> The Christian Ethos alone, through its conception of a Divine Love which embraces all souls and unites them all, possesses a Socialism which cannot be shaken. It is only within the medium of the Divine that the separation and reserve, the strife and exclusiveness which belong to man as a natural product, and which shape his natural existence, disappear.[31]

The measure of our Christian faith in its wide root-meaning, common concern under God, is the measure of our spiritual power; the measure of our spiritual power is the proportion of our democracy; and the measure of our democracy is the proportion of our economic solution.

[31] Troeltsch, *op. cit.*, Vol. II, p. 1005.

CHAPTER IX

The Christian Perspective
on Education

"The art of arts" Gregory Nazianzen called education. Certainly education as the transmission, discovery and reconstruction of what we believe and are, with considered care, shows us what we really believe and want. Our sense of reality and value cannot help being reflected, through and through, in the way we approach this subject, both in theory and in practice. As far as the Christian faith is concerned, there can be no question that Fallaw is right when he writes: "Christendom itself will suffer constriction unless the trend of its education improves."[1] If we really believe that Christianity has the answer to our social questions and strivings, we cannot keep on teaching, for the most part, as we have been, in any realm of life. Obviously there is no easy answer either to the full "what" or to the full "how" of educating. After a lifelong interest in the subject and service of it, Whitehead confesses in his "autobiographical notes" that "the education of a human being is a most complex topic, which we have hardly begun to understand. The only point on which I feel certain is that there is no widespread, simple solution."[2] On the one hand, therefore, we must attack our problem with serious concern, as of utmost importance, and, on the other, with cautious humility as to detailed suggestions. The aim is, within our scale of scope, the fullest and truest possible perspective on education from the point of view of the Christian faith.

[1] *The Modern Parent and the Teaching Church*, p. 86.
[2] In *The Philosophy of Alfred North Whitehead*, p. 6.

In this perspective, education is the elucidation of the Eternal Purpose in its bearing on all areas of life. It is the illumination and direction of all human activities by the light and the power of the Christian faith, according to the degree of its direct or indirect relevance to the subject taught. Education is, consequently, the understanding and application of Agape, whether directly in terms of divine-human relations, or indirectly with regard to the meaning and nature of society as such and of environmental processes.

Comenius rightly scorns our setting up "sparks as torches; a vain endeavor," because we are "ignorant of that other light granted by heaven."[3] Sir Richard Livingston in *Education for a World Adrift* finds the essential fault of education to be the absence of ultimate standards. Calhoun stresses that "man cannot live by culture alone."[4] Cole complains that "in educational circles it almost amounts to a breach of good form to mention the term 'God.' "[5] At the same time his burden of heart is that "an adequate frame of reference for liberal education dare not fall short of a religious world view."[6] Only the Absolute is educationally adequate. The Absolute is God as Agape. The point of this chapter is to illustrate this, by which illustration, in so far as it is satisfactory, the truth of Agape as the answer to our present problems, in this field also, is at the same time verified by a dynamic self-verification, which can, however, never be completely validated except as it becomes translated into actual educational operations, into a *faith* that *works*.

The nature of reality predetermines educational method. Truth is an eternal indicative, conducive to creativity. God's love is "the really real" which must be taught according to its own nature. Meiklejohn is therefore right in the analysis that "always prior to any 'method' is the 'content' out of which it springs, by which it is determined."[7] This content is the Eternal Purpose which is the ground and goal of cosmic process. Eternal Purpose involves cosmic cohesion or coherence. Behind and within all multiplicity

---

[3] Keatings, *Comenius*, p. 30.
[4] "The Dilemma of Modern Humanism," in *The Christian Understanding of Man*, p. 71.
[5] *Liberal Education in a Democracy*, p. 215.
[6] *Ibid.*, p. 228.
[7] *Education between Two Worlds*, p. 17.

and pluralism there is inner unity and integrative meaning. Unless the reality and centrality of this fact of Eternal Purpose are adequately dealt with, according to their degree of relevance, education will lack either inner cohesiveness or elasticity.

The first and most important starting point for the remaking of education is the place of God. Transcendence is needed for what Ulich calls "integralism and directionalism." This transcendence must be as binding as serious reality and social choices, while yet as free and flexible as the need for creative self-fulness. To find this transcendence and to teach it correctly is to begin on the better road of a more adequate education; after that, other problems can be attacked. As T. S. Eliot writes: "Our difficulties of the moment must always be dealt with somehow: but our permanent difficulties are difficulties of every moment."[8] Pestalozzi is eternally right that "the nearest relation of man is his relation to God."[9] Moody maintained that the two necessary conditions for being educated are prayer and love. To be open to God in all our relations to man, according to the nature of the situation, is to have the key to the learning mind and the adaptive life.

Vertical transcendence is necessary. Without it horizontal transcendence loses height of perspective and meaning. Yet vertical transcendence in the Christian faith requires genuine horizontal transcendence, for the Eternal Purpose uses the cosmic process authentically and needfully. Meiklejohn's stress on the "organical theory of society" as necessary to education is not organic enough because it lacks the depth dimension. Comenius was far more profound in his insistence that adequate education involved the unity of knowledge and the unity of mankind within the unity of the purpose of God. God, man and nature were integrally, organically and directionally related in him. How full and wholesome is the aim of his *Didactica Magna*, that we "become learned in the Sciences, pure in Morals, trained to Piety, and in this manner instructed in all things necessary for the present and for the future life."[10] Vertical transcendence is necessary, yet not enough. Horizontal transcendence is characteristic of meaningful process, both

[8] *The Idea of a Christian Society*, p. 3.
[9] Ulich, *Fundamentals of Democratic Education*, p. 34.
[10] Keatings, *op. cit.*, title page.

as regards environmental factors and the sociology of knowledge. Full organic education is rooted in the inseparably involved interaction between the two dimensions of transcendence. Meiklejohn should have followed more fully his observation: "Comenius is a believer who says, "I am a Christian; therefore . . .' Locke is a believer who says, 'I am a Christian, but . . .' "[11]

Education in our modern day has often forgotten that knowledge is mostly "communitarian," to use Walter Muelder's suggestive term. This forgetting has contributed to the disintegration of social cohesiveness, stability, creativity and power. In our own individual learning most of the content becomes taken for granted, pushed into the subconscious and automatic side of life, to make room for further learning and growth. The same must be true of social learning. Brand Blanshard, in *The Nature of Thought,* has pointingly reminded us that the mind is economical of consciousness for our own good. The mistake of much so-called progressive education has been the idea that each person in order to learn must learn everything for himself from the beginning in the way it was originally learned. But there is no going back to beginnings in this sense. Knowledge is never inductive, empirical and individual in this sense. When educators began questioning the learning of mathematical tables and the memorizing of the wisdom of the ages, they failed to understand the wisdom of God in allowing us to learn socially in an accumulative way in order to make further learning possible in the easiest and most efficient manner possible.

Dewey is right, of course, that learning by heart is usually learning by rote, but the answer to that is not the avoidance of memorization, but Comenius' wise observation that "nothing should be learned by heart that has not been thoroughly grasped by the understanding."[12] Whitehead in his *Aims of Education* finds educational wisdom in the constant combination of skill and imagination, learning and understanding. Such learning, too, does not mean personal understanding *de novo,* the way in which the original discoverers saw truth, but the social appropriation of certain vast areas in order that those now living may find their sharp edges

[11] *Op. cit.,* p. 26.
[12] *Op. cit.,* p. 89.

of understanding in the finding of the truth which is now most relevant to them. Creativity lies ahead, not back. The past must be appropriated; the present, achieved; the future, believed.

Horizontal transcendence is what actually gives concrete content within history to the Eternal Purpose. This is the accumulation of insight through the social interpretation of experience which makes integral or directional education possible. John Dewey has stressed growth for growth's sake, or as relative to nothing but itself. Growth, however, is purposive by nature. Desirable growth is within the Eternal Purpose to effect free and full fellowship. Here is where Comenius and Pestalozzi saw the fuller truth. Dewey is right that growth should not be subordinated to external structures foreign to it, not hemmed in by arbitrary authority. Christian revelationalism of the doctrinally rigid type has certainly made it necessary for a great soul and thinker like John Dewey to come forward. Naturalism blows a fresh breeze of protest against the dank walls of closed-in orthodoxy.

Yet the flexible fullness of the Christian understanding of Agape is an authority which is both from an Eternal Purpose, and thus absolute, and from a social background, and thus time-transcending with relation to present choices. Growth is of the essence of God's work in history and must be given free rein, but it can be free only within the Eternal Purpose. Growth itself is within an organic framework, allowing for genuine freedom and self-reality. Such growth becomes molded into certain patterns of wisdom and insight, as well as of learning, which should form the deep and steadying background of all adequate education.

This growth should not only be accepted, within the confines of that which contributes to the common good, but should also be consciously continued through education. Ulich significantly maintains that "true education and character building are possible only when learning is not simply accumulative but is rather an expanding circle of understanding."[13] In this sense education should be both "organic" and "concentric."[14] The past and the present should be pointed in creative unity toward the future. This unity of our heritage is often lacking in modern education. To some extent

13 *Op. cit.,* p. 203.
14 *Ibid.,* p. 205.

Goethe is surely right that "all controversies between the older and younger generation, up to the present times, spring from separating what God according to his nature, has created as a unity."[15] We have definitely a disorganized society and pass on to our children a disorganized heritage. To further growth of significant nature in the future we must establish and pass on a more unified social heritage. Such unity alone can assure the right conditions for maximum educational growth in the future.

Such growth along the free and creative direction of the Eternal Purpose through the social accumulation of knowledge, freely and significantly unified by society, is also the prerequisite for emotional security and intellectual evolution. A disorganized society sows the dragon's teeth of personal disintegration. At least, a disintegrating society prepares the conditions for such personal disorganization. Only when some general unity of purpose is achieved by a section of mankind in general, and by a "creative minority," to use Toynbee's phrase, on a different level of attainment, is there much hope for the ripe conditions which predict a new creative era. Then effort is not wasted and scattered, but focused and significant. This deeper emotional security depends a good deal upon our regaining the vision of knowledge as a social act.

This unified social heritage is also the prerequisite for the further development of intelligence. We are now understanding more of the flexible nature of our natural endowments. They can be changed in their functional capacity. Operationally speaking the intelligence quotient is not a fixed quantity. We may be "in" for a whole new era of intellectual and spiritual evolution, if the resources of the Eternal Purpose are more fully understood and utilized. We turn, then, to the personal response of the individual to this transmissive process whereby the Eternal Purpose becomes largely operative through the historic heritage.

As soon as we touch this topic we meet the conflict between subject-centered and child-centered education. But this is a false contrast. All truly subject-centered education in the plenary perspective of Christian education is completely child-centered. Only when a subject is falsely detached from the fullness of life's mean-

[15] *Ibid.*, p. 41

ing and made an end in itself can there be a subject that is taught without intrinsic inclusion of the child. When the plenary perspective of the Christian faith is rightfully employed, no subject is ever legitimately and adequately taught without full regard to the child who is taught and to the meaning of the society in which this truth is transmitted.

Similarly, no child is ever rightly taught apart from the fullest possible regard and reverence for the subject taught. When the growth of the child becomes our only end, we commit the egocentric fallacy, individualistically or collectively. The true growth of the child is growth in the truth and of the truth in the child. Part of this truth is discovered by the ages and passed on to the succeeding generations. Only when the child learns real reverence for the intrinsic nature of this truth and for the cost of it to mankind can he develop in line with the fullest meaning and power of reality. Augustine scorned the idea that we send children to school to find out what the teacher thinks. Potentially each child contains God, and even actually contains some of Him in terms of the suppressed, yet deeply operative Agape. Each child has the capacity for God formally, and, in content, possesses the beginnings of Christian community. But since this deepest potentiality and actuality are overlaid and tied down by the self-seeking self, no child can grow up to be good by means of his own nature only, whatever the nature of the external stimulus.

Here we run up against a major snag. "Education is an affair of intelligent intercourse between individual and environment,"[16] but part of that environment condemns self-seeking and part approves it. "Ye must be born again," was the verdict of the greatest educator of the human race. Being born from above is having innate capacity for fellowship with God and our fellow man vitalized and empowered to the extent that, by continual dependence on the grace of God, it finds within community its own true dominant freedom and creative zest.

To educate, then, is no drawing out of man of his natural self, but, rather what Kraemer calls the "subversive fulfilment" of human need in the light of the full Christian faith. Modern psychology, particularly of the Freudian variety, has conclusively con-

16 Cole, *op. cit.*, p. 206.

firmed this basic Christian (and Buddhist) insight of man's natural, dominant selfishness. No response to the horizontal alone can, therefore, be adequate by itself, but each child or adult must also stand under the verdict of the Eternal Purpose. That no individual response is adequate is of decisive importance for any discussion of education.

Subject- and child-centered education thus both meet in the need for each child above all to respond to God. Pestalozzi knew that education has to regenerate as well as to inform or to make grow. All education must prepare for and follow up conversion, by the way and in the attitude with which we use what we know in whatever field of teaching or activity. This should be the constant background of the full perspective of the Christian faith on education.

Whether or not this crucial content of truth would ever enter into the subject matter taught would then depend upon the nature of the field. No education can be Christian unless teacher and student respond in this attitude of accepting God's will for the total community. Wherever subject or child becomes an end, there is an idolatrous education at work. This fact should be the conclusive answer to the controversy whether or not it matters what the teacher himself believes or how he lives. Subject matter, teacher and pupil are involved in a total situation of the learning process, and this total learning situation is itself under constant dynamic judgment of its own relation to the plenary perspective of the Eternal Purpose. The final question of education is the question of the faith in terms of which each man and community responds as a total being to the content of his knowledge and its eventual use.

The response of appropriation ought to include several aspects of truth. One is the response of mystery. To have our eyes truly open in a world like this is to see mystery on every hand. When our practical sense, so-called, and the rush of life have made it hard or impossible for us to feel any wonder, we have lost our birthright. Great is God and His ways past finding out. A naturalistic content and attitude in modern education has often seared this sense of mystery. We have become at home in a universe which is not our final abiding place. This life is but a sampling of the fuller existence which God has in store for us. This aura of faith ought to pervade all of our teaching. Our security ought to go beyond historic happenings about which we must ever feel more insecure than those who try to find in them their final security. Besides, as we view the world that we see as we pass through it, the sensitive eye and the lively imagination ought to grow in wonder and gratitude. The education that robs life of its dimension of mystery and explains away or explains falsely our actual smallness of knowledge becomes a burden on our back.

Then, too, education ought to give us deep reverence for the past and genuine gratitude for it. The past does not now exist as something that was. It is flesh, blood and bone of our existence, to think in terms of Unamuno. The past is within us, pushing us, even as the future is within us, pulling us forward. When we remember this fact, we can have no false worship of mere wasness. Nor can we wish to return to it regressively. However great it was, it exists now only as a present obligation and opportunity to make all things new, being corrected by its experience, encouraged by its success, and building on its wisdom. The history of ideas is the royal road to the fullest understanding of any subject, including its present history and possible future. Classical learning is the prerequisite for depth of modernity. The wise educator will have to explore patiently how the past can be reverently appropriated without being idolized or imposing upon us its own frustrations and distortions.

A sense of mystery, received in trust and gratitude because God is love, and a sense of gratitude for the past as a legacy and a challenge, should shape organically the appropriation of the learner, but to these should be added real respect for and understanding of the present society, in its needs, failures and promises. If education is to be Christian, the community must be taken, with genuine seriousness and concern, as primary under God, not, of course, in the totalitarian sense that any man is ever a mere means to it, but in the sense of placing first the needs and opportunities of the full fellowship. Much of the talk of individual counseling and of private tutoring is genuine and to the point. But most of it, perhaps, reflects the disintegrative patterns of an individualistic culture, where knowledge is seldom trusted as a social act and where each individual takes himself and his own knowing far too seriously. Some of it is downright neurotic in nature. The sense of intellectual insecurity and lonesomeness is not due mostly to intellectual factors. It is far more due to the breakdown in community feeling. This lack will not be remedied by the further emphasizing of individuality, but rather by the effecting of real community of living and of learning. All the stress that we have had on individual originality and invidious comparison even in teaching and learning, must be subordinated to the wiser New Testament maxim of being perfected together in the same mind and the same judgment. What we need as primary are fellowship inquiry and fellowship finding.

Only in the context of these three primary factors can we safely proceed to the need for each learner to see the truth for himself and to appropriate it within the organic meanings of his own life and understanding to the maximum possible point. God wants each person to be himself. We should imitate no one in the sense that we should wish to live his life; not even God. Each person is genuinely and uniquely himself, and no one else. There is an inimitable solitariness about each created life. Personality is ever a singular occurrence. All we can share is the stuff of spirit, of meaning, of value, but the inner decision and experience is our very own. Patterns of community there are; but the final inner self is left responsibly intact.

Learning, therefore, must also be the coming to see for oneself as much as possible of this vertical and horizontal transcendence, and of this contemporary community and environment which we experience. Therefore both what we say and what we excite are important. The excitement is deepest and best in relation to the importance of what we say, but what we say becomes dull, unimportant, and fruitless unless we excite a genuine response on the part of the learner. True teaching wins the pupil not only for the truth of the subject, but for the truth of himself. God, the community and the environment become understood and accepted within his experience, and his experience becomes understood and accepted within God, the community and the environment.

As far as the nature of the response of the individual to the instruction from the accumulated wisdom and knowledge of the past is concerned, there are at least four focuses to it.[17] The first is meditation. This meditation is not merely reflection. First of all, it is prayer. Prayer means the acceptance of the purpose of God and a fellowship with God which seeks for, and obtains a new kind of life, both creatively and redemptively. Prayer is the means by which we are delivered from self-centeredness and are made outgoing and objective. Prayer is the revitalizing of the creative energies of the soul by recourse to the Source of all life. Whatever the field which is taught and learned, for its fullest understanding in its fullest context and for its most living use, prayer is one necessary element of response. Prayer is not primarily for the preacher or for special vocations; prayer is the watering of all of human life from above, in order that the parched ground may bear fruit. What difference all education would see if all teachers and pupils knew how to pray in secret and to live openly and naturally the result of such prayer.

Yet meditation means more than prayer. Meditation, in the sense of the quiet pondering of all these things in one's heart, is a significant method of assimilation and maturation. It is the total dwelling on the subject and its meaning, and on the meaning of all life, until through subconscious incubation and through conscious concentration the richest soil possible is prepared for further seeding, while what is sown is nourished in an ever-cultivated soil. Meditation is a prerequisite for mature learning in all areas requiring insight and wisdom.

Secondly, we need memorization. Committing to heart is far more than learning by rote. True memorization is the structural internalizing of the body of the past which can find life only within the bloodstream of the person learning and living. All of us live on a past that is constantly perishing. The fuller that past the more fruitful is life. There is no substitute for hard work in memorization as far as the appropriation of the past goes. Without a broad base of accurate and real knowledge there is little chance for true skill. The medical man, for instance, has to memorize countless facts, functions and formulas. There is real richness in

---

17 This analysis is not chronologically developmental, but systematically analytical. The application of it will have to be existential, adapted to concrete circumstances.

the knowing of history with wisdom and in the learning of classical literature. Memorization is necessary because knowledge is basically a social act.

The transmission of the full culture comes mostly through what Whitehead calls "causal efficacy," the realm of knowledge below explicit awareness, and not through "presentational immediacy" or the present abstractions of consciousness. What we think with is more important than what we think on. We fool ourselves and our children, and are unwise indeed, when we do not encourage them to store in concrete learning the wealth of the past. The richness of the past is the best occasion for the creativity of the present.

Yet personal solitariness before God in meditation and memorization is not enough. There is also, in the third place, the need to share what one learns with others. There is real community in true learning. Often honest talking over material with friends who care and who are deeply interested is one of the best ways of learning. For meditation becomes escapist and memorization becomes mechanical unless in personal appropriation there are vital community reference and consciousness. The discussion method, between class and teacher or within the class in terms of committees or other procedures, is an excellent way of both personalizing and socializing truth. When this takes the place of personal pondering and of hard memorization, education becomes superficial and trivial. When it becomes the follow-through of the other methods, it becomes a good guide to fuller and more intimate understanding. We largely come to know our inner beliefs when we have to express them.

The fourth focus is that of application. Pestalozzi felt strongly that the lie in our whole civilization comes from learning without living. Memorization without the use of that which is learned makes for a deadened personality. We learn by doing, as far as action is open to us. By not applying what can be applied we create in ourselves subtle suppressions which impede further learning. Whitehead has pointed out in *Aims of Education* how even manual skill tends to increase our general intelligence, because we apply our whole self and not merely our minds. Certainly this point need not be stressed in view of the overemphasis it has received in modern activism and operationalism. A certain narrow pragmatism has settled down suffocatingly over much educational method and procedure. Social pragmatism is never operationally sound or adequate unless it makes the spiritual primary.

Pestalozzi felt that the family was the center of education. His works, *Leonard and Gertrude* and *Gertrude Teaches Her Children,* are indicative of his approach. The family is indeed far and away the best teaching agency. Judaism has maintained its solidarity through the ages largely because of its appreciation of the family. The fact that the Jewish crime record is so low has been attributed by a wise Jewish student of penology to this family solidarity. It is astonishing to find how many leaders of men come from ministers' families, or from homes where religion has a prominent and vital place.

Education must be defined not merely as the conscious transmission of learning, but as the whole way in which, in life and thought, we transmit the conditions and emotional climate for the whole-response of our children. The formal teaching of home, church and school has no real power if the children observe that this is external wisdom, but not the real motivational truth by which the parents whom they love and the friends whom they admire live day by day.

When the mother gently and honestly answers the children's questions as they appear from day to day, because she believes genuinely and acts authentically on what she teaches, then children find intellectual integrity and emotional security in that which she teaches. When children observe in the depths of their lives, beyond complete and concrete analysis, that their father not only believes what he tells them, but knows why he believes it, and finds through the believing and living what he teaches, genuine meaning in life and a happiness of an unforced and natural kind, the children imitate in their responses both what is taught in words and what is lived in deed. What is pleasant is learned most easily, as has been observed throughout the history of education. If living for others is the happy and high point of the family life, then the natural egoism of the child finds that the goodness of God, incarnated in the parents, leads them to repentance and to the commitment for themselves to the Christian life.

Yet life, important as it is, is not enough. There must also be the conscious transmission of heritage. The primary part of this transmission is the family devotions. Family meditation is a highway for passing on the best of our historic heritage. Our theology rises no higher, as Douglas Steere says, than our devotion. The family theology, too, rises no higher than its devotion. Devotion, however, demands devotions. Francis de Sales may say that devotions are like the bellows while devotion is like the chimney, yet both bellows and chimney are needed if we are to build a blazing spiritual fire in the life of our children.

Whether in the morning or in the evening, devotions can be held not only as a means for the whole family to do something important together in order thereby to find solidarity, but as the way by which the family becomes a most intimate fellowship through the Eternal Purpose, as the way in which the family finds for itself its reason and meaning for existence. Getting up a few minutes earlier in the morning for that purpose adds rich rewards. Even physical strength is thereby increased. The saints who spent all night in prayer or who arose long before morning found that there is a spring of creative life which can be drawn from no earthly well.

To enrich the devotions the family can appropriate the great heritage of hymns, perhaps, as our family does, by singing one hymn together every day for a week. When different members choose in turn, there is a lively sense of participation, and variety of approach is also assured. The young and the old have different tastes; yet all participate in the one hymn that is chosen. Even the children who cannot yet read can learn from the lips of the older members the great spiritual expressions of the faith and live themselves into the riches of great music as well as of great poetry. Beyond that, however, the Spirit must be present through silent prayer, lest the ceremony become a routine and the words threadbare. Only by the family's living and praying the hymns can they become and remain real.

The Bible, too, should be read every day by the family in a meaningful way. After the reading of the selection—perhaps a paragraph in the Revised Standard Version of the New Testament —comments or discussion often bring out the meaning of that which has been read. Questions or remarks should be open to any member in a free learning situation. Devotional books can be used either as a temporary substitute for or as a supplement to regular Bible reading. During Lent, for example, we always join in reading the *Fellowship of Prayer,* and surprisingly rich and full responses have been made by the family as a whole. The children will offer their suggestions, if opportunity is allowed.

Following the reading, each one can pray according to his own need. Kneeling, while not necessary, is conducive to reverence and attention. It is our custom for the youngest to pray first, and thus not be left to the last when time may grow short or when he may be on the verge of becoming weary. As soon as a child can say words he can pray. Even before this, the child kneels with a parent or an older brother or sister, catching the reverence of the situation and entering into it. One can often feel the searching gaze of the one- to two-year-old, wondering, studying, learning. Woe to the mother who is then not right with God. Woe to the father who has not given over his own tensions and who clings to barriers between himself and others. Certainly no family tension can remain, if the parents live genuinely and constantly to give to their children the best things that life holds and the truth that never disappoints. For better or for worse, this kind of devotions is through and through existential education.

But such devotions are not enough. If the faith is to be strong, there must also be instruction. Here is where we often fail. Wise are the parents who give their children such care. They can read together in a most pleasurable way the lives of the saints, of missionaries, and of other great human personalities, uniting the family on this level. Even the reading of secular stories with the children can give them a sense of security and of being loved. The more the reading combines real pleasure with real instruction, the better it is. We have radio programs, such as *The Greatest Story Ever Told,* that can serve as a focus of inspiration and instruction, even while sitting quietly in a darkened room and watching the flickering fire. Young children can become acutely sensitive to the Christian perspective, and can sharpen and articulate this understanding by the sharing of their reactions with the family circle.

The most important application of the Christian faith for the family is the actual living of the Christian faith in the rough-and-tumble of everyday family life. When the Christian life shines steadily on family attitudes, dispositions and decisions, the most important application of the faith to life is already made. Nothing else can take the place of this actual living. Here the child feels through his whole self the reality of the Christian faith, or else from early childhood the lie in the soul begins to thwart and throttle effective believing and simple acceptance. Yet besides this, the family can do much to apply the Christian faith in concrete ways through which the child appropriates the vertical and the horizontal transcendence.

The family can give generously to a world in need, consistently and wisely. If the child knows that prayers are made for the church, for missions and for the world in need, and yet that very little is given, he senses, in the depths of his being, a discrepancy between faith and life. If, however, all the family give up many things which they could otherwise have together, in terms of possessions or of entertainment, for the sake of regular giving to the church or to agencies of helping and healing, the child knows that he is participating in the reality to which prayer pointed and to which it partially attained. If the child can, furthermore, participate in actual projects, such as the packing of food parcels for overseas, or purchasing a milk goat for Japan, or raising a sum at Thanksgiving and Christmas beyond the amount regularly given, he takes part in direct application of the appropriation through action of the Christian faith. The family, too, can do many small things to make others glad, by refusing to press its own privileges and by heightening the joys of others when good things come to them.

The children and all the family, in addition, can learn to live a life of Christian vocation. If every time that the father has a special task to perform in his business or professional life, the rest of the family remembers his work in prayer, the whole family becomes meaningfully participating in it. Thus a doctor's son prays: "O God, steady my father's hands as he operates today." A preacher's child prays: "God, give Daddy the right words today." Upon the completion of a manuscript by an author, which has been prayed for continually by the whole family that God's will be done through it, a ceremony may be held where the manuscript is lifted up with prayer that it be rightly used by God in His own way. The whole family thus celebrates the divine worship of Christian vocation. When a Christian salesman goes away for a trip, he is followed by prayers that he be led and used to God's glory and kept from the many temptations which beset his life, and be given grace to see his way clear to make Christian choices. Miners pray deep and long prayers as a family, and out of such homes have come rich harvests. Farmers kneel to dedicate their task that they may know the sacredness of the soil. The factory worker finds even routine transfigured when there is a singing joy of family solidarity and a rich prayer life going with him into his work, and his homecoming becomes the occasion for family celebration and creative leisure.

We cannot say too much about the key place of family life for education in the sense of the training of the total self. Around a quarter of the children in the United States are brought up in broken homes. Criminologists tell us that "at least two factors are always present" in crime: family maladjustment and inner conflict.[18] How family solidarity in Christ can eliminate family maladjustment! Only the full Christian faith, with its total supernatural perspective and power, can give the full faith in which we can find the abiding family freedom and fellowship within the family of God, and where our security is beyond what history, as nature and society, can do to us, for we have found our eternal security in God, a security which aids and abets the truest and most real freedom. The Christian family, authentic and persistent, natural and genuinely happy, within the Christian faith, is the answer to the problem of education in this sphere.

The family is the most intimate and intensive community of teaching and learning of all human institutions. The Church, however, is the one community particularly organized around the purpose of the understanding, the accepting and the living of the Eternal Purpose. The Church is, therefore, uniquely concerned with spiritual education, with the most important education of man, which gives perspective and power, authority and motivation, if it is right, to all the rest of life. In one sense, of course, the

18 Atteberry, Auble and Hunt, *op. cit.,* Vol. I, p. 299.

whole life of the Church is educational, for it is the teaching in life and faith of the Eternal Purpose, with all its involvements, as far as is possible and proper. No minister who merely "inspires" adequately serves his people. The good pastor is an able educator. We ought to reread and to take to heart President Faunce's *The Educational Ideal of the Ministry.*

This educational task, naturally, does not take the place of the evangelical. There is no way by which natural man can be taught, as he is, to become good and saved. We must be born again. But good education is patterned after the nature of things, as Comenius, Pestalozzi, and other great educators have pointed out. That means that adequate Christian education is rooted in evangelism and flowers only in the growth of the evangelical faith. Precisely what does this mean? It means that great doctrinal preaching, first, prepares the content to which we must be converted. What happens in decision is not independent of the content in relation to which we are deciding. Secondly, it means evangelism—the announcing of the Gospel, the invitation to accept it, and the persuasion of the hesitant or recalcitrant—is true teaching on the level of whole-response. Thirdly, after decision has been made for God and for the world in Christ, the long, patient, educational process must take over, inspiring, informing, guiding, exciting creative responses both in decisions and in gradual growth. The evangelical faith must become educationally adequate. The tragedy of many congregations is that after a beloved minister has held a church for years, the congregation knows most of its doctrines mainly from chance books or from radio preachers of a more dogmatic and inflexible kind. A great task of the modern minister is the teaching of the faith, by making it both attractive and instructional.

Someone will object to the use of the word "attractive." Yet it is a sound educational principle that what is learned with pleasant associations is more easily and fruitfully learned. Do we, then, thereby reject the preaching of the Cross and the place of suffering in the Christian life? Not at all. We do insist, rather, that it is time that the Christian faith become *the Gospel* in reality. To become that means nothing less than that we can accept the Cross with joy, and can glory in all our afflictions. Christianity is no sacrificial moralism and no grudging acceptance of suffering for others. Christianity is "joy and peace in believing." It is gratitude and acceptance of the gift of grace. Thus true Christian preaching of concern for the world does not come mostly as a duty, or in the primary context of judgment.

Even the celebration of the broken body and of the shed blood becomes the eucharist, the thanksgiving, while we know full well that no thanksgiving is to be had, in a full Christian sense, unless we take up our Cross to fulfill the sufferings of Christ. Unless we find this reality for ourselves, we have no inviting content for conversion, no change of mind which constitutes the heart of the good news for a weary and wounded world. Christianity is the consecration of all of life to God's love, whereby, precisely in the denying of ourselves, we find the goodness of God real, and in redemptive sacrifice we find deep joy and satisfaction. Either this is true in our experience, or we have not yet found Christianity to be real for us. How, then, can we teach it radiantly to others? And unless our faith is radiant, how shall we convince the unbelievers?

Somehow the Church must also take adult education more seriously. Only so can we have parents fit to teach their children. The family can best be unified by concentrating on its meaning and on its responsibility for the children. Parents can best be made to see their obligation and opportunities for Christian living in terms of how they will affect their children. The wise minister remembers this in preparing sermons. He remembers it also in connection with the total orientation of his own work and of the church life. Thus adult classes are organized and put in the perspective of the kind of world which God and we, under Him, want for our children!

But not even here can the minister or the church stop. The whole church becomes focused on the task of educating as fully and as deeply as possible the children of its own care. Church education, or Christian education ("religious" education is a misnomer), must follow the four rules, with whatever adaptations, for transmitting and appropriating the truth which we have already described.

The teacher must first of all be trained in Christian worship, must have committed his life to Christ for the sake of the children, and must radiate the presence of the Holy Spirit because He is actually present. True Christian teaching is always in the Holy

Spirit. If it is out of this perspective and power, the teaching is no longer Christian and fails existentially to do the work it sets out to do. It is good to have trained teachers in content and technique. There is no reason why paid teachers should be more professionalized, surely, than paid ministers! It is well that we have better curriculums for a new and better day in Christian education. It is good to use audio-visual aids and all other means that we can get. But nothing can ever take the place of the praying and the believing teacher who lives his faith. This is the primary requisite for teaching the Christian faith. Nor can anything be more important for the pupil than to come from a home where he has been taught to pray and to accept from God the faith of the Church. Yet the faith of the teacher and the presence of the Holy Spirit should be real and strong enough to overcome the handicaps of much unbelief. Part of Christian teaching even in our ordinary churches (and what a part!) is plain missionary endeavor.

Not only is devotion a prerequisite for the teaching and appropriation of Christian truth, but we need also to observe the necessity of memorization for adequate instruction and learning. Indoctrination is as natural as life. The only question is what we indoctrinate. To commit to memory great Biblical passages is to condition one's consciousness to Christian content. Not to memorize these things is to let the mind either become filled with other ideas, false or lacking, or to appropriate these truths in a vague and confused form. Indoctrination is the internalizing of the depth truths of the past. To use catechetical instruction for the sake of dogmatically and defensively maintaining confessional limitations or traditionalistic theology is to keep our children away from the garden of spiritual satisfaction by roadblocks deliberately put in their way. But in order to avoid such indoctrination we should not neglect memorization. The answer to false indoctrination is not the avoidance of indoctrination, but better indoctrination. Liberalism has played us false in this respect through a lack of understanding of the real problem. What we now need to know is that knowledge is a social act; that deduction is its largest part; that unless we recognize this we shall have no accumulative power for life or creative background for thought.

The creative thinkers are usually those who know enough to relate themselves to what they know from the past in a living way, but who have not sold out their right to think and to create in favor of an unreal awe of the past. The past is no arbitrary standard of truth, but, like the content of all deductive truths, must be open to the test of present thinking and application. Deduction, however weighty in agreement and long-standing in time, is yet ever the servant of induction. That is why we need searching, honest discussion in order that we may try all things and hold fast that which is good. Beyond that lies the creative newness of uncharted seas. God's eternal truth is inexhaustible. More light must break forth from the total Bible of God's unending speech to man. Discussion can become the stimulus, through the fellowship of inquiry, for the fuller fellowship of finding.

Lastly, the church school also needs application. The project method may be best here. Any projects which have to do with everyday living are always best. Concrete action is necessary, since our subconscious can fool us beyond what we imagine. We may learn the eternal and historic truths with avidity. We may commit ourselves to the great indicatives and imperatives of our faith. Yet when something happens at home, in the neighborhood, or at school, we may also fail to see the obvious application of our Christian faith, for we may want not to do so. There are always obvious areas of race problems, the Jews moving in on the street where we live, our relation to other churches and faiths, our supporting certain stands in the community or our giving as a church school class. There are plenty of possibilities for Christian action and witness in relation to nationalism, to war and peace, to class feeling, to maladjusted individuals. Even living on a typical suburban street, if we know our neighbors, affords countless opportunities to enter into their problems in Christian love, wisdom and concrete helpfulness. Church school teachers can be aware of these situations and conceive of projects in terms of visiting and co-operating with different faiths and groups, of giving money and time to agencies of help and healing, and to the continual analysis of local problems, or of typical home and neighbor situations.

The project method is too well known and established to need much discussion. Meditation and memorization without discussion and application become deadening to the spirit and create undigested and unassimilated material. We want a church education that neither goes back to older forms of catechetical instruction nor continues in the present activistic ways, but which combines the two. We complain that we have only an hour a week in which to teach. This can be remedied if we put the need of the child within the center of our Christian concern; but what stares us in the face now is that we are not using to the full even our present possibilities, in terms of consecrated homes, consecrated teachers, and the full gamut of educational perspectives and processes.

Yet individual Christian response, family response, and church response are not enough educationally. Unless the community also is altered there will be strong contrary currents to hold back the Christian flood tide of historic renewal. What power of perspective is evidenced by Fallaw's *The Modern Parent and the Teaching Church* where he binds home, church and community organically together educationally, insisting that the Christian fellowship must redefine Christian community. Obviously we have a depth problem as soon as we even mention Christian community or Christian civilization; even every actual church as a sociological institution is far from Christian, in the vital sense of that word. There is nevertheless a real difference between a community that is informed by Christian presuppositions and that at least honors these in the depths of its consciousness, however it may act below them or contrary to them in the weaknesses of its actual life, and a community that never has accepted them and openly rejects the Christian presuppositions. There is a difference between totalitarian Marxism and Christendom; between rejection of Christian perspectives and even our ordinary civilization which has the Christian tradition as its background and generalized confession. What we are talking about now is not the community of saints, but the community where the saints are honored, at least in theory and in memory. It becomes obvious how much we need to work to change the patterns of our actual community living educationally. There must be real and effective changes, otherwise we contradict the wholeness of life and tend to smother the spirit, however willing it be, by the weaknesses of the flesh. What are some of the aspects of community education which must be changed, if we leave the public schools until our last section?

Obviously the newspapers, the radio, the movies, periodical literature, including comic books, and books in general, need to be basically changed. Words can hardly characterize the baseness and abject poverty of all these media of community education. Here is where people are continually feeding their minds and exciting their imaginations. Understandably, this baseness and poverty are due to our decadent culture and are not only caused by these media of communication of ideas, but also reflect in large measure what people crave, what they want rather than what they need.

The press, the radio, television and the movies ought all to be socialized within a Christian democracy. Kierkegaard claimed in his day that "If the press were to hang a sign out like every other trade, it would have to read: Here men are demoralized in the shortest possible time on the largest possible scale for the smallest possible price."[19] Advertising is skirting indecency and arousing sensuality in unimaginable reaches of conduct. External regulation is hardly enough, of course, while we have the constant pressure of greedy interest appealing to low desires. The press ought to be free of financial bondage and *represent the functional interests of the community in creative co-operation.* The positions on the press ought to be the social reward for social contribution.

Some have suggested that the churches start million-dollar presses, like the *Christian Science Monitor.* Certainly such papers raise the standards, but besides being divisive in nature, they also are involved in the interests of the *status quo* and give little sign of an effective leadership for a new and better world. The different worlds—of art, religion, literature, drama, politics, economics, travel, creative leisure, education—ought to have local activities of a vital nature and out of these worlds ought to come forth the best interpreters of their fields for our daily newspapers. In this way they could all become important educational media in the new world.

The same functional representation of responsibility within a Christian democratic socialism could characterize the management of the radio and television. Already these are sharply supervised, but they are under heavy pressures of private interests and not sufficiently open to the public good. See what is happening in

---

[19] Bretall, *Kierkegaard,* p. 431.

Sweden and in some American cities where the educational advantages of the radio are taken seriously. In no way need we take entertainment off the radio, but we can deliver both the radio and television from the profit pressures of advertising and from the consequent catering to mass taste. If the creative springs of life are opened up, and if enjoyment comes from fullness of life, rather than as a bored escape from world-weariness, we can find ways of enlarging people's horizons, stimulating and carrying on adult education, aiding family, church and community education in measures hitherto quite unforeseen.

The same thing can be said of the motion-picture industry. What possibility for creative education coupled with true entertainment! The screen should be the challenge to a new kind of art and absorb immense creative energy for generations to come. The scope of it can be widened when the resources are the common goods of a concerned community. Individual initiative can surely be stimulated better when the rewards of acting are a higher grade of artistry, a higher grade of appreciation, and the attainment of fuller community feeling and thinking, rather than bloated salaries and cheap notoriety. Many professions could join in creative endeavor in order to produce this transformation. Our jaded age thinks that only immediate self-interest can make people move; when communitarian motivation becomes part of our total pattern of living, from home, church and community, as well as from our national and world pattern, we shall unleash new incentives and surprise ourselves by the discovery of a new dimension of life. The moviegoers each week are multimillions. What can happen when this educational medium is redeemed within the new orientation of genuinely social incentives!

Great civilizations bear great books. Books are the permanent legacy of great living. This educational avenue of books, however, would have to be under public supervision for the common good. Such things as degrading and crime-luring comic books would naturally not be allowed or wanted. It is surprising how utterly exciting *funny* "funnies" used to be to children brought up in a Christian home. They absorbed the child in fascinated wonder. The blasé child of today, for whom no excitement is enough, is not natural, but reflects the deadness of the end of an era. The same is true of books. For better writing there must be truer taste. How this field of educational opportunity should be handled remains, nevertheless, to be tried out in practice, since it is itself creative and unpredictable in terms of any set pattern.

Perhaps the community of tomorrow will be able to do away with our present huge cities and to develop rurban life. Technologically that is now more and more possible. If that comes to be, there ought to be set aside a good deal of community time and planning for the creative side of life, not only for our children but also for all. For the children there can be playgrounds and instructors in various forms of activity, both play and educational. If we can do away with blighted areas and with degrading housing situations, and give room for freedom and faithfulness in fellowship, both through place for privacy and for community activity, we shall have gone a long way toward meeting community needs and preventing the rearing of our present kind of children. This freer world of space and time is where ingenuity can come in, by the way in which we use our modern audio-visual aids and other technological means, whereby education can become an extra pleasure for free time.

As for the adults, there will be more and more time for creative leisure. Man is spirit, mind and body, and as D. Loring Swaim has kept claiming, unless we satisfy all three aspects, we shall never have well and happy people. That means new and larger tasks for our churches. Perhaps they must cease to be our nice little Sunday morning affair and really launch out into a whole new kind of existence, to play a central part in all of life in this new age of increased free time, for all, an age which we now have if we really want it. Perhaps, too, we shall have to satisfy the minds of our people through a whole new kind and scale of adult education for creative leisure, real education in interesting forms from information to practical avocations. And certainly we must teach people to play, to relax and to enjoy life by finding personal satisfaction and peace within relaxed or creative togetherness. The more we have to plan together on the large scale to make this abundance of means for community life possible, the more we shall have to be free and creative within our local circles of community life, in order to infuse and to keep infusing this creative freedom into the warp and woof of our common planning. Christian democracy will greatly depend upon the thoroughness of this kind of community education.

We come, at the last, to the question of the relation between Christian education and our public schools. Obviously the present situation is in need of change. But of what change? Constitutionally, Church and State are separated. With out divided religious situation, this may be well for political purposes. Religion needs freedom from political control and the schools need freedom from religious restrictions, threatened by actually existing organizations. If the question concerned only a functional duality within the community of concern, the situation would not be so bad as it is. Actually there is a division between religion and education, which in the general consciousness amounts to the idea that there is no organic relation between them. To some extent education becomes agnostic, in fact, in the way in which it is understood by adults and children alike. Thus the unity of life is broken and division is made in the human soul. This was avoided while the Church handled education, and regardless of the actual actions of the State, insisted on the unity of all of life under God. Now secularism has nestled into education to the extent that religion *as such* is often treated as a hostile force, as either irrelevant to or as downright threatening educational freedom! Obviously this is not true of many schools and often superintendents or principals, or isolated teachers, make a personal connection between the two, or there is observance of religious customs, and Christian material is read or included in some way in the curriculum. Yet generally there is a tragic rift between the Christian faith, in its full bearing on education, and our public school education.

One way of curing this has been attempted by the so-called released time method whereby pupils have been dismissed an hour each week or so, for religious instruction under church-controlled agencies. Some who have long participated in such programs believe strongly in them. The trouble with this method, however, is that religion becomes a fringe activity of a predominantly secular education, while by definition it must be central to all of life and thought. Psychologically such piecemeal remedies are neither wholesome nor adequate. Besides, they are divisive in stressing actual difference in an outright way in a community of learning which otherwise, for its purpose, is unitive.

There is the answer of the parochial school, and a powerful answer this is. Since all of life must be seen within the perspective of the Eternal Purpose the church is the only agency that can offer whole education. Since secularism and scientism have become rival religions to the Jewish-Christian faith, the only answer is to pull our students out of this environment offering half-truths for whole-truths, and subtly undermining, or even hostilely attacking, the whole-truths by which we must live, if we are to live fully and well. If we had one religion, who knows but this might not be the best answer? Perhaps the public schools are not the appropriate vehicles for this crucial transmission of our total heritage, involving both the vertical and the horizontal transcendence, and the need to understand the latter centrally in the light of the former. The real difficulty with this solution, nonetheless, is that the groups which run parochial schools in several of the forms of our Judeo-Christian stream of life, are isolationist branches, the ones devoted to an exclusive, traditionalistic point of view. Thus there arise through these schools divisive streams of culture and defensive strands of religion.

Even where there is only one dominant form of religion, church schools are often defensive of dogma and afraid to let the new light in through wide and clean windows. Theocracy, or the approach to it, may suffer from a too close identity of spirit, mind and body. Perhaps God has ordained three basic functions for the sake of interaction and creative growth, the church for the spirit, the school for the mind, and the government for the body. During troubled times and for a temporary purpose such parochial schools may play an important role, particularly if they let their limiting shells be broken through and allow their lives free scope within the larger community of learning, free of handicapping pressures or subtle fears, from within or from without.

What other solutions, then, can there be? Our situation is serious. The first act must be the breaking through by our leading thinkers of this false secularism and scientism which keep us from adequacy of perspective and power. Truth must be accepted in its wholeness. That means the open and consistent reworking of all the fields of knowledge in the light of the Eternal Purpose. What this would do to our whole approach and to the total content of our instruction in the various fields is frankly beyond imagination. Again, each teacher, in whatever subject or grade, ought at least to be taught and trained in the best available religious knowledge.

Ideally speaking, God's complete concern for each and for all would then become the eyes through which to look; without "the eyes of faith" and a life dedicated to the common good little can be seen effectively and creatively. In a new age the social patterns should be strongly conducive to each teacher's being Christian *in this inclusive sense of common concern under God.* To be a teacher would then have to be a Christian vocation, in this broad sense, a most meaningful and increasingly important investment of life for the common good, centrally out of God-centered social incentives. All these things can be done from kindergarten to graduate teaching in any school without the infringement of any constitution, because the problem is here not at all of Church and State. If the Constitution or any state regulation should deny the right of religion in the sense of its free study in any institution for the sake of the common good, that Constitution or state regulation should be changed with speed and vigor, for such regulations or interpretations could mean only that secularism had set itself up as a faith, a false god usurping the divine throne, and impoverishing and distorting the truth by which we must live, in order to live in co-operative and creative community for the new age.

Two presuppositions, obvious to any reader of the whole book, lie back of what we are now to say. The first is that we have to have a spiritual rebirth and creative age in which the Church of Christ becomes one organically, whatever be then the means of differentiations in creative and subordinate details of thought and worship. We leave out no church as a possible member. This may seem like unadulterated utopianism, but no church has tougher walls than hell, and even these shall not prevail to protect what is behind them, if the churches confess the love of God in Christ Jesus, in humble and surrendered faith. The Roman branch may find itself up against such reality and power, when the transformed and unified church of the Age of the Spirit moves out conquering and to conquer, in humility and love, that before this inclusive church it will fall into its divinely destined fulfillment. According to our faith it shall be done to us, and if we believe, nothing within the will of God is impossible to us.

Judaism, too, longs for its release, in its subconscious agony, from its ethnic limitations and its arrested development. Its deepest and highest instincts are universal and its interpretation of the law, at the van of its thinking, is dynamic. When God is interpreted as the God of history who is the God of unlimited love, refusing all man-made barriers, and when this becomes a living reality toward Judaism, whether converted or not, Judaism will find an oceanic surge to leave its tragic isolation and find its own fulfillment within its own highest contribution from God to man. Judaism will then come to itself and rejoice with its own heritage. When the teaching concerning Christ is delivered from invidious dogma and defensive doctrine, and is declared to be the love of God in and for history, Judaism will find a door opened to it.

When the humanity of Jesus is accepted, not as a concession, but as a joyous confession, then Judaism will be rid of a false stumbling block, and the Hebrew people will find only the one offense common to us all, that we must be broken through as individual selves by the grace of God in order that we might be remade through faith in Him within the full fellowship love. All this is poppycock, of course, unless we are visited by the dayspring from on high, creating radical newness, which is ours for the believing and the living of it. If only we believe God for an unqualified fellowship, no barrier can be strong enough to withstand Him.

The second presupposition is that producers' capital be socialized and that the school be generally state or federally supported. There ought to be church-related schools which should deal with the creative development of dogma, in its best deductive sense. The vertical direction, in its total meaning and power, ought to be taught in connection with the Church. There could be a kind of combination school for religious research and for the professional training of ministers and church leaders; or there could be the two kinds in separate institutions. In the coming economy of abundance these should be supported out of consumer goods and should be free from political control, ever encouraged to seek for the fuller and more adequate truth of God in His relation to the world. All other schools should be generously supported by the state, whether for general training or for specialized interests like music and art. How, then, can Christian faith be made central?

When we teach subjects dealing with process—science, art, literature, history, etc.—the full perspective and Christian history need not be brought in, but they must, nevertheless, be taught within this perspective. This means that all secularism and all scientism would be eliminated. The subjects would all presuppose, and harmonize with, the Christian teaching at home and in the church. There would be a wholeness of viewpoint without duplication of effort and without making the schools all church schools. Spirit and mind would be functionally distinct in education, but not hostile to each other. They would be complementary and not competing perspectives. The teachers would know the full Christian perspective by being trained in it. The subjects would be taught within this perspective and organically imply and point to it. Growth within the secondary perspectives would challenge growth in the primary perspective and growth in the primary perspective would be the condition for further rethinking of the secondary subjects. Present legal arrangements are not the reason for this suggestion. For the creative community must have vision and strength to change its own blueprint according to newer and better insights. Law exists to be changed for better laws. The Age of the Spirit cannot be fettered to any letter, as permanently thwarting its truer expression. This division of labor, however, would tend to prevent either emphasis on the Eternal Purpose or on the cosmic process from absorbing the other.

Whether or not, however, we get a new level of life, and if the world still stands reliably for education to proceed, we can always teach common concern, which is the very essence of the Christian faith, on any level of education. Whenever our philosophy of life denies this purpose as a total context, it cuts off the flower of civilization from its roots and thus injures its own life. Meaninglessness and meanness are bound to result. Because the Christian faith is true, not only vertically or beyond this world, but as the context and content of creative community, the more it is denied, the more we deny and hurt ourselves. Whatever the situation, the more this common concern is made central, creatively, in cosmos and conduct, the more we build the freedom and faithfulness in fellowship, which we found to be the only thing that can truly satisfy our total lives, as individuals or as a society.

Thus we have come to the end of the chapter. All we have done is to put up a perspective and in its light make a few leading suggestions. Our concern is with the general applicability of the Agape perspective. We now see that the Christian faith as God's creative concern for co-operative community, within the total context of cosmic process, is dynamically self-verifying. The more, in regard to vertical transcendence, this is made the authority and motivation, the more we shall have the perspective and power for a new level of life, which our present corner of history demands. Faith in creative and co-operative life, far beyond our little limits of clan or country, because God has willed it for us and is able to give it to us, is the leverage with which to lift man's history in this fateful hour. For this we need to accept and to know full fellowship by faith in the grace of God, the Eternal Purpose which He purposed in Christ Jesus our Lord, even to declare his complete Concern for freedom and faithfulness in fellowship.

In speaking of "secular" institutions Minear writes, "We are [also] able to trace a positive purpose in those same institutions for us who share now in the inheritance of the new age, for we are participating in the extension of the sovereignty of Christ over all creation."[20] That is it. We must extend Christ's reign, God's love, over all life, inner and outer. No education can ever become adequate that does not pay full attention both to the inner faith of the heart, in its way and place, and to the outer affairs of life, according to their nature, for only thus shall we "diligently search into and set in order both our outward and inward things, because both are of importance to our progress in godliness."[21]

20 "The New Testament Witness and Civilization," in *Theology Today*, Volume V, No. 3, October, 1948, p. 345.
21 À Kempis, *The Imitation of Christ* (Brother Leo ed.), p. 37.

Index